Curbing Clientelism in Argentina

Politics, Poverty, and Social Policy

In many young democracies, local politics remains a bastion of nondemocratic practices, from corruption to clientelism to abuse of power. In a context where these practices are widespread, will local politicians ever voluntarily abandon them? Focusing on the practice of clientelism in social policy in Argentina, this book argues that only the combination of a growing middle class and intense political competition leads local politicians to opt out of clientelism. Drawing on extensive fieldwork, an original public opinion survey, and cross-municipal data in Argentina, this book illustrates how clientelism works and documents the electoral gains and costs of the practice. In doing so, it points to a possible subnational path toward greater accountability within democracy.

Rebecca Weitz-Shapiro is the Stanley J. Bernstein Assistant Professor of Political Science at Brown University. Her research has been published in the *American Journal of Political Science*, *Comparative Political Studies*, *Comparative Politics*, the *Journal of Latin American Politics and Society*, the *Journal of Politics*, and *Latin American Research Review*. She was the recipient of the Sage Prize for Best Paper in Comparative Politics presented at the 2011 American Political Science Association Annual Meeting. Professor Weitz-Shapiro has been a visiting scholar at the Center for Advanced Study in the Social Sciences at the Juan March Institute in Madrid and a Fulbright Scholar in Argentina. She has conducted fieldwork in Argentina and Brazil and has received funding from the National Science Foundation, among other sources. She holds a PhD from Columbia University and an AB from Princeton University.

Curbing Clientelism in Argentina

Politics, Poverty, and Social Policy

REBECCA WEITZ-SHAPIRO

Brown University

CAMBRIDGE
UNIVERSITY PRESS

32 Avenue of the Americas, New York NY 10013-2473, USA

Cambridge University Press is part of the University of Cambridge.

It furthers the University's mission by disseminating knowledge in the pursuit of education, learning and research at the highest international levels of excellence.

www.cambridge.org
Information on this title: www.cambridge.org/9781107423213

© Rebecca Weitz-Shapiro 2014

First published 2014
First paperback edition 2016

A catalogue record for this publication is available from the British Library

Library of Congress Cataloguing in Publication data
Weitz-Shapiro, Rebecca, 1979–
Curbing clientelism in Argentina: politics, poverty, and social
policy / Rebecca Weitz-Shapiro, Brown University.
        pages   cm
Includes bibliographical references and index.
ISBN 978-1-107-07362-3 (hardback)
1. Patronage, Political–Argentina.   2. Patron and client–Argentina.   3. Political corruption–
Argentina.   4. Political culture–Argentina.   5. Local government–Corrupt practices–Argentina.
6. Argentina–Social policy.   7. Poverty–Government policy–Argentina.   I. Title.
JL2098.8.W45   2014
324.2′040982–dc23   2014008093

ISBN 978-1-107-07362-3 Hardback
ISBN 978-1-107-42321-3 Paperback

Contents

Illustrations

Tables

Acknowledgments

In the process of researching and writing this book, I benefited from the support, advice, and assistance of many institutions and individuals. This project took shape when I was a graduate student at Columbia University. John Huber, María Victoria (Vicky) Murillo, and Bob Kaufman served as excellent advisors and have offered invaluable feedback and guidance as this project evolved from a dissertation to a book. Also at Columbia, I benefited from sound advice and comments from Andy Gelman, Lucy Goodhart, Shigeo Hirano, Macartan Humphreys, Pablo Pinto, and Bob Shapiro. Javier Auyero's work on clientelism helped inspire this project, and I was fortunate to have him on my dissertation committee. My fellow graduate students Bernd Beber, Ozge Kemahlioglu, Georgia Kernell, Claudio Lopez-Guerra, Julia Maskivker, Monika Nalepa, Virginia Oliveros, Thania Sanchez, and David Stevens provided valuable comments and camaraderie in equal measure. I owe a particular debt – intellectual and of friendship – to Kate Baldwin, Alex Scacco, and Matt Winters.

The Political Science Department at Brown University has provided a collegial, intellectually stimulating environment in which to complete this manuscript. I would particularly like to thank Linda Cook and Richard Snyder who, in their capacities as chair of the Political Science Department and director of the Center for Latin American and Caribbean Studies, respectively, helped organized a book conference around this manuscript at Brown. Erik Wibbels and Susan Stokes provided excellent, challenging comments at that event that improved the manuscript immensely. Also at Brown, Jeremy Cutting, Elizabeth Bennett, Diego Diaz, Nathan Einstein, Jazmin Sierra, and Miriam Hinthorn provided valuable research assistance at various stages of this project. I also thank the Center for Advanced Studies in the Social Sciences (CEACS) at the Juan March Institute in Madrid, and its director, Ignacio

Sánchez-Cuenca, for hosting me on sabbatical as I was completing revisions to the book.

A number of colleagues, at these institutions and elsewhere, read all or part of this manuscript or provided advice at crucial junctures. Many thanks are due to Sarah Brooks, Ernesto Calvo, Melani Cammett, Kanchan Chandra, Matthew Cleary, Linda Cook, Kent Eaton, Tulia Falleti, Brian Fried, Christopher Gang, Anna Gryzmala-Busse, Mark Jones, Philip Keefer, Stuti Khemani, Chappell Lawson, Steve Levitsky, Pauline Jones Luong, Noam Lupu, Susan Moffitt, David Nickerson, Wendy Schiller, Richard Snyder, Mariela Szwarcberg, Tariq Thachil, Mariano Tommasi, Joshua Tucker, and Cesar Zucco for their thoughtful comments and suggestions. I received valuable feedback at seminars at Yale University, Harvard University, the University of Illinois, and the University of Pennsylvania.

This project would of course not have been possible without the help of colleagues in Argentina, in particular Valeria Brusco, who helped orient me and my research in the province of Córdoba. Jonathan C. Hamner took the excellent cover photo and graciously granted permission for me to use it. Solange Acosta, Matilde Ambort, Paula Bertino, Martín Carola, Erika Decandido, Gretel Echazú, Gabriela Guerrero, Lucas Lázaro, Mariana Macazaga, Ana Perez Declercq, and Denise Priori Sáenz were fantastic research assistants. I am immensely grateful to the many Argentine local government officials who agreed to be interviewed as part of this research.

I received generous funding for this project from three organizations at Columbia University: its Center for International Business Education and Research, the Institute for Latin American Studies, and the Institute for Social and Economic Research and Policy. I also benefited from the generosity of the National Science Foundation, in the form of a graduate research fellowship and dissertation improvement grant number 615547. Ernesto Calvo and Vicky Murillo graciously shared data analyzed in Chapter 6. I thank the Latin American Public Opinion Project (LAPOP) and its major supporters (the United States Agency for International Development, the United Nations Development Program, the Inter-American Bank, and Vanderbilt University) for making data from that project available. Some of the material in Chapter 5 was initially published in "What wins votes: Why some politicians opt out of clientelism," in the *American Journal of Political Science*. I thank Rick Wilson and four anonymous reviewers for their comments. At Cambridge University Press, I thank Lew Bateman for his support for this project and Shaun Vigil for editorial assistance. All errors and omissions are, of course, my own.

In many respects, the intellectual roots of this project date to before I entered graduate school. At Princeton University and at the Universidad Torcuato di Tella in Buenos Aires, I was fortunate to interact with many wonderful friends, teachers, scholars, and mentors. I have happily shared many institutions and fruitful conversations about Latin American politics with Nick Fitch and Miriam Boyer. I thank Jeremy Adelman, Miguel Centeno, Kent Eaton, Amy

Gutmann, Peter T. Johnson, and Gabriel Kessler for encouraging my interest in political science, Latin America, and a career in academia.

Most importantly, I would like to thank my family, whose support I have benefited from since long before I embarked on this project. My parents, Cyndy and Alan Weitz, both modeled and encouraged a love of learning. I am incredibly grateful to them, as well as to my brother Joshua and sister Bethanie, for their love and support. My husband Dan has filled my life outside of work, and I thank him for his patience, prodding, and love. Yael and Natan were born after this project began, but they are now old enough to inquire about its impending publication. I hope one day they will be curious to read it.

I

Accountability, Democracy, and the Study of Clientelism

Stepping off the bus on the main road in Campo Santo, a small, impoverished municipality in Argentina's northwest, it is not difficult to find the town's social welfare office. The office is prominently located near the main entrance to the municipality and, more importantly, identifiable by the sizable crowd of residents waiting outside. The crowd is made up mostly of women, many with small children, joined by a few elderly men. Various staff members from the social welfare office are present, but only a top bureaucrat in the office, Liliana, actually attends to the crowd.[1] The type of requests residents make vary widely: as I arrived on one occasion, an older man asked for help paying for a prescription, while later in the morning a mother came by to pick up a mattress she had recently requested so that her daughter could move out of their shared bed.

These benefits, along with others that Liliana distributes, are funded by the government – municipal, provincial, or federal. However, the treatment beneficiaries receive in Campo Santo is both personal and politicized. Liliana's desk is crowded with photos of herself with the mayor, the governor, and the lieutenant governor. Above her chair hangs a hand-drawn portrait of Juan and Eva Perón, the icons of Argentina's largest political party, the *Partido Justicialista* (PJ), to which both Liliana and the mayor belong. Even more importantly, Liliana treats the distribution of social benefits as a tool for garnering electoral support – one she believes is extremely effective. She described the response of voters to the receipt of social program benefits this way: "At the moment of the vote, it doesn't matter if they're from the other party, they go 'tac' and they vote for the mayor." Campo Santo's mayor also emphasized the importance of individualized exchange in the pursuit of votes.

---

[1] To protect interviewee anonymity, I have changed the names of all nonelected interviewees throughout the book.

In his words, "The typical resident is very clientelist … it's not the best way, but you have to do it."

The municipality of Devoto, in the relatively prosperous bread belt province of Córdoba, seems at first glance vastly different from Campo Santo. Devoto has a low poverty rate and a long tradition of support for Argentina's century-old Radical party, or UCR.[2] At the time of my research, the mayor had just begun his fourth term in office after an election in which the opposition Peronist party did not even present a candidate for mayor. Given the town's relative affluence, the social welfare office did not present the crowded scene described in Campo Santo. Nonetheless, an interview with Graciela, a social worker who held a top position in the town's social welfare office, revealed that the provision of social benefits was highly politicized in Devoto. Graciela was frank about her frustration with how the beneficiary list for a large food distribution program was compiled and maintained. She described how she would like to "clean" the beneficiary list of those not most in need of the benefits, but that the mayor's resistance meant she was unable to do so.[3] Similarly, when asked who had the final say regarding inclusion into the beneficiary list for this program, Graciela's answer reflected the strong influence of political considerations. In her words, the final say over any individual's inclusion would be the result of a dispute between her "professional" criteria and the mayor's "political" criteria. In her own assessment, sometimes the mayor "won" this dispute, while at other times she prevailed.[4]

These brief examples suggest that, in spite of the differences between these towns, political figures in both Campo Santo and Devoto rely on clientelism – the individualized exchange of goods and services for political support – in the implementation of social policy. In doing so, they are not alone; by many accounts, clientelism is an extremely common form of policy implementation in Argentina. However, although contingent, individualized exchange may be the dominant approach to social policy administration in Argentina's towns and cities, it is not the only approach.

About an hour and a half drive from Devoto, the municipality of Río Primero is situated in a similar agricultural zone and enjoys similarly low rates of poverty. At the time of my research, it, too, had a Radical party mayor, although he faced a more competitive electoral environment than his counterpart in Devoto. And in Río Primero, too, a licensed social worker, Carolina, was in a top position at the social welfare office. However, her experience in that office forms a sharp contrast with that of Graciela. In Carolina's words, she and her staff were "not at all ordered around" by the

---

[2]   The UCR, or *Union Cívica Radical*, is in fact not a radical party at all, but a catch-all party founded in the late nineteenth century. It fielded six presidents over the course of the twentieth century and was long the second-largest political force in Argentina, although its fortunes have suffered dramatically since a Radical party president resigned from office in the midst of an economic and political crisis in 2001.

[3]   Author interview, August 2007.

[4]   Research assistant interview, August 2006.

mayor or other political staff in their administration of social programs. She described her office as "very independent" of political considerations. The mayor's own attitude echoed that of Carolina. He claimed to scrupulously avoid using social assistance as a political tool, instead preferring to "let those that want to vote for us ... without any type of exchange."

Uneven Democracy

The experience of these three small Argentine towns reflects two persistent puzzles of the "third wave" of democratization (Huntington, 1991).[5] In the first place, democratic endurance or consolidation has not meant convergence to an ideal-type high-quality democracy. Second, the quality of democracy varies substantially within, as well as across, countries.

Across the world, examples abound of both disappointing democratic performance and subnational variation in that performance. In Eastern Europe, for example, though some new democracies successfully reformed the state inherited from Communist rulers, in others, newly elected officials looted state coffers and weakened state institutions.[6] In Latin America, many of the third wave democracies have come to be characterized as "delegative democracies," wherein once elected, a president enjoys almost free rein to govern as he sees fit – or as best benefits him personally (O'Donnell, 1994). The uneven quality of government performance across subnational units in many new democracies is well established (Bardhan and Mookherjee, 2006c). Brazil's states and municipalities, for example, vary widely in their performance in areas ranging from the provision of basic health care services to extrajudicial killings by the police.[7] Nor is this type of subnational variation limited to the third-wave democracies or the developing world: examples from India to Italy point to the possibility of persistent unevenness in democratic performance within a single state.[8]

Fundamentally, this book is motivated by a desire to shed light on these two puzzles by identifying the conditions under which citizens are most likely to be able to hold local politicians accountable. In other words, what explains variation in the quality of governance *within* democracy? I answer this question through a subnational study of political clientelism. Clientelism, or the individualized exchange of goods or services for political support, undermines a citizen's ability to use her political actions to signal her political preferences or to hold politicians to account. As such, the costs of clientelism for governance are widely recognized. Nonetheless, the literature has paid less attention to

---

5 Both were first brought to widespread attention by Guillermo O'Donnell. See especially O'Donnell (1993) and O'Donnell (1996).
6 See Grzymala-Busse (2007), Hellman (1998), and O'Dwyer (2006).
7 Alves (2012) and Gibson (2012) discuss the former, and see Brinks (2008) on the latter.
8 On India, some recent work includes that by Bussell (2010) and Singh (2010). Works by Judith Chubb, Miriam Golden, and Robert Putnam all point to substantial subnational variation in the quality of Italian government performance.

the links between clientelism and within country variation in the quality of governance. While some countries are monolithic clientelist regimes and others have eliminated clientelism entirely, there is a vast middle ground between these two extremes. This book speaks to those cases in which there is no national-level imperative to reduce clientelism, yet local conditions sometimes create incentives for politicians to eschew clientelistic relationships on their own. By identifying those conditions, a study of clientelism can serve as an apt lens through which to understand paths to accountability within democracy.

Returning to the Argentine context, all three municipalities described in the opening paragraphs are the site of regular national and local elections that are open to interparty competition and take place without violence, ballot stuffing, or overt violations of civil or political rights. Within Argentina, there has been no nationally led attempt to eliminate clientelism from the repertoire of local politicians' appeals to citizens. Yet, at the time of the research for this book, important variation existed. In two of these municipalities – one mostly poor, and one predominantly middle class – mayors relied on clientelism in the implementation of social policy, while in the third municipality, the mayor did not. In a context where clientelism is widespread, it is this second decision – of some politicians to opt *out* of clientelism – that merits particular attention. If we are able to explain this case and others like it, we may be able to illuminate a possible pathway out of clientelism and toward improved local governance in Argentina and elsewhere.

In this book, I argue that it is the combination of high levels of political competition and a large middle class that leads some local incumbents to opt out of clientelism. This argument builds on, yet departs from, two longstanding schools of thought about the determinants of good governance. Modernization theorists since Seymour Martin Lipset have pointed to growing prosperity as crucial for changing citizen preferences and the nature of their demands on government, and thus for achieving good government performance.[9] An equally long trajectory points to the importance of competition – in the form of democracy or within a democracy – for prompting politicians to deliver results to citizens.[10]

I develop the argument that, from the perspective of understanding departures from clientelism, neither condition alone will suffice. This is because of a feature of clientelism that has received little attention to this date: clientelism creates an electoral tradeoff in terms of support from different groups of constituents. That is, though clientelism can lead to increased political support from the poor, it is likely to decrease political support from the nonpoor.[11] The existence of this tradeoff means that, when voters are mostly poor,

---

[9]   See Lipset (1959) and Moore (1966) for classic formulations.

[10] See Schumpeter (2012 [1943]). This approach also draws on insights from economics; see, for example, Barro (1973), Downs (1957), and Ferejohn (1986).

[11] Whereas the former is broadly recognized, the latter observation has received very little attention, though see Banfield and Wilson (1963), Shefter (1977), and Brusco et al. (2006).

high competition can actually strengthen an incumbent's interest in relying on clientelism. This is the opposite of what proponents of the benefits of competition for good governance would expect. At the same time, the mere existence of a large middle class that dislikes clientelism will not necessarily create sufficient incentives for incumbents to move away from clientelism. Limited political competition can insulate incumbents from citizen preferences. It is only when high competition coincides with a large nonpoor population that we should expect incumbents to eschew clientelism. This is especially true for incumbents from parties that normally rely on middle-class support. Under those circumstances, incumbents will both face high costs to clientelism and be motivated to react to those costs by moving away from clientelism.

Employing a subnational comparative approach, I test this theory of clientelism using individual-level and municipal-level data from Argentina. The combination of field observation, a survey of key informants in a sample of more than 125 municipalities, and a mass survey and survey experiment provides an unusually detailed picture of how clientelism works, the attitudes of nonclients toward the practice, and the conditions under which local politicians opt not to rely on it. I provide evidence that the *interaction* between political competition and constituency poverty – particularly in certain partisan environments – is crucial for understanding why some local politicians in Argentina depart from clientelism, thus opening the door to improved governance.

1.1 CLIENTELISM, ACCOUNTABILITY, AND DEMOCRACY

When talking about the quality of government, scholars have a variety of concrete behaviors and measures in mind, ranging from the quality of basic service delivery, to government efficiency in responding to citizens, to the politicization of the civil service, to the control of corruption.[12] This book focuses on clientelism as a practice that directly undermines links of accountability between citizens and those who govern.

1.1.1 Defining Clientelism

Throughout this book, I define clientelism as the *individualized, contingent exchange of goods or services for political support or votes.*[13] My definition

---

[12] See Cleary (2010), Min (2010), Putnam (1994), Bussell (2010), Geddes (1994), Grzymala-Busse (2007), O'Dwyer (2006), and Adserá et al. (2003) for some examples.

[13] Strictly speaking, this is a definition of the practice of political clientelism. Earlier definitions of clientelism within the social sciences emphasized that the practice was embedded in social ties and encompassed the exchange of a broad range of services and support between patrons and clients, which were not necessarily political in nature (Scott, 1972, Eisenstadt and Roniger, 1984). Increases in urbanization, economic development, and the salience of competitive politics in much of the developing world eventually led scholars to shift their attention to examining how these exchange relationships functioned within the context of competitive politics. As early as 1968, Weingrod stated that "patronage in the anthropologists' sense [i.e., about interpersonal relationships] appears to be increasingly a historical phenomenon, while

hews quite closely to an emerging consensus on the definition of clientelism in the most recent wave of writing on the topic.[14] Clientelism is thus distinguished by the *simultaneously* individualized and contingent nature of distribution. By individualized, I mean that clientelism's benefits are targeted at the individual voter, rather than at members of a certain group.[15] By contingent, I mean that in clientelist exchange, a voter's expected utility is tied to her individual political behavior: she believes that she can lose access to valued goods or services if she fails to support a clientelist incumbent.[16]

The term "clientelism" is sometimes used interchangeably with the words "patronage" and "vote-buying."[17] In this book, I define vote-buying as temporally limited to the exchange of small goods in the period immediately surrounding elections.[18] If voters fear their political behavior can be learned, then vote-buying is best considered a subtype of clientelism. If, on the other hand, neither citizens nor politicians expect to be able to identify or punish defectors, vote-buying is better understood as a form of campaigning.[19] I use the term patronage to refer to the exchange of public sector employment for political support or votes.[20] Both patronage and vote-buying can thus be considered subsets of clientelism, and I use this latter term throughout the book.

---

patronage in the political science sense [specific exchange for political support] becomes more relevant to contemporary issues" (Weingrod, 1968, 381).

[14] See, for example, definitions proposed by Chandra (2004), Kitschelt and Wilkinson (2007a), Piattoni (2001a), and Stokes (2009). For a similar conceptualization of the differences between clientelism and other forms of distributive politics, see especially Stokes et al. (2013).

[15] Some definitions of clientelism include distribution to small groups. If groups are sufficiently small and voters continue to believe that access depends on their individual votes, clientelism is certainly plausible in this setting. Given the difficulty of establishing the relevant group size a priori, I prefer a definition that focuses on individuals alone.

[16] Another school of thought in the literature on clientelism suggests that reciprocity, rather than coercion or fear, explains compliance with clientelist exchanges (Finan and Schechter, 2012, Lawson and Greene, 2013). Feelings of reciprocity undoubtedly help explain voting behavior in many settings. However, if reciprocity alone explains voter behavior when individuals receive targeted benefits, it will be hard to distinguish clientelism from constituency service or other noncontingent forms of individualized distribution. Research by Auyero (2000a,b) in Argentina suggests that reciprocity and fear frequently work together to help enforce the clientelist bargain. Given the difficulty of distinguishing these psychological mechanisms, I characterize clientelism as working largely through fear throughout this book. However, the theory of variation in clientelism developed in the chapters that follow does not hinge on this conceptualization.

[17] Some differences in usage are due to linguistic heritage, with "patronage" more common in the Anglophone world, while "clientelism" appears in the Romance languages (Piattoni, 2001a).

[18] Stokes (2009) and Schaffer (2007b) also make this distinction.

[19] For a discussion of this debate in the context of sub-Saharan Africa, see Kramon (2011).

[20] Other scholars have used a similar definition in work with a focus on the North American and European historical experience (Key, 1949, Shefter, 1977, Folke et al., 2011), as well as in some more recent empirical work on Latin America (Geddes, 1994, Gordin, 2002, Kemahlioglu, 2006) and Eastern Europe (O'Dwyer, 2006).

While clientelism may encompass vote-buying and patronage, it is analytically distinct from two other common forms of distributive politics: "pork barrel" politics and constituency service. Pork barrel politics is generally defined as the geographically concentrated distribution of benefits, where the costs are borne by the polity at large. These targeted redistributive benefits can of course be a useful political tool, and there is plentiful evidence that democratically elected politicians use geographically targeted spending to reward faithful constituencies in contexts from Brazil to Italy to the United States.[21] When politicians promise pork to reward their supporters, they are in effect making the distribution of government funds contingent on district level behavior. However, even when the delivery of pork is linked to a group's voting behavior, it cannot be made contingent on the vote choice of an individual within that group.[22]

Constituency service is the distribution of nonmonetary services, in particular facilitating access to the bureaucracy, to citizens on an individualized basis. Constituency service is generally understood to be open to all comers, and it does not carry with it expectations (or implicit threats) that assistance is linked to an individual's political identity or behavior.[23] Instead, constituency service works fundamentally by "generating goodwill among constituents who receive assistance" (Stokes, 2009, 11). Constituency service can have deleterious effects on the quality of government: for example, incumbent politicians who rely heavily on the practice for their reelection prospects might come to benefit from fostering bureaucratic inefficiency.[24] Nonetheless, constituency service (like pork) fundamentally works to get votes in the same way as any other broad-based policy proposal or position – by persuasion.[25]

---

[21] On Brazil, see Pereira and Renno (2003) (though see Samuels (2002) for a different view). On Italy, see Golden and Picci (2008), and Ansolabehere and Snyder (2006) illustrate this phenomenon in the United States.

[22] If that degree of contingency is possible, then clientelism, rather than pork, is a more accurate description. Some literature discusses the phenomenon of "vote banks," wherein politicians give benefits to local elites, who then in turn deliver the votes of a bloc of loyal voters (Bailey, 1963). To the extent that voters believe that future access to benefits depends on their individual voting behavior, we can think of this as "mediated clientelism," a subtype of clientelism wherein local elites capture most of the benefits. If voters receive no benefits at all for their votes, we should instead think of this practice as coercion, rather than an exchange.

[23] When these favors are granted conditional on political support, constituency service then crosses the line into clientelism. This may be the case for Italy – see Golden (2003). On the other hand, some relationships frequently referred to as clientelism may be closer to constituency service (see Baldwin [2013] on Zambia). The fact remains that beliefs about contingency are in the eye of the beholder, which is part of what makes clientelism so difficult to measure.

[24] On the U.S. case, see Fiorina and Noll (1978).

[25] As such, both practices thus fall squarely into the category of programmatic politics. Programmatic linkages include a diverse group of practices that run the gamut from the implementation of universal welfare programs to enacting policies that serve "rent-seeking special interests" (Kitschelt, 2000, 850).

In sum, all three practices – clientelism, pork, and constituency service – may be seen in some way as deviations from an ideal model of politics in which politicians would gain support wholly by advocating the rules-based implementation of policies that benefit the "general interest."[26] Nonetheless, clientelism's singular combination of individual targeting and contingency means that it has unique implications for governance and the nature of accountability relationships between citizens and politicians.

1.1.2 Governance and Accountability

Scholars have focused on two main dimensions of government performance: responsiveness and effectiveness.[27] A responsive government is one that "adopts policies that are signaled as preferred by citizens" (Manin et al., 1999, 9). In other words, responsiveness refers to whether the content of policies matches the substantive preferences of citizens. Effectiveness, on the other hand, refers to whether policies, regardless of their content, are carried out efficiently and effectively.[28] This is more likely to be a valence issue among citizens because irrespective of policy preferences, the vast majority of citizens will want policies carried out without favoritism, waste, or graft.[29]

The existence of strong ties of accountability between citizens and those who govern is crucial for achieving good governance along both these dimensions. When accountability relationships are strong, citizens will be able to differentiate governments that implement desired policies in an efficient manner from those that do not, and then, in the crucial step, reward or punish those governments as appropriate.[30] A politician's knowledge that he can be held accountable for his performance creates incentives for him to be both responsive and effective.

If we accept that strong accountability relationships are crucial for good governance, this then raises the question of what explains the strength of

---

[26] As Piattoni (2001a, 3) states, this is an idealized vision of politics, and even if it were possible to discern the general interest, all democracies cater at least in part to particularistic interests.

[27] See Putnam (1994, 63).

[28] In a number of works, Putnam (1973, 1994) uses the term effectiveness interchangeably with "bureaucratic responsiveness." I employ the former because it more readily encompasses practices like corruption, and it allows us to acknowledge that politicians, not only bureaucrats, can influence how public policies are carried out.

[29] Of course, in some cases, a citizen may prefer that an exception be made to a given policy if that exception will favor her. Nonetheless, if she would condemn that same exception if made for others, this suggests a preference, at least in principle, for the "fair" implementation of policy.

[30] See also Przeworski et al. (1999) and the definition of "electoral accountability" advanced by Mainwaring (2003). In the words of Przeworski, Stokes, and Manin, accountability requires that citizens can "discern representative from unrepresentative governments," and "sanction them appropriately" (Przeworski et al., 1999, 10).

those relationships. Democracy itself is perhaps the most obvious answer.[31] There are many reasons to expect that leaders are more readily held to account within democracies as opposed to other types of regimes. The very definition of accountability requires that politicians can be sanctioned if they do not act in the interest of citizens. Democratic elections institutionalize the communication of preferences and provide a natural opportunity for citizens (at minimal risk or cost to themselves) to exact such a sanction if they so choose.

While admitting that democracy can facilitate accountability, it is a premise of this book that democracy is not sufficient to ensure that citizens can effectively hold leaders to account.[32] There are a number of conditions under which citizens' ability to distinguish good from bad government or to sanction poor performance might be disrupted, even in a well-functioning democracy. At the individual level, learning about the actions of government may be made difficult by lack of political interest or knowledge. Geographic isolation or a sparse media environment can limit access to information, even among those who seek it out. Even where individuals (and the media) are heavily invested in acquiring (and disseminating) information about government performance, a government's actions and motivations are not directly observable. As in a classic principal–agent problem, it is difficult for a citizen to know if a bad outcome is the result of poor decisions taken by the government or by exogenous shocks.[33]

Though some slippage in accountability may be unavoidable, even in a democracy, in other cases, politicians actively engage in practices that are designed to undermine accountability and responsiveness. For example, the practice of using official publicity to reward newspapers allied with the government and punish opposition news sources (Open Society Institute, 2005, Brown, 2011) seeks directly to shape the information citizens have available to evaluate incumbents. Similarly, when national leaders weaken independent auditing or ombudsman offices (Wrong, 2009), they aim to disrupt the flow of unbiased information to citizens. The focus of this book is clientelism – a practice that, at the local level, undermines citizens' ability to act on their judgments of incumbent politicians.

[31] See discussions in Manin et al. (1999, 4) and Powell (2004, 92).
[32] Although not the focus of this book, it is also the case that accountability can be achieved without democracy. Even in the absence of free and fair elections, political leaders may face moral pressures to perform well or fear the sanction of citizens not at the ballot box, but in the streets. For compelling examples of how some measure of accountability can be achieved in nondemocratic contexts, see Tsai (2007) on China and Reinikka and Svensson (2005) on Uganda.
[33] Empirically, phenomena such as persistent corruption (Lambsdorff, 2006), widespread criminality among democratically elected politicians (Della Porta, 2001, Golden and Chang, 2001, Golden and Tiwari, 2009, Vaishnav, 2012), and the reversal of mandates (Stokes, 2001) all illustrate the possibility that democratic government can fail to be responsive or efficacious.

1.1.3 How Clientelism Undermines Accountability

A key requirement of accountability is that a citizen's assessment of the performance of those in power is reflected in her political behavior, including her vote. Clientelism threatens that requirement by reducing the issue space in which some citizens act to the question of access to individualized goods. When clientelism works, citizens believe that their access to highly valued goods is contingent on their *individual* political behavior. When this is the case, the desire to maintain access may become the overwhelming determinant of the vote and other political behavior. As a result, an individual's ability to use her political voice to express her preferences on a government's overall performance will be sharply curtailed.[34] Clientelism in a sense forces clients to become single-issue political actors, and the votes that clients cast "carry little information about their interests" (Stokes, 2007a, 90).[35]

From a normative perspective, we need not be alarmed if some citizens in a democracy make political decisions based on a single issue alone. When undertaken willingly, single-issue voting is not in and of itself detrimental to accountability. However, in the case of clientelism, the belief that access to valued goods can be tied to individual behavior casts doubt on whether such votes are fully free. Clientelism creates a fear of being punished for individual political behavior, and this fear makes possible scenarios where voters might overwhelmingly prefer a challenger and yet continue to vote for an incumbent, thus keeping the latter in power.[36]

By weakening accountability, clientelism is also likely to undermine government responsiveness and effectiveness. Manin et al. (1999, 9) note that responsiveness "is predicated on the prior emission of messages by citizens." When citizens vote, campaign, or turn out at rallies for a clientelist politician, it may be said that they are sending messages that they support his policies and perhaps even the practice of clientelism itself. At the same time, clientelism can lead citizens to take these political actions to maintain access to some valued good, regardless of their views of clientelism or public policy. Considered in this light, the message that clients appear to be sending might be quite different from that they would like to send. If clientelism can coexist with responsiveness, it is surely a diminished form of responsiveness.

Further, by diminishing policy responsiveness to clients, clientelism will thereby increase the relative policy responsiveness to other groups of citizens.

---

34 In fact, Stokes (2005) argues that clientelism actually makes citizens accountable to a clientelist politician for the former's political behavior – she calls this "perverse accountability."

35 Such a vote does, of course, communicate the client's interest in maintaining access to the good. However, the link to individual behavior makes that interest paramount above all others, potentially changing the weight citizens might otherwise attach to various aspects of government performance.

36 I elaborate on this type of scenario in my discussion of the individual client's calculus in Chapter 2. See also Diaz-Cayeros et al. (2003) for a model of this dynamic with reference to Mexico under the PRI (the *Partido Revolucionario Institutional*).

This has particularly important implications because of the sociodemographic profile of clients. While any practice that undermines the secret ballot or free public expression is likely to change the behavior of those who fear their votes might be observed, this need not necessarily alter the content of public policies.[37] Clientelism, however, overwhelmingly targets the poor, a group that is likely to have shared economic and policy interests. As a result, we should expect clientelism to systematically alter the ways in which the interests of the poor are reflected in policy debates and policy design (Stokes, 2007a). Indeed, there are many who argue that clientelism is likely to undermine the implementation of existing public policy and shift the types of policies governments carry out.[38]

Clientelism should also weaken government effectiveness. Whenever ties of accountability are undermined, incumbents will enjoy more leeway to govern *in*effectively. By prompting clients to become single issue voters, politicians enjoy a higher probability of avoiding punishment for failings of any type, from inefficiency to corruption. Clientelism is likely to have a particularly pronounced impact on government effectiveness within the sphere of local politics. The intense personal involvement that clientelism demands from politicians at the subnational level necessarily means that local, clientelist incumbents have less time and effort available to devote to all other tasks of governing. This is not to argue that the absence of clientelism guarantees effective, efficient government. Nonetheless, when clientelism is eliminated, this at least creates the possibility of a more neutral, rule-guided implementation of public policies. In the absence of clientelism, a bureaucrat like Graciela, from the introductory paragraphs of this chapter, would not be engaged in a battle with her town's mayor over the allocation of social welfare benefits. Instead, she might, like her counterpart Carolina, be in a position to implement social policy relatively insulated from political pressures.

1.2 WHY SOME INCUMBENTS OPT OUT

Although a troubling practice from the perspective of democratic theory, the discussion thus far paints clientelism as a useful one from the perspective of an incumbent politician in subnational government. Nonetheless, as the opening paragraphs of this book illustrate with respect to Argentina, clientelism in local governments is widespread, but it is not universal. What might explain that variation – and, more generally, what might explain variation in the use

---

[37] For example, imagine a practice that undermined confidence in the secret ballot for a representative group of citizens. Even though it is clearly a violation of democratic norms, such a practice would have little expected effect on election results or policy outcomes.

[38] See, for example, Medina and Stokes (2002), Fox (1994), and Stein et al. (2006, Chapter 3). On the other hand, note that others argue that clientelism can play a functional role in a democracy, especially from the perspective of regime stability and even redistribution (Valenzuela, 1977, National Endowment for Democracy, 2010).

of clientelism by incumbent politicians within the same country, the same province, or the same political party? The existing literature on clientelism has devoted most of its efforts to understanding the dynamics of clientelism where it is practiced. This book focuses on a prior question: in a context where clientelism is widespread, when should we expect politicians to opt out of the practice? This book argues that the joint presence of high levels of political competition and a large nonpoor population creates incentives for politicians to eschew clientelism. To understand the logic underlying this argument, we have to reconsider *whom* to consider in a theory of clientelism.

Almost universally, scholars of clientelism treat and analyze the practice as an exchange between politicians and their poor clients.[39] In both older and more recent works on clientelism, poverty, either directly or when manifest through income inequality, is cited as a powerful predictor of clientelism.[40] Whether because of their posited shorter time horizons or the greater marginal utility they attach to small material payouts, the poor are overwhelmingly identified as the target of clientelist practices. I concur that the interaction between politicians and poor clients is at the core of clientelism. However, to fully understand politicians' incentives to use clientelism, we need to consider how the practice may affect the voting behavior of nonclients.

Although the nonpoor are not typically a party to clientelist exchange, I argue here that clientelism is likely to engender direct electoral costs – what I call "audience costs" – in terms of political support from these constituents.[41] Previous work has highlighted the possible indirect costs of clientelism along with other redistributive strategies.[42] Most models of distributive politics assume that voters will reward politicians for targeting resources to their own group and (concomitantly, because of fixed budgets) punish redistribution to others.[43] I argue that the use of clientelism in policies targeted at the poor imposes its own electoral costs that are separate from any costs of redistribution per se.

There are two possible sources of these direct costs of clientelism. First, the nonpoor might view clientelism as a negative signal of the quality of

---

39   With respect to a related phenomenon, Shefter (1977) is an exception. In his influential study, he points to the relative influence of two competing groups – a "constituency for bureaucratic autonomy" and a "constituency for patronage" – in explaining differences in the use of patronage across countries. Banfield and Wilson (1963) also develop a similar intuition in their discussion of changes in urban politics in the United States.

40   See, for example, Huntington (1968), Scott (1969), Robinson and Verdier (2002), and Brusco et al. (2004), although see Lyne (2007, 2008) for an exception. This intuition dovetails with the modernization literature that points to the importance of development for good performance in general.

41   I thank Richard Snyder for suggesting this phrasing.

42   For example, Magaloni et al. (2007) argue that, given a budget constraint, spending on clientelist "goods" directed at the poor necessarily decreases the pool of resources available for spending on public goods directed at the middle class.

43   Most notably, Cox and McCubbins (1986) and Dixit and Londregan (1996).

government performance more generally and therefore object to clientelism due to self-interest. Middle-class voters, even if not beneficiaries of the small valued goods and services that may be distributed via clientelism, are consumers of government products and services of many types, ranging from road maintenance to local security.[44] To the extent clientelism serves as a signal of low-quality government performance, these nonclients are unlikely to support a politician who relies on it. Second, middle-class voters might reject clientelism on moral grounds and decline to support a politician who uses it, regardless of whether clientelism has any direct effect on their material well-being. They may believe that it undermines democratic values by preventing clients from enjoying autonomy over their political choices.

Of course, poor voters might share these same moral objections to clientelism or worry that the practice undermines government performance. However, a poor voter faces countervailing pressure to support a clientelist politician when she believes that her future access to valuable goods depends on her political behavior in the voting booth and beyond. It is precisely this conditionality that makes clientelism such an effective vote-getting tool among the poor. In contrast, the nonpoor are unlikely to face such pressures. For these citizens, the drawbacks of clientelism should create strong incentives to vote against politicians who rely on it. Clientelism, then, is likely to create an electoral tradeoff, between votes won from poor clients and lost from the nonpoor.[45]

How will politicians respond to this electoral tradeoff? At the most basic level, demographics may dictate whether the electoral benefits of clientelism outweigh its costs. However, not all politicians will find the tradeoff clientelism creates equally relevant. As V.O. Key noted with respect to the American south, high levels of political competition heighten the electoral imperative and increase politician effort.[46] In contrast, low levels of competition are likely to insulate a politician from these conflicting demands. As a result, I argue that politicians are most likely to opt out of clientelism when the middle class is large *and* when political competition is high – that is, when the electoral imperative coincides with high costs of clientelism. When high levels of competition are paired with a largely poor population – and hence

---

44 I acknowledge that not all of the nonpoor are middle class. Wealthy residents may be able to effectively buy private provision of many government services and thus will not be affected by the quality of those services. In most settings, this group will be numerically small and thus have limited direct electoral impact. In addition, they may still have moral objections to clientelism.

45 Though poor voters left out of clientelist exchange may be another source of opposition, politicians are likely to use a number of strategies to broaden their base of clients among the poor as widely as possible. See the discussion in Chapter 2 of this book and in Chubb (1982) and Szwarcberg (2008).

46 See Cox et al. (1998) for more recent work that builds on Key's insight. More broadly, competition is often associated with improved government performance (e.g., Geddes (1994), Chhibber and Nooruddin (2004), Grzymala-Busse (2007), De la O (2014), and many others).

	Low political competition	High political competition
Mostly poor	Clientelism not related to social structure	*High* likelihood of clientelism
Mostly nonpoor		*Low* likelihood of clientelism

FIGURE 1.1. Competition, poverty, and clientelism: Expectations.

the electoral benefits of clientelism are most pronounced – the incentives for clientelism should be at their highest. In other words, while political competition dampens the incentives for clientelism in some contexts, it can heighten those incentives in others.[47] In contrast, in the presence of limited political competition, constituent demographics are unlikely to be strongly correlated with the use of clientelism. The interaction between poverty and competition is thus at the heart of my theory. Figure 1.1 summarizes my main theoretical expectations.

I also explore how this interaction may itself be modified by partisanship. The dynamic outlined in the previous paragraph assumes that politicians from all parties experience the costs of clientelism – and therefore that the fear of suffering these costs may lead some to abjure clientelism. However, in contexts where party support is closely tied to social class, politicians from certain parties may have only a limited baseline possibility of receiving middle-class votes, regardless of how they perform in office. For politicians from such parties, the incentives to avoid clientelism fostered by high competition and a large nonpoor population may be somewhat muted because of this demand-side dynamic of clientelism. Separately, some parties (but not others) may bring with them entrenched networks that facilitate clientelism and that are not easily discarded (or adopted by other parties). This may affect the supply of clientelism, regardless of levels of competition.[48]

---

[47] My work thus builds on work of a few others who also develop the intuition that the interaction between competition and economic well-being should be important for explaining clientelism (Kitschelt and Wilkinson, 2007a, Magaloni et al., 2007). Both these works have a somewhat different theoretical focus, as they seek to explain the mix of programmatic and clientelist strategies, rather than the reliance on clientelism, or not, by local incumbents. In addition, both explanations rely on the importance of a budget constraint for explaining this interaction, whereas the theory I introduce here relies on the idea of the audience costs of clientelism to generate this interaction.

[48] These two possibilities suggest that partisanship might matter through either a level effect or an interaction effect. See Figure 3.2 in Chapter 3 for a visual depiction of these different dynamics.

1.2.1 Alternative Explanations

The theory outlined thus far draws heavily on two long-standing schools of thought as to the causes of improved government quality and increased accountability within democracies. The first points to political competition as an important source of good governance, while the second has emphasized the role of social structure. My own theory argues that competition and a large middle class jointly provide the impetus for local incumbents to reject clientelism. I also engage with and test, to the extent possible, explanations from three other approaches to the study of the quality of government. These explanations explore how institutions, the state role in the economy, and civil society, respectively, may shape the quality of governance.

Beginning with the first, both political scientists and economists have argued that some institutions facilitate accountability more than others, although precisely which institutions are best for accountability remains an unsettled question. For example, there is an ongoing debate about which national-level electoral institutions are most conducive to citizen control over politicians.[49] Similarly, a substantial body of theoretical and empirical work reaches mixed conclusions about whether institutions that increase power outside of the center state – like federalism and decentralization – improve accountability or not.[50] The subnational empirical approach I adopt in this book allows me to hold institutions largely constant. The task of exploring the extent to which institutional design can explain variation in clientelism at the local level might ultimately build on multiple subnational studies of the type carried out in these pages, or on empirical work within a country with more substantial subnational institutional experimentation.

Other explanations of the quality of government have focused on the role of the state in the economy. A long intellectual tradition rooted in economics argues that the larger the state role in the economy, the greater the opportunities for the state to exploit citizens and block paths to accountability.[51] These types of arguments have resonated with other social scientists whose work focuses more directly on issues of clientelism and patronage. Kanchan Chandra, writing on India, and Kenneth Greene, focusing mostly on Mexico, both argue that state control of resources helps incumbents cultivate and maintain clientelist relationships with their constituents.[52]

---

49   See contributions by Persson et al. (2003), Kunicova and Rose-Ackerman (2005), Chang and Golden (2006), and Tavits (2007).

50   See Weingast (1995) and Rodden and Rose-Ackerman (1997) for different perspectives on this debate. Bardhan and Mookherjee (2006c), Wibbels (2006), and Treisman (2007), provide excellent summaries of the literature.

51   For theory and evidence on this point, see de Soto (1989), Goel and Nelson (1998), and Fisman and Gatti (2002).

52   See Chandra (2004) and Greene (2007). Note that other scholars have argued the opposite – that a larger state that offers more generous benefits is more likely to be able to marginalize local power brokers engaged in particularistic politics (see Wolfinger (1972) for this argument

Finally, a group of scholars call attention to the possibility that non-state actors can help citizens control the state and improve its responsiveness to citizen preferences. The mechanisms through which civil society might improve governance range from its role in disseminating information and making legal claims to the more indirect path of moral pressure.[53] The argument that civil society can serve as the driver of good governance was notably advanced in Robert Putnam's 1994 volume, *Making Democracy Work*, where he tested this hypothesis against subnational data from Italy. An important stream of the literature on civil society has maintained this subnational focus, and the argument has also gained traction with policy makers focused on improving service provision to the poor (World Bank, 2004). Both of these factors mean that this book provides a particularly compelling empirical setting in which to test this hypothesis.

To test my own theory against these alternative explanations, I rely on original data on the implementation of an important social welfare program across a sample of Argentine municipalities, along with the analysis of a large national survey and an original survey experiment of Argentine residents. To preview my findings, I find no evidence that political competition or social structure in isolation can explain differences in the use of clientelism across the municipalities in the dataset. In contrast, my data analysis offers substantial support for the hypothesis that these are important predictors of clientelism in *interaction* with one another. I find no evidence for the claim that the state role in the economy structures clientelism and some limited evidence to support the claim that a stronger civil society will decrease the incidence of clientelism.[54] Even controlling for these possible effects, the empirical analysis presented in Chapter 5 continues to support the theory's main hypotheses. Next, I explain my empirical approach in more detail.

1.3 A SUBNATIONAL APPROACH IN ARGENTINA

Subnational political dynamics are more important now than ever before. As has been amply documented elsewhere, recent decades have seen a marked increase in the power and relevance of local governments across the world.[55] As Treisman (2007, 1) puts it, "[f]or anyone who might not yet have noticed, political decentralization is in fashion." This fashion is particularly

in the context of U.S. politics). I return to this debate in the conclusion, where I use a comparison of the Argentine case with that of Brazil and Mexico to speculate on how state size might be related to clientelism.

53 For evidence from Brazil, Mexico, and Latin America more broadly, see Peruzzotti and Smulovitz (2006), Ferraz and Finan (2008), and Cleary (2010).

54 Data limitations mean that my measure of the state role in the economy is a very imperfect proxy; I discuss this in more detail in Chapters 4 and 5.

55 See, for example, Burki et al. (1999) on Latin America and World Bank (2005) on East Asia, and various cites in Treisman (2007, 2–4).

pronounced in Latin América, in spite of its longstanding centralist tradition (Velíz, 1980). The third wave of democratization in the region that began in the 1980s was followed by meaningful decentralization in many countries, including those – such as Argentina, Brazil, and Mexico – that had been federal in name only for long periods of their histories. In Latin America as a whole, fiscal decentralization has advanced rapidly; the subnational share of expenditures for a group of eight countries increased from 16% in 1980 to 29% in 2000 (Falleti, 2010, 7). A growing literature on the causes and consequences of decentralization attests to the importance of the phenomenon in the region.[56] Fiscal decentralization was accompanied by political and administrative decentralization, as well. Mayors and governors throughout Latin America are now directly elected and in many cases exercise real political power.[57]

The increased budgetary, decision making, and political power exercised by subnational politicians is widely believed to have significant consequences within and beyond the local sphere.[58] Nonetheless, most of the existing literature focuses on the economic or fiscal dimensions of decentralization. We still know very little about the conditions that affect how newly empowered local officials will exercise their power in other arenas or the consequences of decentralization for the quality of local democracy. This is especially true of the municipal level. With a few important exceptions within and outside Latin America, most work on decentralization has focused on the state or provincial level, rather than on municipalities.[59]

Substantively and methodologically, a focus on subnational politics has advantages for a study of clientelism that go beyond the typical benefits of subnational comparative work.[60] Clientelism is inherently a local-level phenomenon. Recall that clientelism is different from pork and other forms of distribution because of the individualized, contingent nature of clientelist exchange. As a result, clientelism requires that voters are in personal contact with those offering them goods or services in return for their support. Perhaps inevitably, such communication transpires at the local level. Even when clientelism is part of a national-level electoral strategy, it is very likely that local elected officials and political brokers are those who are in direct contact

---

56 See, among many others, Willis et al. (1999), O'Neill (2003), Montero and Samuels (2004), and Eaton (2004).

57 See Falleti (2010, 6–11) for a concise summary of these trends in the region, with particular attention to Argentina, Brazil, Colombia, and Mexico. As she points out, not all decentralization reforms actually empower local government officials.

58 See, for example, Remmer and Wibbels (2000), who show how subnational policy choices affect prospects for national economic adjustment, and Weitz-Shapiro (2008b), who demonstrates a correlation between local government performance and citizen satisfaction with democracy and government as a whole.

59 Important exceptions include Grindle (2007), Pasotti (2009), and Falleti (2010).

60 See King et al. (1994) and Snyder (2001) for clear statements of the general advantages of a subnational approach.

with voters. In addition, subnational measurement improves the ability of a researcher to accurately code cases (Snyder, 2001). This is especially useful when the phenomenon of interest is, like clientelism, hard to measure and sometimes purposefully hidden from view.

Consistent with clientelism's inherently local character, many studies of clientelism to date have been site-specific, and in that sense subnational.[61] However, this subnational focus has rarely been simultaneously comparative. With a few recent exceptions, studies of clientelism have not focused their attentions on variation in the practice across subnational units within a single country.[62] A study of clientelism that is *both* subnational and comparative in nature can thus advance our understanding of how and why politician reliance on clientelism can vary, even within a single country context.

The choice of that context – Argentina – is in many ways a natural one for the study of clientelism. Since the resurgence of the academic study of the phenomenon in the last decade, clientelism has received greater attention in Argentina than in any other single country.[63] This attention may reflect the relative pervasiveness of the practice in Argentina. Although cross-country measures of clientelism are scarce, in a new cross-country dataset, Argentina is ranked as highly clientelist using a variety of metrics.[64] Similarly, Argentina typically ranks comparatively highly on other measures used to proxy for clientelism, such as corruption.

Both historical and institutional circumstances contribute to the widespread reliance on clientelism in Argentina. The country's two largest parties

---

[61] Work by Dianne Singerman on exchange relations in Cairo's slums (Singerman, 1995), Judith Chubb's work on patronage and clientelism in Naples (Chubb, 1982), and Javier Auyero's analysis of clientelism in a large city on the outskirts of Buenos Aires, Argentina (Auyero, 2000b) are all illustrative.

[62] Those exceptions include work by Susan Stokes and coauthors and Mariela Szwarcberg. An alternate comparative approach to clientelism would be to focus on cross-national, rather than within-country, variation. Some recent studies of clientelism have moved in the direction of large, cross-national studies of the type analyzed by Keefer (2007) and developed by Kitschelt and his colleagues (Kitschelt et al., 2009). To achieve broad geographical coverage, these efforts measure clientelism using proxies (such as corruption or rule of law) or expert opinions on the behavior of national parties and politicians. This macro-level approach to data collection allows for the geographic comparison precluded by site-specific subnational studies. However, national-level approaches to clientelism are by definition removed from the site of exchange relationships between voters and politicians. Such approaches also ignore the possibility of within country variation in clientelism and, given data sources, likely reflect practices in capital cities and prominent regions.

[63] See, among others, Auyero (2000b), Levitsky (2003), Calvo and Murillo (2004, 2013), Brusco et al. (2005), Stokes (2005), and Szwarcberg (2008).

[64] See Kitschelt et al. (2009). As the data from that project are not yet publicly available, this is based on assessment of the visual presentation of their data in that paper. Using innovative survey techniques, Calvo and Murillo (2013) compare the extent to which access to partisan networks mediates distributive expectations among voters in Argentina and Chile. Although they find variation both within and across countries, their results confirm the widely held belief that clientelism is more widespread in Argentina than in Chile.

throughout the twentieth century – the Peronist, or Justicialist Party (PJ), and the Unión Cívica Radical (UCR) – are catch-all parties with clientelist origins and no clear ideological profile (Calvo and Murillo, 2004, 2010).[65] This is especially true of the Peronist party. The PJ has long been associated with the use of nonprogrammatic appeals to voters, both charismatic and through the individualized distribution of material goods.[66] In the 1990s, the individualized distribution of material goods gained importance, as the PJ relied on clientelism to maintain the party's appeal to poor voters in the face of a shift toward neoliberal economic policies and the decline of labor influence within the party (Levitsky, 2003). In addition, institutionally, Argentina is one of the few democratic countries that has not adopted the Australian ballot.[67] That is, although voters cast their ballots in secret, parties continue to produce their own ballots. These party-produced ballots may be distributed in advance of election day, which facilitates *quid pro quo* exchanges (Stokes, 2005).

While this book builds on the existing research on clientelism in Argentina, it uses the Argentine context to ask a new question about clientelism – what explains variation in the reliance on the practice within a single country? The apparent pervasiveness of clientelism in Argentina means that it poses a "hard case" for identifying pathways out of clientelism. If we can establish the conditions under which politicians will opt out of clientelism in Argentina, this suggests that these same conditions should be sufficient to prompt a departure out of clientelism in other contexts, as well.

Although clientelism may be more pervasive in Argentina than elsewhere, in other respects, the country's political practices share much with those of other relatively young, middle- and lower-income democracies. In recent years, scholars of these contexts have paid increasing attention to the weakness of formal institutions and the importance of informal institutions in structuring political behavior and outcomes.[68] Democratic "consolidation" in many of these countries has not meant the elimination of informal institutions and practices like clientelism, police violence, and illegal campaign finance. Argentina is no exception, and, as Levitsky and Murillo (2006, 14) argue, its history of "unstable and weakly enforced institutions" is typical of many countries outside of the long-standing wealthy democracies.

Argentina is also a particularly useful case for identifying and explaining *within* country variation in the power and persistence of informal institutions.

---

65 The data in Calvo and Murillo (2010) show quite strikingly the amorphous ideological identity of both parties in the current period. Note that, in spite of its long history, the UCR has suffered from decreasing political relevance in recent years, under pressure from the growing hegemony of the PJ, as well as younger parties from both the ideological left and the right.

66 On charisma, see Torre (1990) and McGuire (1997), while Plotkin (2002) elaborates on the historical role of indivdiualized distribution.

67 Some provinces in Argentina adopted the Australian ballot (or what in Spanish is referred to as the "boleta única") for the first time in the 2011 elections.

68 Levitsky and Murillo (2006), Helmke and Levitsky (2006), O'Donnell (1993, 1996).

O'Donnell (1993) calls attention to the fact that in many young democracies, "blue" areas, where the rule of law governs, are juxtaposed with so-called "brown" areas, where informal institutions actually rule.[69] Although O'Donnell's aim is not to offer a comprehensive explanation of when and why such brown areas persist, he suggests that they are often found in countries' economically and geographically peripheral areas. A similar intuition has been applied to the case of Argentina, where Gibson and Calvo (2000) contrast government practices in "metropolitan" versus "peripheral" regions. In this book, I use the Argentine case to test more nuanced predictions about the conditions under which one particular informal institution, clientelism, is most likely to persist or to become less prevalent. I argue that the interaction between poverty and competition, rather than peripheral status per se, explains differences in the quality of government across municipalities. Within Argentina, Chapters 2, 4, 5, and 6 draw on fieldwork and an elite survey in more than 125 municipalities in three provinces. These three provinces, Córdoba, Río Negro, and Salta, are drawn from both the country's historical "core" and its "periphery," and they were selected to represent a mix of social and political conditions. The municipalities within these provinces similarly reflect a range of political and economic realities.[70]

Finally, Argentina provides an excellent setting for exploring the subnational dynamics of clientelism within the realm of social policy. The recent rise of targeted social safety net programs in lower and middle-income countries has been accompanied by praise for a few prominent programs that have broken with traditions of clientelism in social policy through technocratic, centrally run administration.[71] Though this focus on top-down administration offers one model for improving governance, it leaves aside the question of what to expect in the many countries where national governments lack the political will or capacity to constrain clientelism in social policy in a top-down fashion. A focus on Argentina allows us to explore whether an alternative, subnationally driven path toward accountability in social policy can exist, and if so, under what conditions.

1.4 IMPLICATIONS FOR UNDERSTANDING THE QUALITY OF GOVERNMENT

The research described in the chapters that follow is deeply rooted in the empirical experience of small and medium-sized municipalities in Argentina. The range of empirical evidence afforded by a single country study points to

---

[69] His observation has resonated with scholars of South Africa (Munro, 2001), Colombia (Boudon, 1996), and Brazil (Brinks, 2003), among others.

[70] I discuss the selection of municipalities in detail in Chapter 4. Chapter 6, which tests the key assumption that non-poor voters reject clientelism, uses data from a large in-person survey and an original survey experiment, both of which drew respondents from across the country.

[71] Programs in Brazil and Mexico have received the most attention from scholars and policymakers. See Chapter 7 for a longer discussion.

broader conclusions with respect to the role that social structure and political competition play in shaping the quality of government performance. It also yields implications for how scholars might approach the study of decentralization and distributive politics theoretically and across a range of empirical settings.

Development and Governance

As noted previously in this chapter, the view that development and a growing middle class is good for the quality of democracy has been a dominant one in modern social science since the publication of Lipset's well-known contribution in 1959. The precise pathways that link development to accountability, however, remain unclear. This link may be due to the changing preferences of the middle class or the growing costs of providing discretionary goods to an increasingly prosperous public.[72] My work suggests another mechanism through which a growing middle class can create incentives for improved governance: the middle class reacts negatively to manipulative strategies used vis-à-vis the poor. In developing the idea of the audience costs of clientelism, I build on the work of a previous generation of scholars who highlighted the dislike of the middle class for related practices, such as patronage, and I provide the first systematic empirical evidence of these attitudes. Even while reinforcing the relevance of development, this work also suggests the need to exercise caution when making monotonic predictions about the consequences of development for accountability. I argue that it is not enough for the costs of clientelism to exist, but that they need to become relevant for politicians – something that is most likely to occur when political competition is high and within the context of a hospitable partisan environment. Increased prosperity matters for good governance only in interaction with other factors. Thus, this book suggests a new understanding of the conditions under which development can strengthen accountability.

The Limits and Opportunities of Competition

This book also engages with the large literature that posits that increased political competition improves performance. While I build on the long-standing idea that increased competition heightens politician incentives to get votes (Key, 1949), I highlight the fact that the desire for electoral success can have mixed consequences for the quality of government performance. On the one hand, this book reinforces the importance of elections as creating an opportunity for change in accountability relationships.[73] In the presence of a large middle class, intense political competition should provide the impetus for a departure from clientelism. At the same time, I argue that, like development, competition is not a panacea for problems of governance. When the middle class

---

[72]   Magaloni (2006) and Magaloni et al. (2007) emphasize this second point.
[73]   Magaloni (2006) makes this point with respect to elections under the authoritarian PRI rule in Mexico.

is small, competition and clientelism can easily coexist. This book thus contributes to a new literature that points to the limits of competition for improving accountability relationships between citizens and politicians.[74]

Distributive Politics

This book also makes two related contributions to the study of distributive politics. First, the theory and findings suggest that to understand the electoral implications of public policy, we must examine *how* policies are implemented, above and beyond what they distribute, how much, and to whom. In the empirical case that is the focus of Chapters 4 and 5, the very same benefits – boxes of food – are distributed in all the Argentine municipalities under study. This apparent uniformity in the distribution of private goods in all locations masks important variation. The manner through which distribution takes place – whether poor citizens' access to these goods is linked to political behavior or not – varies across space and has implications for the political behavior of recipients and non-recipients alike. Anticipating the potentially negative reactions of nonpoor voters, mayors who face high competition and have a large group of nonpoor constituents are much more likely than their counterparts to abandon the practice of clientelism. This is especially true for mayors from political parties that rely on the middle class for support.

My focus on the methods of policy implementation reinforces the long-standing view that voters consider more than a single dimension when casting their ballots. In particular, this study suggests that, in addition to ideology, voters may take into account politicians' competence, efficacy, or fairness in implementing policy.[75] In doing so, it recalls the admonitions of scholars of other policy arenas to look beyond the most readily available measure to understand the content and politics of public policy.[76] It also highlights that important variation can emerge in the de facto, rather than de jure implementation of policies, reinforcing the importance of informal institutions (Helmke and Levitsky, 2006).

On a second, related point, this book suggests the importance of broadening the range of actors we consider when evaluating the political causes and implications of public policy. I provide a theoretical framework and empirical evidence in support of the claim that nonpoor voters care about how policies directed at the poor are carried out. This appears to be the case even when

---

74 See Golden and Chang (2001) and Golden and Tiwari (2009), among others.
75 See Stokes (1963) for an early statement of the critique of unidimensional voting models, including an argument for the importance of valence issues in voter decision-making. Since that time, many theoretical models of voting have incorporated some dimension that is unrelated to the content of policy proposals – see, among others, Londregan and Romer (1993) and Ansolabehere and Snyder (2000). Though these models do not define valence as the extent to which policies are implemented "fairly," such a definition would fit into this existing framework.
76 On the politics of the welfare state, see Esping-Anderson (1989), Castles (2002), and Mares (2004), among others.

the budget for these policies is fixed and funded by other levels of government, and thus policy implementation does not impose clear direct costs on nonpoor voters.

In other words, certain policies and methods of policy implementation have "audience costs." In the literature on international relations, this term is used to denote the domestic political costs that leaders incur when they fail to carry through on military threats (Schelling, 1960, Fearon, 1994). I argue that even domestic policies may have an audience that may be willing to punish a politician not for the substance of a policy, but for how it is carried out. This framework also raises the possibility that a policy's "audience" – that is, not its direct targets – may reward a politician for particularly effective implementation, just as they may punish him for poor implementation.[77] These two points of emphasis – on the method of policy implementation and on the existence of audience costs – also suggest an alternative mechanism that can help explain prior findings that identified the sometimes null or negative electoral effects of spending on patronage and social programs.[78]

Advancing Theories of Decentralization

The resurgent interest in decentralization described in this section has also revived interest in two schools of thought concerning the consequences of decentralization for the quality of government and democracy.[79] On the one hand, beginning with the classic works of Tiebout (1956) and Oates (1972), scholars have advocated decentralization and the empowerment of subnational governments on the basis of economic efficiency and local governments' presumed superior ability to match voter preferences with policies. More recent work has expanded on the possible positive consequences of decentralization to include improved political accountability, as well.[80] At an extreme, some authors argue that decentralization may have positive consequences for such wide-ranging aspects of government performance as "transparency, accountability, responsiveness, probity, frugality, efficiency, equity, and opportunities for mass participation" (Crook and Manor, 1998, 2).

In contrast, others are more cautious about the political and economic consequences of decentralization. Campos and Hellman (2005) and Bardhan and Mookherjee (2002, 2006a), for example, highlight the importance of local conditions in shaping the consequences of decentralization. In some cases, the local political arena may empower entrenched elites or special interest groups. As O'Donnell (1993, 1359) describes it, in many young democracies,

---

77 Zucco (2013) provides one example of such "audience benefits." He shows that nonpoor Brazilian voters may have rewarded the incumbent party for its competent administration of a large social policy.
78 Brusco et al. (2006), Calvo and Murillo (2004).
79 See Manor (1999), World Bank (2004, 89–90; 186–191), Treisman (2002), and Bardhan and Mookherjee (2006b, 8–10), and for similar formulations of this well-known tension.
80 See Dillinger (1994) and Crook and Manor (1998).

subnational political dynamics are characterized by "personalism, familism, prebendalism, clientelism, and the like." In such contexts, decentralization can hardly be expected to improve democratic functioning or strengthen accountability.

This book addresses the need – identified by Campos and Hellman (2005) and Bardhan and Mookherjee (2006c), among others – to document not only the diverse possible consequences of decentralization, but to explain the conditions under which decentralization will have positive or deleterious consequences for the quality of governance. This book offers a novel theory and support for the claim that decentralization is most likely to improve accountability in localities that enjoy *both* competitive local elections and a large middle class.

1.5 A ROADMAP

The next chapter illuminates the dominant, clientelist mode of social policy implementation in Argentine municipalities. In doing so, it sets the stage for understanding the empirical and methodological approach taken in the remainder of the book. The chapter draws heavily on interviews and observational data to illustrate the strategies many local officials use to make clientelism work effectively as a vote-getting strategy among the poor. It also shows the range of activities that may serve as indicators of clientelism in the day-to-day administration of public affairs.

Having thus established how clientelism can and does work in many Argentine towns and cities, the rest of the book turns to the development of a theory and empirical testing of the book's central question: what explains variation in government accountability? Chapter 3 lays out the book's central argument, that a joint decrease in poverty and increase in competition creates incentives for politicians to opt out of clientelism. It also calls attention to the role of partisanship – from either a demand or supply side – in triggering those costs. Chapters 4, 5, and 6 then offer the main empirical tests of the theory. Chapter 4 lays out the rationale for a focus on social policy within the context of Argentina, provides details about a particular social program, and concludes with some initial empirical support for the theory. Chapter 5 presents various statistical analyses of original cross-municipal data to test the argument's predictions, as well as alternative explanations, with respect to variation in clientelism. It is here that I present the most direct evidence that the *interaction* between competition and poverty, in a hospitable partisan environment, is most strongly associated with incumbent departures from clientelism. I then turn to the theory's crucial assumption that the nonpoor will punish clientelism in Chapter 6. That chapter employs new evidence from two surveys – a large citizen survey and an original survey experiment focused on the middle class – in support of the claim that clientelism creates electoral costs.[81] The final chapter of the book turns to the comparative context and the macro-level determinants of clientelism. It seeks to understand how other countries in Latin America have succeeded in curbing clientelism in social policy even while Argentina has apparently failed to do so. It then offers some final reflections on the relationship between the nature of the state and prospects for government accountability.

[81] The former relies on data collected and generously shared by Ernesto Calvo and Victoria Murillo.

2

Making Clientelism Work: Politician Behavior and Voter Beliefs

A rich ethnographic literature has provided detailed and engrossing depictions of clientelism in a number of settings (Chubb, 1982, Lande, 1983, Auyero, 2000b). This chapter does not set out to replicate such an enterprise. Instead, it makes a distinct contribution to our understanding of clientelism by articulating the behaviors that must be carried out by politicians, and the beliefs that must be held by citizens, for clientelist exchange to be viable. With respect to the former, politicians must establish their identity as personal gatekeepers for benefits and goods funded by the government. In the first part of this chapter, evidence from field work in small towns and cities in Argentina illuminates how politicians facilitate clientelism by claiming credit for, and heightening a sense of scarcity around, the goods and services they distribute. The description of the range of behaviors this entails lays the groundwork for the original measure of clientelism employed later in the book. With respect to the latter, clientelism succeeds when citizens are willing to vote (or engage in other acts of political expression) on an instrumental basis, and further when they believe their political behavior can be monitored by politicians. The second half of this chapter draws on secondary data from a variety of settings to show that these conditions can be, and are frequently, met.

The empirical examples employed here focus on how politicians facilitate clientelism when distributing state-funded social assistance. This complements existing scholarly work that examines clientelism in the context of the distribution of small material goods immediately before elections (Brusco et al., 2004, Weber Abramo, 2004, Gonzalez-Ocantos et al., 2012) and public employment (Robinson and Verdier, 2002, Calvo and Murillo, 2004, Oliveros, 2013). Although all three types of goods can be and are deployed in clientelist exchange, state-funded social assistance should hold particular appeal for clientelist politicians. This is because clientelism is most likely to be a viable electoral strategy when the goods or benefits that can be exchanged are (1) valuable to citizens; (2) available to a relatively large number of citizens;

and (3) ongoing, yet reversible. To consider each in turn, a good must be of considerable value to a citizen if she is to consider access to that good the basis for her political behavior. Second, it must be fairly widespread if it is to serve as a vote-getting tool on a mass scale.[1] Finally, the temporal nature of a good is relevant to its usefulness for clientelism. From the perspective of a politician who uses clientelism, the ideal good is potentially ongoing – which increases its value and allows for the development of over-time exchange – and yet easily revocable, so that a client fears losing access to it.

State-funded social assistance is likely to meet the three criteria mentioned above. State-funded social assistance can take a variety of forms, including cash, food, and subsidies for access to health care or educational services, all of which address basic needs. Although the same type of benefits might be distributed in a one-time exchange immediately before an election, when they are distributed by an incumbent on an at least potentially ongoing basis, this further increases their value to recipients. This is especially true for those in structural poverty or those who face the likelihood of long-term unemployment and economic hardship.[2] Furthermore, although these benefits are valuable to recipients, they are relatively inexpensive from the perspective of the state. Their low cost means that they can be widely distributed and hence are relevant to a politician's vote-getting calculus.[3] Finally, social assistance funded out of state coffers also has a temporal nature that is particularly amenable to clientelism, as these benefits tend to be *potentially* ongoing and yet also subject to the possibility of withdrawal. As I illustrate later in this chapter, many citizens receive repeated assistance from their local elected leaders, whether through established programs or more informally, that does not come with assurances of continuity. This is especially true for informal

[1] In some cases, select benefits may be distributed to intermediaries who in turn organize mass support. In Argentina, for example, public employment is distributed to party activists who use their government positions to fund their actual full- or part-time employment doing party work (Auyero, 2000b, Szwarcberg, 2008, Oliveros, 2013). Nonetheless, even this type of intermediary requires that some other benefit or good be made available to larger numbers of citizens.

[2] In a context of poverty, regularity itself is of great value. On the negative consequences of income volatility for poverty traps and investment, see Dercon (2003), Fafchamps (2003), and Rosenzweig and Wolpin (1993). See also Wood (2003) on how the search for reliable income can encourage clientelism and other types of relationships of dependency.

[3] Data I collected from a subset of municipalities in the province of Córdoba in Argentina illustrate the difference in scale between safety net programs and public employment. In a sample of twenty-three municipalities, the average town distributed food from a large safety-net program to five residents for each resident employed at the municipality in any capacity. When we consider only temporary employees, whose positions are much more amenable to political manipulation, there are about thirteen food program recipients for each temporary employee. These data are from the first twenty-three municipalities (ordered alphabetically) in Córdoba included in the sample used for the elite survey described and analyzed in Chapters 4 and 5. Data on employment were collected from the provincial office in charge of municipal affairs until the head of that office restricted access to the data.

assistance, which can be withdrawn on a whim, but it can even be true for benefits from established social programs. All of this suggests that a focus on clientelism in the distribution of ongoing social benefits, including social programs, will help paint a more complete picture of how clientelism works.

2.1 THE IMPORTANCE OF POLITICIAN DISCRETION

Although subnational incumbents can use the distribution of social assistance as a medium for clientelist exchange, it also presents some challenges for them to do so successfully. Clientelism depends fundamentally on voter belief in politician discretion, and government funded social assistance – and in particular, social safety net programs – may challenge that crucial belief for a number of reasons. First, politicians are in fact likely to enjoy less discretion over public monies, which are almost always subject to at least some minimal controls, than over their own private or party funds. With respect to social welfare programs in particular, these are generally destined for certain populations; if this targeting is specific and strictly enforced, it will limit a politician's freedom to select beneficiaries using a political logic. At an extreme, it might eliminate a politician's discretion entirely. Second, especially as compared to the distribution of benefits funded privately or by political parties, voters who receive government-funded benefits might be more likely to perceive these benefits as entitlements that cannot be easily withdrawn.[4] In some cases, voters might believe that decisions about how to allocate – and withdraw – government benefits are largely technocratic or insulated from the whims of the politician of the moment. Combined, these sorts of perceptions mean that a voter is less likely to believe that a local politician is responsible for her benefit or to fear that this benefit could be withdrawn in retaliation for political behavior. Maintaining these beliefs is crucial to the functioning of clientelism – regardless of what is distributed.

In light of these challenges, local politicians can take certain actions to increase the likelihood that voters believe that politicians are responsible for granting and withdrawing valuable benefits. In particular, politicians who rely on clientelism can effectively claim credit for the goods they distribute by concentrating decision making and politicizing nonelected officials. They can also foster a sense of scarcity around these goods that makes their future distribution appear uncertain by making access unpredictable and irregular. I draw on observations from field work to illustrate how politicians in small and medium-sized Argentine towns and cities pursue each of these strategies.

---

4 Nelson (2000, 56), for example, refers to the role of "entitlement psychology" in the case of pensions, and we might expect that many government programs create some sense of entitlement.

2.1.1 Credit Claiming

Observers of clientelism in diverse settings emphasize the crucial role that credit-claiming plays in clientelist exchange. Voters are most likely to change their political behavior in return for some valued good when they believe that a given politician is in fact the gatekeeper who controls access to that good. To establish their identity as gatekeepers, politicians must effectively appropriate credit for goods they do not personally fund and, perhaps, whose distribution they do not control. Drawing on his work in Malaysia, but writing about clientelism more generally, James Scott describes the politician's point of view quite eloquently. In his words, "[e]very government decision that benefits someone represents an opportunity for someone to use that act to enlarge the circle of those personally obligated to him. To the extent he succeeds in representing his act as a personal act of generosity, he will call forth that sense of personal obligation that will bind his subordinates to him as clients" (Scott, 1972, 95, footnote 21). One observer of Italian politics in the postwar period suggests that Italian politicians shared a similar goal and aimed to claim credit personally for government policies: "[i]t is never the State or the national community that appropriates sums for this or that project, for the construction of house or schools, for the realization of public works or industrial programs: it is always thanks to the interest of this or that local deputy or the local secretary of the DC" (Tarrow [1967, 327], cited in Chubb [1982, 75]). Although he describes individualized benefits, Javier Auyero's description of how poor recipients attribute responsibility for what they receive in a large suburb of Buenos Aires echoes these words (Auyero, 2000a, 71, emphasis added):

The organization that grants a pension, offers a job, or gives out medicine or a food package is not the local, provincial, or national government but Matilde or Juan ... *[I]t is not the state that is perceived as the distributing agency but Matilde or Juan or some other broker.*"

Given the centrality of personalized credit-claiming to clientelism, we know surprisingly little about how it is achieved. How is it that a government official in Malaysia, Italy, or Argentina is able to successfully claim credit for what he does, creating the perception that he personally, rather than government as an institution, is responsible for the benefits or goods that he distributes? Desposato (2007, 105–107) suggests that the very fact of distributing private goods, such as scholarships or baskets of food, rather than public goods, such as roads or hospitals, makes credit claiming easier for politicians. Though this may be the case, private goods may also be distributed through large government programs not tainted by clientelism. Food stamps, scholarships, or cash transfers may be distributed through standard procedures by neutral bureaucrats and seem quite disconnected from recipient political behavior. The difficulty of appropriating credit for government programs should be especially acute for local incumbents when they administer programs that are funded by higher levels of government.

At the most basic level, a politician may directly (either privately or publicly) claim ownership and responsibility for the benefits he distributes, regardless of the origins of those benefits. Sometimes this credit claiming can be quite bold. Turning again to Judith Chubb's work on Italy, she reports that the fulfillment of long-deferred requests around election time is often accomplished with a note from a candidate claiming credit for the accomplishment. She quotes from one such note as follows: " 'I am pleased to inform you that – as a result of my personal interest in your problem – you will receive a subsidy of 5,000 lire. Vote DC' " (Chubb, 1981, 172). Such brazen credit-claiming occurs in the Argentine context as well. In 2001, for example, a public scandal emerged when the then-governor of the province of Buenos Aires distributed 800,000 pairs of shoes – imprinted with his signature on the tongue – to needy children.[5]

Of course, politicians are not always so direct in their credit claiming efforts. Clientelist mayors can also use a variety of other tactics to appropriate credit for social benefits in an individualized fashion. The workings of the municipality and the distribution of social programs can be structured so as to maximize the effectiveness of clientelism. In particular, concentrated decision making and the politicization of administrative personnel help Argentine mayors claim credit for the social benefits they distribute.

Concentrated Decision Making

In many of the small and medium-sized cities I studied, mayors (and their close political appointees) personally receive and decide on requests for inclusion into valuable government programs and other forms of social assistance. In my visits to such cities across the provinces I studied, I frequently sat in line with city residents waiting to be attended by either the mayor or, in cases where there was a close connection between the mayor and the top official in charge of social policy, by the head of the social welfare office. (I discuss the politicization of these officials in more detail in the following pages.) While waiting I noted repeatedly that, although other employees were present, residents had to wait to make their request to one of these two individuals. By concentrating the receipt of requests for benefits in their own hands, rather than allowing line bureaucrats or lower level officials to receive such requests, mayors thus become the public face of these benefits. When a mayor, or a top aide who is closely associated with him, receives a request for aid directly

5 Interestingly, the governor, Carlos Ruckauf, defended his action by comparing himself favorably to other politicians who "keep the footwear to distribute it during elections." (His distribution did not take place in an election year.) In another example, the mayor of San Fernando, in the province of Buenos Aires, distributed eyeglasses to children with his name printed on the sides of the glasses (Alconada, 2009).

from a constituent and immediately provides a response, he puts himself in a position to claim credit for this aid as an individual, rather than as a representative of government as an institution.

The town of La Merced, in the province of Salta, is illustrative of how this extreme personalization can shape the way social welfare benefits are distributed. When I arrived to the town on three separate occasions, all at mid-morning, a number of individuals were waiting to makes requests to Elena, a top official in the municipality's social welfare office (this number varied from about five to about twenty on different occasions). In general, the three staff people who sat in an area with two desks outside her office seemed mostly occupied with keeping track of the order of the line. Though they occasionally asked new arrivals the nature of their request, none of them began to actually evaluate or process those requests. Each resident had to wait to talk to the head to make his or her request directly. Up the stairs, a similar scene played itself out outside the mayor's office.

The concentration of decision making in very few hands requires, not surprisingly, an extensive time commitment from those few people (generally the mayor and his close associates) who are able to grant assistance. The apparent availability of mayors in these municipalities is sometimes so extreme as to seem almost absurd. In the town of La Merced, mentioned earlier, a large sign hangs in the main stairwell in the municipality building, which leads from the main courtyard to the second floor, where the mayor's office sits. A photograph of the sign is reproduced in Figure 2.1. It reads: "Mayor. Attention to the Public. Tuesday, Wednesday, Thursday and Friday. 7:30 to 12:30. Monday, 3pm to 7pm."[6] Although La Merced may be unusual in the fact that it advertises extensive mayoral availability so graphically, the degree to which this mayor was potentially accessible is not unusual. In an interview, the mayor's chief of staff in Villa San Lorenzo, a nearby town, estimated that the mayor of that town spends about 80% of his time "in contact with the residents," receiving requests of various types. In municipalities where the mayor personally receives requests for inclusion in various social welfare programs, such extensive availability to the public should not be surprising; in fact, given the concentration of decision making, the absence of such availability would make it nearly impossible for program benefits to be distributed and allocated.

This concentration of decision making power is likely to have profound effects on voter beliefs about how social aid is distributed. The line staff of municipal social welfare offices in Argentine municipalities may be permanent civil servants who retain their positions regardless of who is elected at the local or national level. A reliance on these employees to distribute benefits could foster the impression that the benefits are not tied to any specific administration

---

6 Mayors in the cities I visited rarely stuck to firm schedules (this is true of this municipality as well, in spite of the sign), further contributing to the sense that they maintained discretion over benefits, as I detail in the remainder of this section.

FIGURE 2.1. La Merced.

or individual. In contrast, depending almost exclusively on political appointees and the mayor himself blurs the lines of responsibility between the government as an institution and the particular politician in power at the moment. Especially in a setting where information about the national policy environment is scarce, the concentration of decision-making power in the person of the mayor and his close associates will encourage voters to believe that their present and future receipt of benefits depends on the whims of the politician, rather than on institutional rules or even anonymous bureaucrats. This belief is further reinforced by the frequent waiting and uncertainty about when requests can be made (let alone the extent to which they will be satisfied) that naturally accompanies the concentration of decision making in very few hands.

Politicization of Nonelected Officials

As elected officials, mayors are necessarily political actors. We can imagine that, in municipalities where these officials take center stage in the distribution of social welfare goods, voters are likely to believe that their continued receipt of such goods is a political decision. However, these mayors sometimes also rely on close officials to complement their own strategy of personalization and to reinforce the perception that government benefits are linked to political behavior. In many of the municipalities I visited, officials who headed the social welfare offices used a variety of tactics to signal the existence of a link between social welfare benefits and political behavior.[7]

---

7 It is still possible, although more difficult, for a mayor to use clientelism when nonelected officials are not politicized. Recall, for example, the town of Devoto, described in the

FIGURE 2.2. Campo Santo.

Some of these signals were visual, and hence apparent to any visitor to the social welfare offices. As described in the introduction, the office of Liliana, the head of the social welfare office in Campo Santo, displayed a large drawing of Juan and Eva Perón. This drawing, reproduced in Figure 2.2, was joined by photos of herself with the mayor, governor, and lieutenant-governor, all visible to anyone who sat across from her, as residents would regularly do in order to make requests for aid. Her office also prominently displayed a calendar with the campaign photo and motto of the lieutenant-governor, who was

introduction. In that case, mayoral intervention into program administration took place over the objections of Graciela, the social worker who held a top position in the social welfare office.

then running to succeed the serving governor, who was barred from reelection because of term limits.

In their interviews with me, top bureaucrats in these municipalities and others like them often emphasized their long history of interaction with and personal "closeness" to the mayor, as well. In Malvinas Argentinas, a municipality in Córdoba, both the mayor and a top bureaucrat in the social welfare office emphasized to me that they had worked together for a long time in the same faction within the Radical party before the mayor was elected. When I inquired how the bureaucrat and mayor resolved conflicts that might come up, the bureaucrat replied that "it's very rare that we don't agree" (Author interview, August 2006). In a small group of municipalities, at the time of my research, the head of the social welfare office was actually related to the mayor, an even clearer signal of the relationship between elected officials and the distribution of social benefits. In fact, the mayor and the top bureaucrat in the social welfare office of Malvinas Argentinas were also cousins. In other cases, familial connections were even closer. For example, in another municipality (San Lorenzo, in Salta), the mayor's brother headed the municipal social welfare office.

Placing a relative in charge of social welfare distribution is a clear signal of the mayor's involvement in social assistance, although it is not the only way to signal that involvement. So, for example, in the town of Cachi, in Salta, when the head was asked whether she was related to the mayor (as part of the survey analyzed in later chapters), she said no, but then explained to the interviewer that she and the mayor were neighbors. In Campo Santo, as mentioned in the introduction, the head of the social welfare office had previously worked for the mayor, when he was a provincial legislator, and said she had known him for twenty years, since she was seventeen years old. Residents of the small and medium-sized towns included in this study are likely to be well aware of these sorts of connections. This closeness, combined with the prominently displayed political paraphernalia in certain social welfare offices, sends a clear message to town residents who come to these offices asking for assistance. It also suggests that direct mayoral involvement in the administration of social policy and close ties between a mayor and head of social welfare are typically complements, rather than substitutes.

Although these various strategies broadcast the link between social welfare and politics, it is impossible to know whether, in their private conversations with beneficiaries, public officials in such municipalities claim that the mayor is personally responsible for government programs. Nonetheless, the extreme personalization of distribution in these places seems likely to foster such beliefs among residents. In addition, interviews with the head of the social welfare office in towns where this type of distribution prevailed suggests that the political nature of this exchange is indeed understood by voters. Though social welfare officials rarely claimed they initiated the exchange of goods for votes, a number of them made comments indicating that, at the very least, they were receptive to such exchanges. For example, a top official in the social welfare office in the municipality of Salsipuedes in Córdoba recounted to me a case in which a resident who came to ask to be included in a social welfare program pointed out that he came from a household with four voters. In response, the head related, "you start to think, well, four plus five … " before trailing off (Author interview, August 2006). Four votes from a single household, when combined with others like them, could make a difference in an election in a small town. In clientelist municipalities, mayors and their closest associates use the individualized distribution of social welfare assistance to claim credit and gain political support.

2.1.2 Manufacturing Scarcity

For clientelism to work, poor citizens must not only believe that politicians and their closest associates are personally responsible for the distribution of social assistance, but also that they are in a position to withdraw future assistance in retaliation for noncompliance with the clientelist bargain. These two beliefs are obviously linked, as a politician who exercises complete discretion over who receives benefits is by definition also in a position to decide who does *not* receive benefits. Voter beliefs about the loss of benefits are likely to be affected by the extent of their distribution. Where goods are scarce (or citizens believe them to be) this should heighten the plausibility of threats that they may be withheld at some point in the future. As a result, voters should be more likely to comply with their end of the clientelist bargain.

Once again, we can turn to the work of Judith Chubb to highlight the importance of scarcity to clientelism's effectiveness. In one emblematic quote, she cites the words of a national deputy from the Italian Christian Democrats as he explains the importance of "recommendations" (*raccomandazione*) for placement in the civil service. In his words, "I receive an average of 1000 *raccomandazione* per year. The important thing, however, is not to place 1000 persons per year – that is impossible and would be in any case counterproductive. You must place only 1 out of 20, 50 out of 1000. In this way you keep in subjection the 950 from the previous year together with the 1000 new supplicants of the current year" (Chubb, 1982, 91). Chubb argues that successful clientelism relies not on the widespread distribution of largess but, as this deputy suggests, in the skillful management – and even purposeful manufacture – of scarcity.

Encouraging voter belief in scarcity can be accomplished in a number of different ways. In fact, belief in scarcity can coexist with widespread assistance, as even where most poor individuals receive some form of government assistance, this assistance is unlikely to address their needs completely. In addition, belief in scarcity could also be the product of an unpredictable policy environment at the national level (regardless of the current extent of distribution).[8] Where the continued distribution of benefits is uncertain, the fear of losing benefits might prompt individuals to behave so as to maximize their chances of holding onto benefits at a future time period where benefits may no longer be so widespread. Here, I focus on two patterns of behavior at the local level that serve to reinforce a belief in scarcity. When access to decision makers is unpredictable and distribution of benefits is intermittent or irregular, voter perceptions of scarcity will be heightened.

Unpredictable Access

As already discussed, where mayors and their closest associates monopolize the receipt and granting of requests for social assistance, this facilitates the personal appropriation of credit for government programs. Where power is this concentrated, it should not be surprising that some mayors claim, as in the case of La Merced, to be available to the public for up to five hours on a daily basis.

Nonetheless, the mayor's actual availability in these towns is not as extensive as these signs would lead us to believe, and, even more importantly, tends to be highly unpredictable. Using as an example the case of La Merced, although a large sign in the municipal office building states the mayor's "office hours" in clear terms, and by the mayor's own accounting he spends much of his time receiving requests for aid from local residents, his actual availability does not match that publicized by the municipality. In trying to arrange an interview with him, I witnessed firsthand some of the delays a resident of the town might experience. On an initial visit to the town, I was unable to meet with the mayor, but his chief of staff informed me that he had placed me on the mayor's list of appointments for the next morning. He told me to arrive before eight o'clock the next day (the mayor's habitual arrival time) to maximize the probability that I would be able to meet with him. When I arrived at a quarter to eight the next morning, there were already eight people in line waiting to talk to the mayor. The mayor himself had already arrived, but was in meetings with different officials and was not yet receiving members of the public (myself included) who had come to have an "audience" with him. At 8:45, he finally began meeting the public, beginning with those individuals who had been held over from the previous day's list (courtesy of the mayor's chief of staff's efforts, I was among them). At 9:45, I was the third member of the public that the mayor spoke to that day. Before I went in to speak to the mayor, his secretary announced to those waiting that the mayor would be leaving early that day, and that those whom the mayor did not have time to meet with personally would be able to make their requests to his chief of staff instead. Those who

---

[8]   In the case of Argentina, national policy uncertainty in the realm of social policy is undoubtedly high. See Spiller and Tommasi (2003, 2007) for excellent discussions of the broader origins and consequences of Argentina's uncertain policy environment.

wanted to speak directly to the mayor would have to return another day to try again.

This type of unpredictability was typical of many of the municipalities where I conducted fieldwork. In La Merced, Campo Santo, and the other municipalities I discuss here, residents who wanted to request aid did not make appointments in advance, but instead they were free to simply show up at any time and wait. Though flexibility may have some advantages, it means that individuals have no way of anticipating how crowded an office will be when they arrive, or whether the head of social welfare or the mayor will happen to be available at the time they arrive to make their request.

This contributes to the type of scene I witnessed the first time I arrived for my scheduled interview with the head of social welfare policy in the city of La Merced. On that morning, about twenty people stood in the hallway outside the head of social welfare's office, waiting their turn to make requests.[9] This very public waiting is a feature I observed in many clientelist cities in Argentina. Surely a byproduct of the extreme concentration of decision-making power, it is also likely to foster a sense of resource scarcity among the poor. Long lines mean that those requesting aid must queue for long periods of time surrounded by others who are seeking the same or similar benefits, thereby accentuating the sense of competition for limited resources and perhaps concomitantly increasing the perception that other factors (such as political behavior) are relevant in the allocation of benefits.

It is difficult to establish intentionality in this context, and I do not claim that clientelist politicians purposefully seek to create long lines with the express purpose of fostering the perception among voters that political actors enjoy discretion over who receives government benefits. Nonetheless, long waits have a variety of consequences for voters' anxiety, perceptions of self-worth, and their assessments of the value of the awaited good.[10] Beginning with this last item, according to Brock's (1968) "commodity theory," unavailability (or scarcity) increases the value of products to individuals. Schwartz (1975) argues that long waits make those waiting feel unimportant and are associated with low social status. Maister (1985) highlights how different types of waiting affect anxiety, noting, for example, that uncertain and unexplained waits will increase anxiety more than certain and explained waits. As described in this chapter, the waiting common in clientelist settings is typically of the anxiety-inducing type. This anxiety is likely to be accentuated by the fact that, in

---

9 This is in a town with a population of about 8,000 residents, so 20 people is a substantial crowd.

10 Making others wait is also an expression of power; see Bourdieu (2000) on this point. Other authors have touched on the role of waiting in the context of the welfare state. Focusing in particular on the consequences of waiting for self-perception and political participation in the United States, see Lipsky (1980), Sarat (1990), and especially Soss (2002, Chapter 5). Auyero (2011) presents a compelling ethnographic account of waiting for welfare benefits in the city of Buenos Aires.

making repeated visits to government offices to request benefits, individuals are unlikely to know the extent of available resources and are bound to spend their time waiting along with others who are making similar requests.

As this case illustrates, concentrated decision making, combined with unpredictable access, greatly increases the amount of time residents must wait to make requests for social welfare aid. Residents sometimes make multiple trips to the municipal office with no guarantee that they will succeed in even *requesting* assistance, let alone that their request will be satisfied. The experience of repeated visits and public waiting that result from the unpredictability of access undoubtedly fosters a sense of scarcity around these valued goods.

Irregular Distribution

Another tactic available to foster a sense of scarcity is the reliance on the intermittent, irregular distribution of small benefits outside the structure of large social programs. Argentine provinces and municipalities frequently organize and fund social assistance to supplement that offered by the national government (Smulovitz and Clemente, 2004). The choices local politicians make about how to use the funds at their discretion also shape the extent to which a given municipality leads its residents to believe that welfare benefits are scarce.[11]

In municipalities where clientelist distribution is the norm, I observed that officials emphasize the distribution of small, low-value goods to individuals in response to specific requests. By handing out small goods to individuals in response to requests, municipalities in effect require poor residents to make numerous visits and repeated requests for aid. Returning to the case of La Merced, I conducted an interview with a top official in the office of social welfare during the course of a morning when she was receiving residents in her office. To illustrate the nature of the aid the municipality distributes, she explained to me the situation of the woman who had left her office immediately before I entered. According to the head, the woman had come in earlier in the day asking for some foodstuffs, in particular formula for her baby. The head showed me the copy of the purchase order she had written out for the resident, which authorized her to buy the formula, along with a few other items, at a local grocery store. The woman had returned to the office (right before my arrival) because the purchase order did not specify her preferred, name-brand formula, and the store owner would give her that brand only if it was listed on the purchase order. The resident had returned to the office to ask the head to add the brand name to the purchase order, which she did. In addition to her repeated visits in a single day, this woman would likely visit the municipality

---

[11] Nationally funded programs, although supposed to be more regular, sometimes take on an intermittent character, as well. For example, bureaucratic and funding delays mean that, although benefits from the food program analyzed in subsequent chapters are supposed to be distributed every forty-five days, actual distribution is far from consistent.

again within the month. After all, her baby was only four months old, and the purchase order authorized only a small amount of formula; she would undoubtedly return asking for more in the future.

This anecdote highlights the ways in which an "aid on demand" policy can heighten voter awareness of a politician's discretion. By distributing only small amounts of aid at a single time, this approach all but ensures that the very needy will make repeated visits to the municipality's social welfare office. Owing to the informality of the benefits, some, like the woman I saw in La Merced, will make repeated visits in a single day. More commonly, however, those in need will make multiple visits over the course of many months, frequently asking for a very similar type of aid. This will create longer lines and waiting times, perpetuating an air of scarcity among poor residents. Furthermore, this type of informal policy means that at each visit, the resident is subject anew to the politician or his associate's decision about whether or not to grant her aid – a decision that could have important consequences for the individual's well-being. As discussed elsewhere, even beneficiary lists of formally organized national and provincial social programs can and are frequently revised, and current beneficiaries are by no means guaranteed continued support. This ability to withdraw benefits is even more pronounced where no formal program exists. In that situation, a politician need not make any formal changes at all – from one month to the next, or one visit to the next, a politician or bureaucrat could plausibly stop distributing a benefit with no explanation at all.

Finally, note that the intermittent distribution of goods has the added benefit (from the perspective of a clientelist politician) of allowing these politicians to spread benefits widely while simultaneously manufacturing scarcity. Intermittent distribution allows politicians to help many more voters than would be possible if they were committed to the regular, consistent distribution of benefits to a single set of voters.[12] In open-ended interviews in municipalities that I categorize as relying on clientelism, the comments of political appointees and politicians repeatedly highlighted the ways in which intermittent distribution of benefits was compatible with the widespread distribution of benefits. So, for example, the Secretaria de Gobierno of La Merced estimated that "100%, or 99%, of the requests [for help from poor residents] are satisfied." He explained that not all requests are satisfied fully, but that residents who

---

[12] Szwarcberg (2008) documents two other strategies that serve the same goal of fostering widespread distribution while manufacturing scarcity. The first is the use of a "stand-by" list for public assistance – a list of potential beneficiaries who are expected to attend political rallies and provide political support in exchange for the chance to become actual beneficiaries at some time in the future. The second is the practice of rotating benefits among clients, taking individuals on and off the welfare rolls over time. Note that both strategies suggest that, rather than restricting distribution to a small group of supporters, clientelist politicians and their agents cast a relatively wide net among the poor in their search for clients. They do so by pursuing strategies that simultaneously spread benefits widely and foster an appearance of scarcity.

ask for help "are given a solution one way or another."[13] This intermittent
distribution to a wide variety of voters makes it possible for incumbents to
keep "in subjection" (to return to Chubb's terminology) a large number of
citizens at a relatively low cost.

2.2 CITIZEN BELIEFS AND BEHAVIORS

The previous sections have shown how local incumbents use government
funding – through structured social programs or informally – to make public
benefits compatible with clientelist exchange. Successful clientelism, however,
also requires certain assumptions about citizen beliefs and behaviors. In
particular, clientelism works when individuals are willing to use their political
voice instrumentally and believe that their political behavior can be monitored.
Beginning with the former, I argue that logic and evidence support these two
assumptions at the municipal level in Argentina. Note that I focus largely on
voting behavior as the key measure of expressed political support. Clientelism
frequently takes place in the context of long-term relationships where citizens
may fulfill their end of the "bargain" by displaying their political support in
a number of ways – including attending political rallies, publicly "declaring"
their preferences, convincing others to vote as well as, of course, in their voting
behavior.[14] In what follows, I focus mostly on voting behavior because it sets
a high bar for demonstrating my point; this is especially true with respect to
a citizen's belief in the possibility of monitoring, because most other political
behaviors are inherently observable. Furthermore, voting is of special interest
because it is the key political act in a democracy and the crucial one for
clientelism to succeed as an electoral strategy.

2.2.1 Instrumental Voting

As already noted, clientelism works when citizens are willing to exchange
their votes and other expressions of political support for material benefits or
services, even when this results in behavior at odds with a citizen's "true"
preferences. In other words, we must assume that, for many poor voters, the
value of material benefits will outweigh the value they attach to expressing
their ideology or partisan identity at rallies or other public settings, and, ultimately, at the ballot box. Given the long-standing interest in political science
in understanding both the expressive and instrumental components of voting
(Fiorina, 1976), an assumption that instrumental concerns will outweigh
expressive ones for poor clients deserves some explanation and elaboration.

---

[13] Author interview, August 2007. Although these claims of comprehensiveness of assistance
     should clearly be taken with a grain of salt, it is worth noting that these claims were
     concentrated in municipalities where other indicators also suggested that the mayor relied
     on clientelism.
[14] See Auyero (2000b), Szwarcberg (2009), and Nichter (2009) for examples.

It is worth noting that most early models of voting assumed the act had an instrumental character. Downs (1957), for example, posits that voters cast their ballots for whichever party yields them a more preferred policy platform, and that voters actually turn out to vote when the probability of affecting the outcome of an election, multiplied by the benefit an individual receives from victory of one party over the other, exceeds any possible costs of voting. As other scholars pointed out, given the near impossibility of affecting the outcome of an election in a modern democracy, this purely instrumental depiction of voting was at odds with the behavior of millions of citizens. In grappling with this apparent contradiction, a large literature emerged that highlighted the many ways in which voting might yield expressive utility.[15] As Fiorina (1976, 393) states, many voters in long-standing democracies vote for reasons as varied as the desire "to express solidarity with one's class or peer group, to affirm a psychic allegiance to a party, or simply to enjoy the satisfaction of having performed one's civic duty."

Although the term "expressive voting" is used mostly to explain why citizens turn out to vote at all, it can also be usefully applied to models of how voters choose candidates once they are in the voting booth. Note that even as models of vote choice have become more complex and acknowledge the multidimensionality of the voting decision, most still assume that, at the moment of casting his ballot, a voter acts as if he were the pivotal voter. Given the extremely small probability that a given voter in a modern polity will in fact be pivotal, we can think of the voter's decision as a type of expressive voting. This is true even when a voter's decision is driven by the desire for a material payoff targeted at some group of which he is a member. For example, Dixit and Londregan (1996) assume that voters consider both ideology (or partisan attachment), as well as consumption (the result of parties' "tactical redistribution") in deciding how to vote.[16] However, in their model, in contrast to the framework I rely on here, those tactical rewards are received by each member of a targeted group, regardless of his or her individual behavior. In other words, citizens vote for the party or politician they want to win the election out of a genuine desire to see their party (or politician) implement its platform and policies.[17]

This perspective is clearly useful for explaining voting behavior in many places. However, we should bear in mind the settings in which such models emerged – developed, long-standing democracies where most forms of particularistic politics were presumed to have fallen by the wayside. The need to emphasize expressive voting emerges from the fact that, in such a setting, an

---

[15] This literature is far too extensive to summarize here, but see Riker and Ordeshook (1968) for the classic statement.

[16] Similar multidimensional models of voting are presented in Persson and Tabellini (2000) and Lindbeck and Weibull (1987), among others.

[17] Stokes (2005) is an important exception to this type of modeling, as her model links individual consumption to individual voting behavior.

individual's vote has an almost zero likelihood of affecting her own material well-being. That is, this approach assumes that democracies are programmatic in the sense employed by Kitschelt (2000). Although benefits may be targeted to certain groups of voters through pork or other redistributive tactics, voters do not believe that the implementation of government policies is tied to *individual* behavior in the voting booth.

In contrast, in contexts where individual well-being is in fact tied to individual voting behavior (or where voters believe this to be the case), there is no reason to resort to expressive voting to explain citizen behavior. In fact, we should expect instrumental concerns to frequently dominate expressive considerations, including ideological preference or party loyalty. As Chandra (2007, 91) convincingly argues, expressive benefits pale when compared with concrete material aid that is crucial for subsistence: "[t]he ephemeral expressive benefits provided by the act of voting are overshadowed by its utility as an instrument through which to secure the protection, services, and opportunities at the disposal of elected officials."

In other words, wholly expressive voting may be a luxury that belongs to those settings where voters do not believe that politicians can mete out individual-level punishments or rewards for voting behavior, and further to those individuals who are not dependent on government assistance. In the many democracies where these conditions do not hold, understanding political behavior as predominantly instrumental makes sense. Indeed, the literature on these cases frequently adopts precisely that assumption. Desposato (2006, 59) summarizes a view articulated by many scholars when he states that "poor, risk-averse voters may well prefer private goods rather than policy promises." Ethnographic work from throughout newer democracies (and some long-established ones) repeatedly highlights the fact that many poor voters view politics and elections as presenting an opportunity for individualized enrichment – or, conversely, as posing a risk of individual economic or material losses if they vote the "wrong" way. As Kerkvliet (1991) relates for the case of the Philippines, voters view offers of particularistic goods from politicians as "practically their only opportunity to get anything from the government" (cited in Schaffer and Schedler [2007, 26]). Especially for those citizens who are barely able to satisfy their basic subsistence, it surely makes sense to try to use their political behavior for material advantage. In the words of a poor client in a city on the outskirts of Buenos Aires, the consequences of political behavior (in her case attending a political rally) can be substantial: "if I do not go to her [the politician's] rally, then, when I need something, she won't give it to me" (Auyero, 2000b, 160). In a similar vein, Nichter (2009, 18) relates the clearly instrumentalist view of voting adopted by a citizen in Brazil. This interviewee describes how the possibility of needing assistance at some point in the future enters into his voting calculus: "I even vote foreseeing a need [for assistance from a politician] ... . I think that the poor need to vote well because, if we're poor, at any time we need them [the politicians] too."

In contexts where, as Chandra (2007, 91) says, "the vote is the currency through which individuals secure ... goods for themselves or their micro-communities," and especially for the poorest citizens, precisely those most likely to be targeted via clientelism, instrumental voting makes sense.

Instrumental voting might even make sense in contexts where the contingent direct exchange of benefits for votes is not widespread. The work of Gerber and colleagues on vote secrecy and instrumental voting is worth quoting at length. As they say, "when weighed against the vanishingly small chance of casting a ballot that decides an election, if a citizen believes that there is even a very slight chance of her choices being disclosed and that this disclosure may have personal repercussions, concerns about secrecy can have an influence on her voting behavior that easily overwhelms her own preferences over which candidate should hold office" (Gerber et al., 2009, 1). The authors do find some evidence of this practice in the United States, especially among voters who believe their vote choice might be learned by others. So, for example, "those in union households who are concerned that the ballot is not secret ... were substantially less likely to vote for the Republican presidential candidate in 2008 than union members who thought their choices were protected" (Gerber et al., 2009, 4). As I go on to argue in Section 2.2.2, doubts about ballot secrecy are likely to be widespread among the poor in many parts of the developing world. In such contexts, we should not be surprised if instrumental concerns dominate expressive ones for many poor voters.

2.2.2 Monitoring

Even if voters are willing to act instrumentally, they will do so only if they believe there is some likelihood, however small, that the clientelist exchange can be enforced. The ongoing character of many clientelist relationships and the inherently public nature of some political acts (such as attendance at rallies) obviously facilitates enforcement. Monitoring of actual voting behavior is a more difficult task. Much of the existing literature on clientelism treats politician monitoring of voter behavior as crucial to the practice's success, and, as a result, expends significant energy in trying to demonstrate that monitoring can coexist with the secret ballot.[18] Here, I emphasize that it is a voter's *belief* that her vote may be monitored, rather than actual monitoring, that is crucial for clientelism's success. Other scholars have also pointed to the importance of voter perceptions of violations of the secret ballot, rather than actual violations. As Chandra (2004) highlights in her study of clientelism in India, "[t]he *perception* that voting procedures are subject to the same type

---

[18] Alternately, some who believe the monitoring assumption is too strong have turned their focus to practices that are more readily observed, such as voter turnout (Nichter, 2008, Stokes and Dunning, 2008). Although there may be a role for turnout buying, I argue here that even when monitoring is far from perfect, traditional clientelism may persist.

of discretion as other policies should deter cheating and encourage the sale of goods and services in return for votes just as if the ballot were in fact not secret" (53, emphasis in the original). In the paper mentioned previously that examines perceptions of ballot secrecy in the United States, Gerber et al. (2009) also refer to the importance of what they call the "psychological secrecy" – as opposed to the actual secrecy – of the ballot.

Before discussing perceptions of monitoring, I summarize the evidence of actual vote monitoring in a variety of settings. Among tactics that have been used in the United States in the past, oft-cited examples include voting machines rigged so that split ticket voting registers a different sound than voting the party line and the practice of accompanying disabled or illiterate individuals in the voting booth because of their need for "assistance."[19] Another tactic that allows the secret ballot to be violated in democracies is chain voting, which has gone by names as evocative as "the caterpillar," "the shuttle," and the "Tasmanian dodge." Whatever its name, this tactic relies on the cooperation of voters, who, once in the voting booth, deposit a premarked ballot they have brought with them and retrieve a blank one to deliver to a party operative as evidence of their cooperation (see the descriptions in Cox [2010, footnote 1] and Schaffer and Schedler [2007, 23]). In other contexts, election observers who are charged with maintaining the integrity of the electoral process in fact monitor individuals or groups of voters at polling places and possibly infer their choices. For example, partisan observers in present-day Argentina can monitor voting stations to see who arrives to vote and how long they stay in the booth and then, at the end of voting, get vote tallies for each voting booth (Szwarcberg, 2007). Similarly, Chandra (2004, 139–140) describes how, before electoral reforms in India in 1994, partisan observers were able to empty ballot boxes frequently and count ballots in the order in which they were cast, allowing for the reconstruction of the choices made by groups of voters over the course of the day. Although the spread of new technologies such as electronic voting may impede some of these efforts at monitoring, other technologies, especially cell phones with cameras, may facilitate quite accurate monitoring of vote choice at the individual level (Schaffer and Schedler, 2007, 23). Violating the secret ballot in a modern democracy may be difficult, but it is certainly not impossible.

Voter *belief* in monitoring will obviously be buttressed in contexts where actual ballot secrecy is violated, even if only occasionally. However, even in contexts where an individual's vote is rarely subject to actual monitoring, politicians and their agents can engage in a number of practices that foster voter skepticism about ballot secrecy. Political acts outside of voting, such as attendance at campaign events or rallies, are quite readily observed. The practice of visibly monitoring attendance at these events (as documented in

[19] See Kitschelt and Wilkinson (2007a, 15–17) and the references therein, as well as Wolfinger (1974), Keyssar (2009), and the examples in Stokes (2005).

the Argentine case by Auyero [2000b] and Szwarcberg [2008]) is likely to undermine voter confidence in the confidentiality of political preferences and other political practices, including the vote itself.

Even where the ballot is not observed, voters themselves might share information about their vote choice with others. Gerber et al. (2009) refer to this as the "social secrecy" of the ballot. In the United States, the focus of their research, revelations of one's vote choice are likely to be voluntary. However, in clientelist settings, voters might anticipate pressure to "volunteer" their vote choice to political actors or they may be asked directly by political brokers and operatives how they voted. As Gerber et al. (2009) relate, research from psychology suggests that "individuals find social interactions involving lying less pleasant (DePaulo et al., 1996) and that such discomfort increases and lies are told less frequently with individuals one is closer to (DePaulo and Kashy, 1998)." When voters are embedded in social networks with political actors, lying to these individuals should be especially hard.[20] Similarly, engaging in some public act of support for a candidate (such as attending a rally) in view of friends and neighbors may make it more difficult for a voter to act differently in the voting booth. These social and psychological mechanisms can further increase a clientelist politician's vote share even while not, strictly speaking, violating ballot confidentiality.

Separately, politicians may more directly seek to undermine voter belief in the secret ballot. Holzner (2010) cites the example of a local branch of the PRI (the *Partido Revolucionario Institutional*, Mexico's long-ruling party until the year 2000), that distributed farm animals to voters who turned in a copy of their voter ID cards and signed a petition saying they were members of the PRI. According to the author, the party's goal was "to make people think the PRI had their personal information and could use it to find out whether they had actually voted for the PRI" (Holzner, 2010, 157). Holzner claims that both the PRI and the PRD (*Partido de la Revolucion Democratica*, a leftist party), use strategies like this throughout Mexico. Even more directly, one observer relates the threats made by the government candidate to voters in low-income neighborhoods in the Brazilian state of Piauí in the 1980's: "whoever does not vote for our candidate will not drink from my well. Whoever does not vote for our candidate will be fired ... If you doubt me just try it"(Teixeira [1985, 128] cited in Desposato [2006, 63].)

There are a number of reasons to believe that these varied strategies to undermine ballot confidentiality will be especially powerful among the poor. The poor are more likely to be dependent on the state for subsistence and, as a result, to rely on what Auyero (2000b) calls "problem-solving networks" that include politicians and political brokers. Gaining access to state resources targeted at the poor usually requires demonstrating one's need – either informally or through a formal evaluation. In the course of demonstrating their

[20] Brusco et al. (2004) provide some nice illustrations of this with respect to the Argentine case.

need, the poor must invite government officials into their homes and give political actors detailed descriptions of their work, family, and personal lives. Even if not their intent, these actions are likely to undermine an individual's belief in the secrecy of his private actions – including the vote. In some cases, political brokers are a constant presence in poor neighborhoods and communities and are residents of the community themselves, leading these brokers (and presumably citizens) to believe that they "know who's with you and who's not with you" (Brusco et al., 2005, 76). In addition, to the extent poverty is correlated with lower levels of education, poor voters are also less likely to be aware of institutional protections that exist to maintain the secrecy of their ballots.

The available empirical evidence on voter beliefs about ballot secrecy suggests these types of tactics are effective. Data from various countries in Latin America – as well as the United States – show that voter skepticism about ballot secrecy is relatively widespread. In Argentina, for example, a 2003 survey carried out in four provinces found that 37% of respondents responded in the affirmative when asked if a political party operative is able to find out how "a person in your neighborhood has voted," with an additional 12% answering that they did not know whether or not such a vote could be learned (Stokes, 2005, 318). In other words, only 50% of those sampled were fully confident that their votes were secret. In a separate survey, Oliveros (2013) asked municipal employees in three medium-sized Argentine cities whether they believed the government or political parties could learn for whom they voted. Even among this group, which is more educated and enjoys higher income than recipients of social assistance, affirmative responses ranged from 11% in one city to about 31% in the two other locations.[21] Moving to data from elsewhere in Latin America, Gonzalez-Ocantos et al. (2012) find that more than one-third of Nicaraguan respondents to their survey believed that the government or political parties could find out how they had voted.[22] In Mexico, through a series of semistructured interviews in the early 2000s, Holzner finds that fully two-thirds of his interviewees believed their vote choice could be learned by others (Holzner, 2003).

Although this type of skepticism about the secrecy of the ballot is presumably more widespread in younger or more fragile democracies, recent evidence suggests that voter doubts about ballot secrecy are not limited to these types of polities. In a survey of voters in the United States, Gerber and his colleagues find that one-quarter of respondents do not believe their vote choice is kept

---

[21] Municipal employees were interviewed in the municipalities of Santa Fe, Tigre, and Salta, respectively.

[22] And, importantly, this belief is highly correlated with the incidence of reported vote-buying. Gonzalez-Ocantos et al. (2012, 211–212) report that only 6% of respondents who believe in the secrecy of the ballot report receiving a targeted good in exchange for their vote, whereas that figure rises to almost half among respondents who doubted ballot secrecy.

secret, and 40% of respondents believe it would be "not at all" or "not too" difficult for employers, politicians, or union officials to learn their vote choice (Gerber et al., 2009, Table 1). The authors also find that doubts about ballot secrecy are more widespread among the poor and the least educated, precisely those groups that are typically the subjects of clientelist offers and exchange.[23] Considering the limited doubt cast on the integrity of the ballot in the modern United States by experts, this level of skepticism about ballot secrecy is almost shocking, and it suggests that undermining voter belief in ballot secrecy will be relatively easy in many younger democracies.

2.3 THE VOTER'S DECISION-MAKING CALCULUS

In a setting where politicians come to individually own credit for government programs and poor voters are highly dependent on these benefits, we should expect clientelism to be a very powerful vote-getting tool. Given the assumptions about voter behavior and beliefs laid out here, how will clientelism work to get votes?

A voter faced with these circumstances will expect her future utility to be tied to her *individual* behavior in the voting booth, not only to the outcome of elections. Imagine, for example, a situation where an incumbent uses clientelism, and a challenger does not. Assume also the voter does not believe herself to be pivotal; her vote choice will not sway the outcome of the election. The voter receives some valued benefit from the incumbent, and, in the event the incumbent is reelected, believes that her future receipt of the benefit depends on whether or not she has voted for the incumbent. In other words, if the incumbent wins, and she has voted for him, she expects to continue to receive the benefit.[24] If the incumbent wins, and she has not voted for him, she expects – with some likelihood – to be denied the benefit. In contrast, her expected utility from a challenger victory will not be correlated with her behavior in the voting booth. Thus, even if she truly prefers the challenger, once we assume instrumental preferences and no expressive utility, the voter is always better off casting her ballot for the clientelist incumbent.

Figure 2.3 displays visually the voter's decision-making calculus. As it makes clear, a voter's utility from a challenger victory is unrelated to her vote choice. Compare nodes 2 and 4 in the figure. Regardless of how she casts her ballot, the voter receives only an ideological benefit (or loss) from a challenger victory. In contrast, if the clientelist incumbent wins, the voter's utility depends on how she behaved in the voting booth. Compare nodes 1 and 3. If the incumbent wins, and she has voted for him (node 1), she gets the valuable

---

[23] The authors also find decreased confidence in ballot secrecy among non-Whites and those with less political interest.

[24] For simplicity, I present this as a one-shot exchange, but most clientelist exchanges are carried out in the context of ongoing relationships.

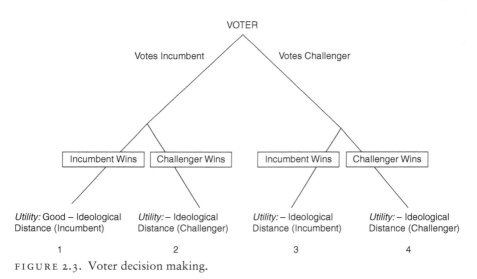

FIGURE 2.3. Voter decision making.

good and some ideological utility. In contrast, if the incumbent wins and she has not voted for him (node 3), the voter gets the same ideological benefit or loss, but, with some nonzero probability, no valued good.[25] If the incumbent wins, the voter is always better off having voted for the incumbent. Given that her vote choice does not affect her utility from a challenger victory, clientelism creates quite a powerful inducement to vote for the incumbent. Note that this remains true even if the challenger were to run on an anti-clientelism platform or even if he were to credibly promise universal distribution to all voters. As long as future utility is potentially linked to individual vote choice in the event of an incumbent victory, but not in the event of a challenger victory, each client will find it in her interest to vote for the incumbent.[26]

Ethnographic work and popular accounts suggest the widespread, and effective, use of clientelism as a vote-getting tool in Argentina. Nor are scholarly observers and journalists alone in attributing unique power to clientelism in Argentina. Politicians and their close associates tend to share this view. To repeat the words of Liliana, a top bureaucrat in the social welfare office in Campo Santo, "[a]t the moment of the vote, it doesn't matter if they're from the other party, they go "tac" [making a motion of putting a ballot in a

[25] We need not assume that the incumbent is able to reward or punish with 100% certainty for clientelism to work. In the scenario described here, as long as the probability of receiving the good in node 1 is greater than it is in node 3, and the expected utility from nodes 2 and 4 remains unchanged, the voter will be expected to cast her ballot for the incumbent.

[26] For a number of reasons, including access to government resources (Wantchekon, 2003), it is reasonable to expect an incumbent politician to have an advantage in the use of clientelism. In a setting where a challenger uses clientelism as well, a voter's calculus may be altered. In that case, a voter's decision should depend on the value of the promised benefit as well as the expected probability that each candidate will be elected.

ballot box] and they vote for the mayor" (Author interview, August 2007). This chapter articulates the conditions that allow these types of beliefs – and the practices they support – to be pervasive. In particular, it emphasizes the compatibility between targeted social assistance and local clientelism, and it documents how local incumbents can claim credit for government benefits and foster a sense of scarcity around them, thus making the clientelist manipulation of these programs possible. It also calls attention to the voter beliefs and behaviors that facilitate clientelism. This chapter thus shows how politician behavior and voter beliefs combine to make clientelism "work" in present-day Argentina.

3

Curbing Clientelism: Why Some Politicians Opt Out

Chapter 2 illustrated how clientelism can work as a vote-getting tool on a mass scale. Local incumbents who so choose can claim credit for the distribution of valued benefits, and citizens, worried about future access to goods crucial to their well-being, will be willing to exchange their political support for these benefits. However, though there are many strategies Argentine mayors can use to make clientelism work, not all local incumbents rely on clientelism in social policy. As the anecdotes that began this book suggest, clientelism in Argentina is widespread, but it is not ubiquitous. Officials in a minority of towns and cities explicitly deny personal responsibility for government programs and opt not to make political ties or behavior a precondition for receiving government benefits. In this chapter, I seek to understand these exceptions: within a single national political environment, why do some local incumbents opt out of clientelism?

My answer to this question relies on what I call the "audience costs" of clientelism. Although clientelism is typically targeted at the poor, there are other, nonpoor citizens in the political environment. The reactions of these nonclients to the practice of clientelism will affect a politician's incentives to rely on the practice.[1] I argue in this chapter that the non-poor are likely to punish clientelist politicians in the voting booth. As a result, clientelism creates a heretofore unexplored electoral tradeoff – while clientelism garners support among the poor, this comes at the cost of lost electoral support from nonpoor voters.

---

[1] Throughout this book, I refer interchangeably to the "poor" and "clients." Although obviously a simplification to assume that all clients are poor and all of the poor are clients, this is a fairly good approximation of reality in the Argentine case. As noted in the previous chapter, clientelist incumbents can use a variety of tactics to spread benefits widely among the poor. Even if not all of the poor are on the receiving end of concrete benefits, many will view themselves as *potential* beneficiaries and hence potential clients. As Judith Chubb has argued, even nonrecipients can become part of clientelist networks through the "constant anticipation of possible future favors" (Chubb, 1982, 167).

Of course, the mere existence of an electoral tradeoff does not assure clientelism's decline. At the most basic level, the costs of clientelism will be increasing in the share of the population that is not poor. However, clientelism is likely to diminish only when those costs exist and politicians are sensitive to them. I argue that politicians are most likely to be sensitive to the costs of clientelism in the presence of high levels of political competition, with these effects perhaps being further contingent on the existence of a hospitable partisan environment. The theory I develop therefore argues that the *interaction* between political competition and poverty, rather than either alone, creates incentives for politicians to opt out of clientelism.[2] Furthermore, these incentives may be strongest for incumbents from political parties with a legitimate reason to fear losing middle-class support. Before elaborating on this theory, I provide some more examples of an alternative, nonclientelist model of social welfare provision.

3.1 AN ALTERNATIVE TO CLIENTELISM

The town of El Carril, in the province of Salta, is located just down the road from La Merced, a municipality discussed at length in the previous chapter. Although residents of both towns rely heavily on seasonal employment in the tobacco industry, El Carril is also the site of a tobacco processing plant, which creates more jobs and lends greater prosperity to the town. While La Merced has traditionally been a Peronist party stronghold, at the time of my research, El Carril's mayor was a member of the Partido Renovador de Salta (PRS), a province-level conservative party. The manner in which social welfare benefits were provided presents another point of contrast between the two municipalities. A top official in El Carril's social welfare office detailed her interaction with residents. In her words, "I explain to them [the beneficiaries] that it [the PNSA] comes from the national government. [I] never ... take the program and grab it as my own ... it's not ours" (Author interview, August 2006). This attitude was reinforced by the other ways in which social programs were administered in this town. In contrast to most of the municipalities described so far, El Carril had a clear division of labor between the mayor's office and the social welfare area, as well as among the staff in the social welfare office. The top bureaucrat in the office explained that all social welfare aid is distributed from that office, and so residents who go to the mayor's office to ask for aid are instead redirected to her office.[3]

---

[2] See Kitschelt and Wilkinson (2007a) and Magaloni et al. (2007) for other theories that explore the possibility that the interaction between competition and demographics might help explain clientelism, though both pieces focus on a different dependent variable – the mix of clientelism and programmatic politics.

[3] Notably, the social welfare office was distinct from the municipal building in El Carril, rather than integrated into it.

More broadly, the way in which social welfare provision is organized differs between typical clientelist and nonclientelist municipalities. When describing their efforts to supplement national programs, officials in cities not characterized by clientelism tended to advocate (in interviews, at least) more systematic assistance oriented around distributing a particular type of aid for a discrete period of time rather than the constant, but unpredictable model of "aid on demand" that is dominant in clientelist municipalities. As an example of the former, the municipality of El Carril runs a program to distribute shoes to school-age children immediately before the start of each school year. By delimiting the time of year (the beginning of the school year) and target population (school-age children), the municipality likely minimizes the type of unanticipated visits over the course of the year that characterize a town like La Merced. Following a similar logic, the head social worker on staff in Colonia Caroya, a prosperous agricultural municipality in the province of Córdoba, specifically told me that they organize a schedule they use to attend to public requests to encourage individuals receiving or requesting aid of different types to come at different times. By establishing and following a schedule, the staff thus minimizes unnecessary trips to the municipal offices and the extra waiting time that entails.

Note that this behavior does not necessarily reduce the actual scarcity of benefits distributed. In fact, in interviews, incumbents and bureaucrats from nonclientelist settings were more frank about the existence of scarcity and were less inclined to offer assistance to all of the needy than officials and politicians in clientelist towns. The attitude of the head of the social welfare office in El Carril was typical. In her words, "well, we can't get to everyone, right? We try to identify the most critical cases."[4] Nonetheless, it is important to note that in this setting, politicians and their top appointees, in contrast to those who rely on clientelism, do not take actions that artificially heighten this sense of scarcity.

Finally, mayors and their closest associates are much less central figures in social welfare distribution in these cities when compared to those discussed earlier. In Colonia Caroya and Río Primero, two municipalities where I did not find evidence of clientelism, neither mayor reported spending much time on social welfare requests.[5] Of course, even when mayors are removed from day-to-day decision making, this does not preclude the possibility that some residents may still request aid with a political exchange in mind. So, for example, in an interview with the mayor's chief of staff in Río Primero, he recounted an exchange that he had with a local resident before the most recent elections. The resident came to the chief of staff to explain to him that her husband did not have any sneakers, and she told him that "if you don't give him sneakers, he is not going to go vote." According to the chief of staff, his

4 Author interview. August 2006.
5 I was unable to interview the mayor of El Carril.

own response to her was as follows: "Fine. Go ahead, don't vote." This explicit delinking of social welfare aid from political behavior is a sharp contrast with the attitude of officials in clientelist municipalities. In the remainder of this book, I seek to understand what explains these very different models of citizen–politician engagement within a democracy. My answer focuses on the ways in which the interaction between voter demographics, political competition, and political party shapes the incentives of local incumbents.

3.2 THE AUDIENCE COSTS OF CLIENTELISM

Although the electoral benefits of clientelism have been well studied, the possible costs of the practice have received relatively limited attention. Some authors do point to the redistributive consequences of clientelism. Magaloni et al. (2007) argue that, given a budget constraint, spending on clientelist goods necessarily decreases the pool of resources available for spending on public goods that might gain middle-class support. Similarly, most models of distributive politics assume that voters will reward politicians for targeting resources to their own group and (concomitantly, because of fixed budgets) punish redistribution to others (Cox and McCubbins, 1986, Dixit and Londregan, 1996). However, these authors examine only the costs of the redistribution, rather than any possible costs of *how* that redistribution takes place. Clientelism is defined by the nature of the relationship between patrons and clients, not by the substance of what is distributed. In fact, the same benefits can be distributed to the poor via clientelism or not. In contrast to existing work, I argue that the use of clientelism in policies targeted at the poor imposes its own electoral costs above and beyond any costs of redistribution itself. In that sense, this works builds on, and develops more fully, insights dating back to those of Banfield and Wilson (1963) and Shefter (1977), whose work on the United States and Western Europe has previously pointed to the disregard with which middle-class voters view patronage, clientelism, and related practices.[6] However, this view has received very little attention in the more recent wave of writing on clientelism.[7] In some cases, scholars have simply ignored any potential role of the middle class in the dynamics of clientelism (Auyero,

---

6 Writing on American cities, Banfield and Wilson (1963, 46) compare what they label the "middle class ethos," which favors "efficiency, impartiality, honesty . . ." with the beliefs of immigrants and the poor, "who are far less interested in the efficiency, impartiality, and honesty of local government than in its readiness to confer material benefits of one sort of another upon them." My explanation for different patterns of behavior differs from that of Banfield and Wilson. I argue that the poor may share a concern for government performance, but that material needs and politician behavior lead the poor to act as if they cared only about material benefits.

7 Within recent work, Brusco et al. (2006) provide an important exception. In interpreting some puzzling results, these authors point to the possibility that patronage and the manipulation of social service provision might cause dissatisfaction among some voters. They speculate that

2000b), while others have suggested that the middle class may actually prefer clientelism when compared with possible alternatives.[8] Why, then, might middle-class voters punish clientelism?

3.2.1 The Perspective of Nonclients

Nonpoor voters might reject clientelism for reasons of two different types. First, these voters might view clientelism as a negative signal of the quality of government performance more generally and therefore withhold support for a clientelist politician for largely self-interested reasons. Second, they might reject clientelism on moral or normative grounds and therefore punish a politician who uses it, regardless of whether clientelism has any direct effects on their material well-being. If either view is widespread among nonpoor voters, it should create audience costs to the practice of clientelism.[9] I examine each of these in turn.

Nonpoor voters, even if not consumers of the targeted social programs or other small favors typically distributed as part of clientelist relationships, are consumers of government products and services of many types, ranging from road maintenance to local security. Note that this is not true of all of the nonpoor: especially in the developing world, there may be some portion of the nonpoor population that sends its children to private schools, lives in neighborhoods with privately maintained streets and private security, and so on, effectively buying its way out of dependence on many government services. While these voters may in fact not care about the quality of government services, in most settings, this group will comprise a very small share of the electorate.[10] The vast majority of the nonpoor are deeply affected by how well their government carries out its day to day tasks. As such, if clientelism serves

---

these costs will be minimized when a program is funded from the outside, whereas here I argue that the audience costs of clientelism can exist even when voters bear no fiscal cost.

[8] For example, writing on Argentina, Levitsky (2003, 118) suggests that the Peronist party's shift away from reliance on unions to more professional politicians (the so-called "jacket and tie Peronism"), and the corresponding increased reliance on clientelism, was actually appealing to middle-class voters.

[9] Of course, we should not expect a distaste for clientelism to wholly determine the voting behavior of this group. Nonetheless, if nonpoor voters are less inclined to support clientelist politicians, all else equal, then information about clientelism will lead at least some citizens to change their voting behavior.

[10] For example, only about 7% of Argentines fall into the "upper" or "upper middle" classes (categories ABC1, using the most commonly employed measure of social class) (Mora y Araujo, 2002). On the other hand, there are obviously other ways, outside of their voting power, through which the elite can influence elections, and this group may even prefer clientelism if it dampens calls for more substantial redistribution. For different approaches that highlight the role of landed elites in stunting national-level democracy, see Rueschemeyer et al. (1992) and Acemoglu and Robinson (2001). I set this elite group aside for the purposes of the framework developed here, which focuses on the electoral incentives surrounding clientelism.

as a signal of low-quality government performance, these voters are unlikely to support a politician who relies on it.

There are a number of reasons to think that clientelism does serve as such a signal. At the most basic level, the personal time and attention clientelism demands necessarily reduces the time available to devote to other areas of administration. As highlighted in Chapter 2, "successful" clientelism requires that incumbents personally appropriate credit for benefits and programs that are, in fact, funded by the state. Perhaps the most natural way for an elected politician to accomplish this is for him to personally receive requests for, and decide on, the allocation of assistance to individual citizens. As I document in the case of small towns and cities in Argentina, the degree to which some clientelist politicians make themselves available to citizens can verge on the absurd. To the extent that time spent on a task is positively correlated with the quality of outcomes, time politicians spend cultivating and maintaining clientelist relationships will decrease the quality of services they offer in areas of greater direct interest to nonpoor constituents.

More broadly, we can think of a politician's decision to adhere to principles of good government, or general public-minded management, as a reflection of that politician's interest in administering government funds efficiently and fairly, without waste or favoritism. By definition, clientelism entails threatening citizens (implicitly or explicitly) with the withdrawal of government-funded benefits or other vital assistance if they fail to reciprocate with political support. It frequently means that a politician distributes government funded goods in a way that departs from formal criteria that can be defended in public.[11] As such, when a politician uses clientelist practices, he demonstrates a willingness, in at least one area of administration, to deviate from implementing public policy in a way that is faithful to its design or to formal rules. Clientelism can then serve as a signal of inefficient or abusive use of public funds in other areas. Although cross-national data on clientelism are quite limited, that which exists supports the claim that clientelism is correlated with other forms of malfeasance. Using a new cross-national dataset that employs expert surveys to evaluate the nature of citizen–politician linkages (Kitschelt et al., 2009), Singer (2009) examines the relationship between clientelism and corruption. He finds that countries where clientelism is more prevalent also suffer from greater levels of "grand" corruption.[12] To the extent this is true at the subnational level, as well, nonpoor voters may quite rationally dislike clientelism out of concerns for their own material self-interest.

---

[11] On the importance of public defensibility for distinguishing between different forms of distributive politics, see Stokes et al. (2013, Chapter 1). Of course, some government policies are explicitly designed to benefit certain groups in a way that other groups view as unfair. In this project, I am concerned mostly with policy implementation, rather than with policy design.

[12] That is, theft or other distortions by elite politicians, as opposed to petty corruption by bureaucrats.

Wholly apart from concerns that originate in self-interest, the nonpoor may find the conditional distribution of goods or services for political support morally or normatively distasteful or otherwise "take offense" (Kitschelt and Kselman, 2012, 7) at the practice. Democratic objections to clientelism may take a variety of forms. Citizens may object to the concentration of power in the hands of resource-holders who are able to command large numbers of votes through clientelist relationships. In addition to diluting the principle of "one person, one vote," voters outside of these exchanges may resent the fact that the practice of clientelism can minimize the power of their own votes.[13] Citizens who attach a high value to the integrity of the democratic process may also object to the fact that clientelism exploits poor voters and prevents clients from enjoying autonomy over their choices at the ballot box. Of course, poor voters might share these moral and normative objections to clientelism. The practice can nonetheless be an effective tool for garnering political support among the poor when the goods distributed via clientelism are sufficiently valuable to them and they believe that their political preferences and, ultimately, their vote choices, might be learned and monitored. This is precisely the power of clientelism. In the case of the nonpoor, however, clientelism does not offer any countervailing inducements or appeal to override its drawbacks.

Note also that both mechanisms are distinct from any direct costs of redistribution itself. Separately, of course, voters might prefer redistribution to themselves and those like them and resent distribution to other groups in society. Regardless of redistributive preferences, the costs of clientelism are a result of *how* those in power relate to a subset of the citizenry. This distinction is important because it implies that the costs of clientelism are likely to exist even in the absence of direct monetary costs of redistribution to the citizens who make up clientelism's "audience." So, even in contexts where tax evasion is rampant, or when redistributive programs are funded at no cost to taxpayers – say, by an international organization or with a party's private funds – the practice of clientelism may still lead the nonpoor to withdraw support from a clientelist politician.

How Does the Audience See?

Before turning to the conditions under which incumbents will be most sensitive to the costs of clientelism, I first highlight a basic assumption of the theory: that the nonpoor can indeed learn about clientelism. Citizens must be able to learn about clientelism if they are to punish politicians for it. Given the political costs of clientelism, politicians face incentives to hide clientelism from those citizens who are not a party to the practice, but who make up its potential audience. There are three main channels through which the nonpoor may learn about clientelism: direct observation, opposition effort, and the reports

---

[13] This normative objection thus also incorporates self-interested concerns.

of other actors in society. Their relative importance will depend on population size as well as the existence and trustworthiness of these sources. As long as one of these channels is available, we should expect the costs of clientelism to be activated and, conditional on political competition and a hospitable partisan environment (as detailed below), these costs to affect local incumbent behavior.

The simplest and most straightforward way a nonclient may learn about clientelism is through direct observation of an incumbent's actions that signal clientelism. As detailed in the previous chapter, clientelism relies on the extreme personalization of credit claiming, manifest through the concentration of decision making and the politicization of nonelected officials. In small towns and cities, it is quite realistic to assume that the fact that a newly appointed bureaucrat is the mayor's relative or neighbor, or that the mayor makes himself directly available to requests from the poor many hours of the week, will be widely known. In many of these places, municipal offices are contained in a single building. Middle-class voters who come to the municipality to pay property taxes or renew a driver's license can easily intersect with their neighbors who may be seeking government assistance. In the cases that are the empirical focus of this book, direct observation is likely to be the main mechanism through which the nonpoor gain information about clientelism.

Of course, the ability to directly observe the trappings of clientelism is unlikely outside of small towns. In other contexts, opposition party candidates or nonparty organizations are most likely to disseminate information about clientelism. In the case of opposition parties, the incentives to spread information about clientelism are clear. Whenever some voters will punish clientelism, an opposition party may stand to gain from disseminating that information. These same incentives may lead certain voters to be skeptical about the veracity of such accusations, but opposition parties are likely nonetheless to be an important source of information about incumbent reliance on clientelism.[14] Other actors, such as the news media, nongovernmental organizations (NGOs), and in some cases independent government auditing agencies, might also provide information about clientelism in contexts where direct observation is impossible or unlikely.[15] As long as these sources are deemed sufficiently reliable, they will enable non-clients to learn about clientelism, thus triggering the electoral costs of the practice.

In summary, a full accounting of the effects of clientelism needs to consider two types of voters. The first, poor clients, are the direct beneficiaries of

---

[14] For an account of the dissemination of information about government malfeasance by opposition parties in Eastern Europe, see Grzymala-Busse (2007, Chapter 3).

[15] Ferraz and Finan (2008) provide evidence from Brazil on how information about municipal corruption from federal government audits reduces incumbent support in the subsequent election. They also illustrate how different sources of information about malfeasance can interact: in the Brazilian case, punishment for corruption was more pronounced in municipalities with local news media.

clientelist relationships and are likely to deliver their support to their patrons as described in most of the literature. The nonpoor, although not directly involved in clientelist exchange, make up clientelism's audience and are likely to be turned off by the phenomenon. In other words, clientelism creates a tradeoff: while it may reap electoral gains from poor voters, it is likely to decrease electoral support from the nonpoor.

3.3 MAKING COSTS RELEVANT: POLITICAL COMPETITION

For clientelism to become less common, is it not enough for the audience costs of clientelism merely to exist; they must become relevant to an incumbent's electoral calculus. At the most basic level, numbers count. As the share of the population that is nonpoor increases, so will the share of voters who are willing to punish clientelism. This is consistent with the basic intuition of modernization theory and also with existing arguments that increased development should decrease the incidence of clientelism (Kitschelt and Wilkinson, 2007b, Stokes et al., 2013). Alone, however, an increase in the number of nonpoor constituents is unlikely to be sufficient to induce a departure from clientelism in a context where the practice is widespread. Instead, I point to the importance of a high competition environment, in conjunction with a sizable nonpoor population, in making the costs of clientelism relevant.

3.3.1 Competition, Clientelism, and Government Performance

Interparty competition is the starting point for many explanations of government performance.[16] Much of this literature focuses on the salutary effects of political competition, and scholars have argued that increased competition improves government performance for a range of outcomes. In contrast, the literature on clientelism has made mixed predictions about the links between competition and the propensity for clientelism. Here, I highlight the fact that these literatures draw on similar logics but vary in their conceptualization of the identity and preferences of citizens. As such, a theory that explicitly considers the preferences of different groups of voters will better explain the relationship between competition and patterns of politician–citizen linkages.

Political Competition and Government Performance
Students of corruption and government performance in general argue that increased competition and opposition presence improves that performance and decreases corruption by making politicians more responsive to voter

---

[16] For the purposes of this summary, I touch on works that operationalize competition in many different ways, including scholarship that focuses on the effects of democratic political competition as opposed to authoritarian regimes, as well as work that examines the possible effects of increasing electoral competitiveness or opposition presence within a democracy.

preferences.[17] Theoretically, the link between political competition and political responsiveness has been long recognized. In Federalist 57, for example, James Madison referred to the "restraint of frequent elections" that would prevent elected members of the House of Representatives from a possible "degeneracy" away from the interests of the people (Madison, 1788). The argument that the imperative to win votes prompts politicians to be responsive to voter preferences in the design and implementation of public policies is common in contemporary times, as well. Perhaps the most basic distinction can be drawn from the comparison of democratic systems with their nondemocratic counterparts, which by definition lack a political opposition that is able to compete on a level playing field with the governing party. As Bueno de Mesquita et al. (2002, 2003) argue, the need to maintain the support of a larger portion of the population in a democracy (in their terminology, because of the increased size of the winning coalition as a share of the selectorate) forces leaders to compete through the provision of public, rather than private, goods.[18] This creates more public-regarding policies and greater incentives to root out corruption. Cross-national empirical evidence is mixed on this point – although democracy is not clearly linked to reduced corruption in the short term, a long history of democracy is associated with lower levels of corruption (Treisman, 2000, Lederman et al., 2001, Adserá et al., 2003, Gerring and Thacker, 2004).[19]

If open competition for office decreases corruption and improves responsiveness, it is a small step to surmise that the more intense the competition, the better the outcomes. Both theory and evidence support the claim that increased levels of competition can lead to improved governance within democracies, as well. Examining the relationship between competition and corruption in her classic study, Rose-Ackerman (1978) argues that intense competition should decrease corruption.[20] In a study of the use of civil service patronage and party competition in Latin America, Geddes (1994) finds that there is a link between the intensity of interparty competition and civil service reform.

---

[17] Although see Cleary (2007), Golden and Chang (2001), and Golden and Tiwari (2009) for partial exceptions. Golden and Chang emphasize the importance of intraparty competition for certain types of malfeasance. I do not address the substantial literature that examines the effects on corruption of different types of electoral systems (see Persson et al. [2003] and Kunicova and Rose-Ackerman [2005], among others).

[18] Although, as the authors point out, democracy commonly involves a number of different institutions, they focus on the effects of the use of competitive elections to select leaders.

[19] Democracy has also been associated with other broad measures of "good" government performance, most notably economic performance, both theoretically and empirically. A discussion of this literature is beyond the scope of this work, but see for example Olson (1993) and Rodrik (1997), among others.

[20] Within her framework, while high levels of competition make a bribe less attractive to the briber and hence less likely, successful bribes are likely to be larger in size. So though competition may decrease the number of bribes that are made, the anticipated effect on the amount of money that changes hands through corrupt exchanges is indeterminate.

Similarly, Grzymala-Busse (2007), writing on the post-Communist states of Eastern Europe, finds that competition in the form of a "robust" political opposition improves governance and reduces state capture. There is evidence for the salutary effect of competition at the subnational level, as well. Beer (2001) shows that increased subnational competition improves legislative institutionalization in Mexico, and Wibbels (2005, Chapter 6) and Remmer and Wibbels (2000) find that political competition in Argentine provinces is associated with increased fiscal responsibility and rapid economic reform.[21]

Political Competition and Clientelism

In contrast to the enthusiasm for interparty competition in general, the literature on clientelism does not make clear predictions about the expected relationship between political competition and the prevalence of the individualized exchange of goods for political support. On the one hand, it is sometimes argued that clientelist practices go hand in hand with political monopoly and low levels of effective electoral competition (Fox, 1994, Rodríguez and Ward, 1994, Ward, 1998, Medina and Stokes, 2002, Hale, 2007).[22] This fits with our image of clientelism as a "backward" political practice characteristic of the developing world or the least developed parts of wealthier countries (Stokes, 2007b). It is also consistent with findings that increases in political competition prompt improvements in government performance more generally.

On the other hand, many discussions of clientelism and competition suggest an entirely different logic. The very fact that clientelism is treated as a vote-getting strategy suggests that some level of political competition is a prerequisite for clientelism. As Nyblade and Reed (2008) argue, political competition "may actually encourage politicians to abuse their position to attempt to hold on to their office."[23] The view adopted by authors who take this approach suggests that higher levels of competition should be associated with greater incentives to use clientelism because the votes clientelism can provide become increasingly valuable in competitive electoral environments. Scott (1969), for example, characterized clientelism as a strategy politicians pursue when they can no longer rely on either traditional loyalties or outright fraud to ensure the votes of an emerging mass electorate in developing democracies. In more recent work, van de Walle (2007) predicts that as

---

[21]   In the case of Remmer and Wibbels (2000), these authors, similar to Geddes (1994), highlight that balanced political competition (as opposed to highly fragmented or hegemonic competition) is associated with better outcomes.

[22]   Kitschelt and Kselman (2012) present a somewhat more nuanced view, positing that although the relationship between democratic experience and clientelism should be negative "in the aggregate," there may be a curvilinear effect at low levels of democracy. They find mixed support for this empirically.

[23]   Empirically, Nyblade and Reed (2008) look at both vote-buying and self-enrichment by Japanese legislators and find that increased interparty competition dampens corruption (what they call "looting"), while greater intraparty competition increases vote-buying (what they call "cheating").

electoral competition increases in Africa, clientelism targeted at the mass electorate will become more widespread. Keefer (2002) makes a similar argument about Indonesian politics after the fall of Suharto, and Krishna (2007) argues that increased political competition in India has made local brokers capable of delivering votes even more valued actors than in the past. Studying local government in Mexico, Grindle (2007, 75–76) finds that clientelism continued to be used in elections even in cities where competition increased and the hegemony of the PRI declined. Even among authors who do not place political competition at the center of their analyses, clientelism is often treated as a tool particular to competitive political systems. For example, in her examination of clientelism and ethnic parties in India, Chandra (2004, 54) argues that "the more dependent the voter is upon the state, the more likely he ... uses his vote as a means through which to extract material benefits from *competing candidates*" [emphasis added]. All these analyses suggest that clientelism and political competition can indeed coexist.

Increased Effort, Disparate Outcomes

So, while most scholarly literature assumes that democratic political competition improves the quality of governance and accountability, the literature on clientelism stands out for its lack of clarity on the consequences of political competition for the phenomenon, with arguments made on both sides. What explains this difference? Though the particularities of the arguments put forward vary, these diverse literatures share a crucial assumption: that increased competition creates incentives for politicians to take actions that maximize their political support. In other words, harkening back to V.O. Key's classic work on voter turnout in the American south, greater electoral competition increases politician effort (Key, 1949).[24] They come to different conclusions, then, largely because of different assumptions about the *form* that increased effort takes. In the case of interest to us here, the form this effort takes can either be accountability decreasing (continued reliance on clientelism) or accountability enhancing (a departure from clientelism). In turn, this disagreement about the form that increased politician effort takes itself stems from the emphasis by different authors on different sets of voters with different preferences.

Scholars of government performance more broadly tend to assume that the voting public uniformly dislikes corruption, government malfeasance, and other forms of "bad" performance, and that if voters discover evidence of this, they are likely to punish the implicated politician. This perspective is widespread, and, for example, motivates the emphasis of Adserá et al. (2003) on the importance of information and the media in controlling corruption: if voters learn about corruption, the authors assume that they will punish

---

[24] For more recent theory and evidence on increased elite mobilizational effort in close elections, see Cox and Munger (1989) and Matsusaka and Palda (1993) among others, for the U.S. case. Cox et al. (1998) provide a fuller summary of the literature as well as evidence from Japan.

politicians for that behavior.[25] This prompts politicians in competitive environments (measured in Adserá et al. [2003] by a country's level of democracy) to minimize corruption. Geddes' (1994) work on civil service reform suggests that voter preferences for "efficient" government are an impetus for reform in this area, as well, and she argues that the expectation that some voters prefer a professional, not patronage-based, civil service creates incentives for parties to advocate reform to attract their support. Similarly, Grzymala-Busse (2007) posits that an active and critical opposition makes incumbents fearful that grabs for state resources will be revealed to the voting public, leading to moderation of their behavior.[26] Her argument also rests on the assumption that, if they become aware of these practices, voters will punish an incumbent party that tries to exploit state resources for private gain. These assumptions about voter preferences, especially with regard to corruption, seem quite reasonable: corruption's costs may be spread across many voters, but with few exceptions, the vast majority of the voting public does indeed suffer these costs. All else equal, we would not expect a voter to prefer a corrupt candidate to a noncorrupt one. Within the literature on clientelism, those who posit that competition decreases the incidence of clientelism seem to have a similar dynamic in mind.

In sharp contrast, another strain of the literature on clientelism has focused on the fact that particular voters – mostly the poor – do receive clear benefits from clientelism, in the form of individually targeted private goods. Thus, unlike the expected negative attitude toward corruption, the voters who are the focus of much of the literature on clientelism are expected to view clientelism as a benefit, rather than a cost.[27] The theoretical literature on clientelism focuses almost exclusively on the effects of these exchanges on the voting behavior of poor clients, and on the whole presumes that the mix of benefits and threats that clientelist politicians deploy leads to a net gain of votes for the politicians who use clientelism (see, e.g., Stokes [2005]).[28] For those who adopt this perspective that clientelism gives a valued benefit to usually

[25] Not all authors make this assumption about voter preferences. Bueno de Mesquita et al. (2002), for example, suggest that the relatively lower costs of providing public versus private goods as the size of the winning coalition increases is what prompts greater public good provision in competitive electoral environments.

[26] As noted previously, Grzymala-Busse (2007) also argues that a large opposition is more likely to be able to uncover and reveal information about malfeasance to the public.

[27] Of course, whether or not clientelism creates a net benefit for the client is disputed; in a deeper sense, clients' "true" preferences with respect to public policy issues might be ignored when they cast their ballots in order to ensure continued access to small, material benefits (Stokes, 2007a). Here, though, I refer to those concrete material benefits they receive that consequently shape their voting behavior.

[28] The chapter by Magaloni et al. (2007) in Kitschelt and Wilkinson (2007b) is an important exception in that the authors examine the tradeoffs between providing private and public goods. The authors assume that politicians can "mix" over the provision of public goods and clientelist practices, simultaneously appealing to middle classes with the former and capturing votes of the poor with the latter. In their framework, although clientelism and has no direct costs in terms of votes, it does incur indirect costs, because any funds devoted to clientelism

poor clients who cannot be assured the receipt of that benefit otherwise, the intuition that competition should increase incentives for clientelism follows naturally. If clientelism yields additional votes for the politician who relies on it, then, as competition increases, and politicians invest more effort in winning elections, that effort should be manifest in an increased likelihood of relying on clientelism.

These different assumptions about just who benefits (and loses) from corruption and clientelism help explain the different predictions about the relationship between political competition and these phenomena. Corruption, self-enrichment, and other similar practices are generally understood to impose costs on all voters, and thus scholars predict increased competition should decrease incumbent reliance on such practices. In contrast, many scholars of clientelism have focused only on the poor, treating clientelism as a benefit for these voters alone, without considering the possibility that it imposes any costs on other voters. This perspective lends itself to the view that increasing competition actually increases the incentives to use clientelism.

What should this mean for our expectations regarding the likelihood that an incumbent mayor will opt out of clientelism? The previous section argued that the use of clientelism will create audience costs that will diminish a politician's support among the nonpoor. Clientelism thus creates an electoral tradeoff between political support gained from poor clients and lost from the nonpoor. This section's focus on political competition and politician effort suggests when that tradeoff will be most relevant: in the face of high competition, the presence of a large middle class should create incentives to abandon clientelism. In contrast, clientelism should continue to be electorally appealing even when competition is high if it is also the case that large numbers of voters are poor. In other words, the interaction between political competition and voter poverty, rather than either alone, is likely to explain why some politicians depart from clientelism. Finally, note that where political competition is low, the model has no clear expectations about whether politicians will reject clientelism, although we should not expect constituent demographics to be an important predictor of clientelism.[29] These predictions are summarized in Figure 3.1.

3.4 PARTISANSHIP AND THE COSTS OF CLIENTELISM

While a focus on how political competition and citizen poverty interact to shape politician incentives for clientelism adds complexity to existing

---

limit the supply of public goods. In contrast, by treating clientelism as a signal of general government performance, I argue that clientelism may have direct costs in terms of support lost from middle-class voters. Also, I treat clientelism as a mode of policy implementation, rather than an end to which funds are allocated. In the framework developed here, "mixing" over the use of clientelism is unlikely to prevent a politician from incurring its costs, as long as nonpoor voters become aware of the practice.

[29] I discuss possible scenarios at low levels of competition in more detail later.

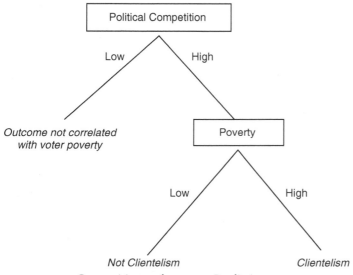

FIGURE 3.1. Competition and poverty: Predictions.

explanations of the phenomenon, it remains simplified in other respects. In particular, thus far, I have treated local mayors as isolated agents making a one-time choice. There are some theoretical reasons to adopt this approach as a useful shorthand when predicting departures from clientelism. On the other hand, it is also the case that clientelist exchange is frequently enmeshed in ongoing, long-term relationships, many of which have a partisan character.[30] The theory developed thus far is silent on the role of partisanship: it treats political parties as interchangeable, assuming that politicians, regardless of party, will respond similarly to the incentives created by competition and voter demographics. In this section, I expound on how partisanship may constrain departures from clientelism through two main channels that reflect supply-side and demand-side considerations. Chapters 5 and 6 then test these hypotheses about whether and how partisanship matters using both municipal-level and individual-level data.

Beginning with the supply side, political parties may, in a number of ways, constrain politicians' willingness and ability to engage in clientelism or to depart from it. Networks of intermediaries are typically central players in clientelist exchange, serving as the direct connection between parties on the one hand and voters on the other.[31] These networks are generally understood

[30] The emphasis on the role of parties in clientelism is particularly strong in two prominent cases in the literature: the PRI in Mexico (see, e.g., Magaloni et al. [2007], Magaloni [2006], and Greene [2007]) and the PJ in Argentina (see, among others, Auyero [2000b], Levitsky [2003], and Stokes [2005]).

[31] See Auyero (2000b), Wang and Kurzman (2007), and Krishna (2007) for excellent descriptions of the role of intermediaries in Argentina, Taiwan, and India, respectively. Stokes

to be constructed slowly over time – in the words of Kitschelt and Kselman (2012), "the result of long, hard organizing efforts" – and are often associated with a particular party. The historically developed, party-bound nature of these networks could constrain politicians who otherwise face incentives to act against their party type. A politician from a historically "nonclientelist" party who wants to engage in clientelism, for example, may find it difficult to quickly assemble a network that would allow him to convincingly engage voters in clientelist relationships. By the same token, a politician from a historically clientelist party may find it hard to abandon the practice if it means alienating brokers and other intermediaries who have been central to his success in the past (and may come to be again in the future).[32] Even in settings where networks are less important, the partisan "supply" of clientelism may vary nonetheless if politicians from different parties have systematically different tastes for clientelism. Knowing that party labels can serve as a signal of candidate characteristics and behavior in office (e.g., Cox and McCubbins [1993] and Aldrich [1995]), politicians may self-select into a particular party based in part on that party's reputation for employing clientelism. In some parties, budding politicians who show a talent for cultivating clientelist networks are rewarded with higher ballot positions on closed lists (Szwarcberg, 2009), and thus are more likely to continue to advance in the party and should have a higher chance of eventually obtaining a candidacy for executive office. Whatever their origins, these supply-side dynamics suggest that the likelihood of relying on clientelism could vary systematically by party.

Partisanship may also shape the incidence of clientelism through what I label demand-side dynamics. The two crucial assumptions of the theory developed in this chapter are first, that nonpoor voters dislike clientelism, and second, that political competition prompts politicians to be more sensitive to the tradeoff clientelism generates between political support lost and gained. This generates the prediction that the combination of high levels of competition and a large middle class creates incentives for any individual politician to reject clientelism. Although presented in a partisan-neutral fashion, it is possible that this interaction might depend on an incumbent's partisan affiliation. For these incentives to be meaningful, politicians must fear the possible loss of support from nonpoor voters. This, in turn, implies that politicians enjoy at least a modicum of support from this population in the first place. If parties systematically differ in the extent to which they enjoy support from the nonpoor, then the relevance of the threat of the loss of that support will differ across parties, too. A politician cannot fear the loss of support that he does not have. Incumbents from parties for which the middle class are core

---

et al. (2013) provide a comprehensive theory and empirical treatment of the role of party intermediaries (brokers) in clientelism across a range of cases.

[32] I thank a reviewer for highlighting this point and encouraging me to expand my consideration of partisanship more generally.

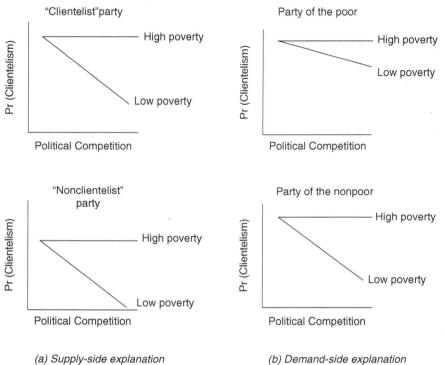

(a) Supply-side explanation   (b) Demand-side explanation

FIGURE 3.2. Partisanship and clientelism.

supporters have more to lose from alienating those voters. Unlike supply-side factors, which could operate orthogonally from class and competition, demand-side explanations that incorporate partisanship are essentially inter-active. Politician concerns about voter attitudes toward clientelism are more likely to be triggered as political competition increases.[33] Thus, if partisanship shapes sensitivity to the costs of clientelism through demand-side effects, this should be most evident in settings of high political competition.

To clarify how partisanship might alter the predictions laid out above, Figure 3.2 presents these two possibilities visually, in a schematic manner, by imagining how the relationship between poverty, competition, and clientelism could be altered once we take incumbent partisanship into account.[34] The four graphs share a number of characteristics. In each case, the y-axis shows

[33] In the same vein, it is worth noting that the supply-side dynamics elaborated on here could operate for any type of party, whether organized around class, ethnicity, region, or some other dimension. In contrast, the demand-side explanation is most likely to hold when parties have clear class bases.

[34] These graphs do not rely on any data; they are intended solely to provide a visualization of the theoretical possibilities described earlier.

the probability that an incumbent would rely on clientelism, while the x-axis shows political competition, running from low to high. In each graph, there are two lines, marking the expected probability of clientelism when poverty is either high (the top line) or low (the bottom one), as competition runs from low to high. Recall that the theory developed here makes no prediction about the likelihood that an incumbent will rely on clientelism when competition is low. For simplicity here (and because it matches the data for the Argentine case quite well), I depict levels of clientelism as at least relatively high whenever competition is low: that is, in the absence of electoral pressures, clientelism is quite common. Each figure includes two graphs, with the top depicting expectations for an incumbent from a party with a greater affinity for clientelism (whether for supply or demand reasons), and the bottom depicting expectations for an incumbent from a party with less affinity for clientelism.

The left-hand side of Figure 3.2 illustrates how our expectations might change across a clientelist versus nonclientelist party if differences are mostly driven by supply-side factors: the party's "taste" for providing clientelism. If this is the case, then mayors of all parties are sensitive to the costs of clientelism (the slopes in the two figures are the same), but mayors from the party depicted in the top graph simply have a stronger preference for the practice than those in the bottom figure. Thus, at all levels of competition, and when poverty is high or low, the probability of observing clientelism for a nonclientelist party is simply shifted downward. Empirically, in a regression analysis, this would be captured by an intercept effect.

In contrast, the right-hand side of Figure 3.2 depicts a situation wherein the likelihood of using clientelism is affected by partisanship as a result of demand-side considerations. In this scenario, the top graph depicts the behavior of a prototypical party that has mostly poor constituents and struggles to attract middle-class support. Its low levels of support from the nonpoor also means that it has less to fear from losing that support. In this case, as competition increases, and when poverty is low, the likelihood of observing clientelism decreases, but at a slower rate: the bottom line in the graph is downward sloping but relatively flat. In contrast, we can imagine that the party depicted in the bottom half of this figure depends on the support of the nonpoor, and thus will more rapidly move away from clientelism as competition increases, as long as poverty is low. Empirically, in a regression analysis, this would be captured by an interaction effect, rather than an intercept effect.

Finally, while both supply- and demand-side considerations point to ways in which partisanship could constrain politicians from freely choosing to rely on or reject clientelism, other theoretical traditions and empirical findings suggest some reasons to set partisanship aside in developing a model of clientelism. Most fundamentally, as Mayhew (1974) eloquently stated with respect to the United States Congress, a politician's first-order preference will always be to get reelected, as the achievement of other goals is contingent on remaining in office. Particularly with respect to the role of partisan brokers and broker networks in facilitating clientelism, we should be cautious that we do not overstate the importance of parties. Recent work from settings as disparate as Argentina and India illustrates how in some cases broker networks can be rapidly constructed with sufficient monetary inducements (Levitsky, 2003, Chapter 5), and that brokers may switch fairly readily between parties (Krishna, 2007). The importance of partisan identity and broker networks may be especially attenuated in the local government arena. In general, local governments are responsible for the delivery of many services that can be treated as valence issues and, as such, are less likely to divide constituents along traditional party lines.[35] In small and medium-sized towns and cities, politicians may more readily engage in direct contact with voters, further reducing dependence on brokers and the partisan networks in which they may be embedded. If party does not matter, then we would not expect to see the differences depicted in Figure 3.2a and b. I will test these possibilities in the chapters that follow.

3.4.1 Low Competition: Diverse Possibilities

Before turning to the empirical evidence, I conclude this chapter by noting that the theoretical framework developed here, whether abstracting from parti-sanship or incorporating it, does not predict what to expect where political competition, which is the main motivator of politician effort in this theory, is low. What it does offer is a contrast with our clear predictions about the power of constituent demographics when competition is high: where competition is low, any link between constituency poverty and politician behavior should be relatively attenuated.

What, then, might explain clientelism or its absence when competition is low? When strong electoral incentives are lacking, an incumbent enjoys more freedom to choose to use clientelism – or opt out – as he sees fit. If the supply-side explanation elaborated on earlier is correct, partisanship might provide one answer: a politician's partisan identity can shape the likelihood that he will use clientelism, even in the absence of intense competition.[36] Otherwise, historical factors, factors external to the local context, or even a politician's social-psychological characteristics should become more salient in predicting clientelism in low-competition settings. Empirically testing many of these explanations would require a longer historical purview and a different research design than that adopted in this book. Nonetheless, here I briefly

---

35 The view that the quality of local government can be evaluated on a single, performance dimension explains efforts in many parts of the world to make local elections nonpartisan. As of 2004, for example, twenty-one of the thirty largest American cities hold nonpartisan elections for local officials (National League of Cities, 2005).

36 A demand-side explanation of the role of partisanship, on the other hand, modifies the theory's predictions in settings of high competition, but offers no new insight into what to expect where competition is low.

reflect on the ways in which past conditions and behavior may affect politician attitudes toward clientelism in low-competition settings.[37]

A situation of low competition could come about as a result of a number of different processes. I first consider the possibility that competition is itself a result, at least in part, of past choices with respect to clientelism. This book largely treats political competition as independent of clientelism. At the same time, the framework developed here acknowledges that clientelism affects the competitiveness of elections at the margins – that is, after all, why the choice of clientelism is electorally relevant. Indeed, one of the purported advantages of clientelism as described elsewhere in the literature is its ability to lock in the votes of clients and thereby limit political competition (Magaloni et al., 2007). In predominantly poor municipalities where there is little cost to clientelism, a politician who relies on the practice at any given point in time should expect to be rewarded with more limited competition in the future. A politician who attributes at least some of his current electoral security to clientelism might continue to rely on the practice in an effort to stave off increases in competition. Therefore, in some low-competition, high-poverty municipalities, the use of clientelism could be understood as the result of the enduring nature of a decision about electoral strategy made at an earlier time.

Of course, clientelism is not the only factor that shapes future competition. This should be especially true at the municipal level, where the popularity of provincial and national copartisans, economic growth, and other factors independently affect the competitiveness of elections.[38] In Chapter 5, I return to the question of endogeneity in a bit more depth by exploring some empirical patterns in the cross-municipal dataset I analyze. There, I find little evidence that would support the claim that poverty and clientelism necessarily lead to a low-competition equilibrium. Thus, though a history of clientelism should reduce competition at the margins, past clientelism is no guarantee that competition at some future time will be low, even in predominantly poor areas.

In settings with little competition and a large middle class, the appeal of clientelism may also depend on a municipality's history, though endogeneity is less of a direct concern. Imagine a predominantly poor municipality with limited competition where a commodity boom markedly increases income

---

[37] I thank Susan Stokes for encouraging me to think about different historical trajectories.

[38] The outcomes of subnational elections are rarely understood as a pure reflection of local political considerations. For example, on the effects of gubernatorial coattails in Brazil, see Samuels (2000). In the empirical case explored in this book, which uses political competition to explain clientelism, the existence of coattails and other related phenomena offers the advantage of ensuring that local political competition is at least partially exogenous to the behavior of local political actors. Note that the same is true of levels of poverty. Clientelism can depress growth and, at the margins, lead a municipality to have greater levels of poverty. Nonetheless, the importance of provincial and national economic processes ensures these effects will not be determinative.

rather suddenly, but where competition remains low. A mayor in a municipality like this one might continue to act like his counterparts in less prosperous
settings. For at least some mayors, this will mean the use of clientelism. On
the other hand, in a historically prosperous, competitive municipality that
undergoes a sudden drop in competition, clientelism is unlikely to have been
used in the past, and we would not expect to see it emerge just because of a
sudden decrease in competition.[39]

There are, of course, many possible paths by which a municipality can arrive
at a situation of low competition, regardless of its demographic makeup. The
death of an opposition leader or a mayor's strong personal charisma, among
other factors, might explain why any given politician enjoys high security
in office at any given point in time. In these cases, an incumbent's decision
about whether to use clientelism may depend on the broader costs and benefits
of clientelism. Some mayors might in fact relish the personalized nature of
assistance that is inherent in clientelism and take advantage of the absence of
electoral pressures to engage in clientelism, while others will find it a difficult
or distasteful task they avoid unless electorally necessary. The relationship
between local government officials and higher levels of government may also
shape the perceived costs of clientelism in a low-competition setting. Mayors
with close ties to higher level officials might benefit from the financial resources
these officials can offer.[40] National or provincial allies may be able to provide
mayors with funding to increase the number of public employees who can be
used for political work, facilitating the use of clientelism.

To the extent possible, I test these hypotheses alongside the theory's main
predictions in the chapters that follow. Chapter 4 lays out the empirical
context, makes the case for the importance of studying social policy in
Argentina, and introduces a new measure of clientelism. It also includes
some initial evidence on patterns of clientelism across space that is consistent
with the theory. Chapter 5 then turns to a much more rigorous test of the
theory developed here, including its partisan variants, as well as of alternative
explanations. Chapter 6 uses a large in-person survey, along with an original
survey experiment, to test the core individual-level assumption of the theory:
that nonpoor voters will punish clientelism electorally.

---

[39] The data I use for empirical analysis in the following chapters are cross-sectional, so they do
      not allow for an empirical test of these possible trajectories.
[40] This should be especially important in contexts where municipalities have limited autonomous
      tax collection capacity.

4

Clientelism, Social Policy, and Measurement

As illustrated in Chapter 2, local incumbents and bureaucrats engage in a range of behaviors that help make clientelism work as a political strategy. The breadth of these practices, and the difficulty of observing them directly, makes the task of developing a measure of clientelism a difficult one. To make measurement tractable, as well as because of its inherent importance, I measure and explain clientelism in the realm of social policy. In this chapter, I review the recent rise of new forms of social policy throughout Latin America and their relationship to clientelism, and I explain why Argentina is a particularly interesting case in this light. Next, I offer details about the social program on which I focus and explain a new and innovative measure of clientelism across municipalities. Finally, I present some initial evidence for the theory developed in Chapter 3.

4.1 SOCIAL POLICY AND THE RISE OF SAFETY NETS IN LATIN AMERICA

Any review of the history of the welfare state in Latin America focuses on two salient facts.[1] First, in many countries in the region through the late 1970s, social spending was minimal, making it difficult to speak of a "welfare state" at all.[2] Second, regardless of the size of the welfare state, social spending in Latin America has historically been quite regressive (Lindert et al., 2006). A disproportionate share of social spending has been devoted to

[1] See Mesa-Lago (1978), Huber (1996), Segura-Ubiergo (2008), and Haggard and Kaufman (2008) for excellent and detailed descriptions of the evolution of the welfare state in Latin America.

[2] In fact, Segura-Ubiergo (2008, 29) reserves that term for a small group of countries that exhibited relatively high welfare state effort before the 1980s: Uruguay, Argentina, Chile, Costa Rica, and Brazil. Others, including Mesa-Lago (1978), identify three groups of welfare state performers.

funding generous pensions and other benefits for small, elite groups of workers (such as civil servants), while workers in other sectors, particularly the large informal sector, were largely neglected, either through policy decisions or their "self-exclusion" because of their failure to make contributions to the system (Huber, 1996). As Lindert et al. (2006) show for a sample of countries in the region, higher income groups tend to enjoy a greater rate of coverage by social insurance and receive greater resource flows per capita as compared to lower income groups.

The decades since the 1980s have seen a marked shift in social welfare policy throughout Latin America. The debt crisis of the early 1980s and the subsequent shift to neoliberal economic policies as prescribed by the "Washington Consensus" (Williamson, 1990) in the 1980s and 1990s created, on the one hand, enormous pressure to tamp down on government spending, and, on the other hand, increased demand for greater assistance from the state from many sectors of the population. Traditional social welfare benefits, even though far from comprehensive, were extremely expensive, and governments in the region were not in a position to expand them. It was in this context that many countries embraced a new form of social policy: social safety net (SSN) programs. These programs are generally defined as "non-contributory transfer programs targeted in some manner to the poor and those vulnerable to poverty and shocks" (Milazzo and Grosh, 2008, 1).[3] Examples of SSNs include cash transfers, of which conditional cash transfer programs (CCTs) have received the most attention from international policymakers and scholars (among others, see Fiszbein and Schady [2009], De la O [2013], Zucco [2013]), as well as noncash transfers, including food and workfare programs. These programs distribute limited benefits that are highly targeted at the poor, which allows governments to address some social needs with a relatively limited fiscal impact.

As Grindle (2000) describes, these policies appeal, for different reasons, to a broad range of actors, including economic policymakers on the ideological right, as well as democratization advocates and leaders of civil society and NGOs from the ideological left. The broad appeal of social safety net programs has been buttressed by the growing advocacy and availability of implementation advice from international organizations (e.g., Grosh et al. [2008]; Fiszbein and Schady [2009]). The World Bank devoted more than eleven billion dollars in lending for SSNs between fiscal years 2000 and 2010 (Independent Evaluation Group, 2011). Over that period, Latin America received about 60% of total World Bank lending in this area, which speaks to the particular importance of these programs in the region. Haggard and Kaufman (2008,

---

3 Even though I focus on Latin America, the rise of SSNs has not been limited to this region. This is particularly true of conditional cash transfer programs, which have spread throughout lower and middle-income countries, and have even been piloted in New York City (Fiszbein and Schady, 2009).

265) describe the general trend in social welfare policy in Latin America this way:"[O]ver the course of the 1990s and early 2000s, reforms of core social insurance programs, efforts to expand basic social services, and the adoption of anti-poverty programs constituted a 'modal pattern of social policy.' " In addition to being widespread, there is ample evidence that at least some SSNs are effective at improving health and educational outcomes for beneficiaries (Rivera et al., 2004, Adato and Hoddinott, 2010). It is thus not surprising that some supporters have adopted the view that these programs – in particular CCTs – may serve as a "magic bullet" (to use the words of Nancy Birdsall, head of the Center for Global Development) for solving the problem of the intergenerational transfer of poverty in Latin America (Dugger, 2004).

4.1.1 A Magic Bullet for Accountability?

What are the implications of this new form of social policy for government accountability and responsiveness? In a number of cases, SSNs not only have been lauded for their direct effects on schooling and health, but they also have been credited with eliminating clientelism, favoritism, and other deviations from "fair" distribution historically linked to social assistance targeting the poor. The possibility that targeted social programs can eliminate these practices is perhaps best epitomized by the two largest and most praised social safety net programs: Bolsa Familia in Brazil and Progresa/Oportunidades in Mexico. Numerous evaluations by scholars and policymakers highlight the extent to which program administration has been insulated from the day-to-day pressures of politics.[4] By most accounts, Mexican and Brazilian beneficiaries access these programs based on need, understand these resources are funded by the state, and they do not believe that their continued access to benefits is linked to individual political behavior.[5] Although the question of exactly how and why these programs have succeeded in breaking with clientelism is not a settled one, they seem to have successfully limited clientelism through top-down initiative.

Safety Nets Outside of the Model

While Brazil and Mexico provide examples of how social safety net programs can avoid becoming enmeshed in the exchange of benefits for political support, there are many other countries in which the rise of social safety net programs targeted at the poor has not been accompanied by the decline of clientelism

---

4 These programs are of course not apolitical in the broader sense; in fact, their success has been a boon to the political fortunes of those responsible for them (Zucco, 2013, De la O, 2013). However, the political rewards for these programs are those of programmatic politics, not clientelism.

5 Lindert et al. (2007), Hall (2006), De la O (2013, 2014), Levy (2006), Diaz-Cayeros et al. (2012). I return to a discussion of these programs in the conclusion.

or more overt political manipulation. In her comprehensive review of CCT programs in Latin America, De la O (2014) pays particular attention to their operational guidelines (both in writing and as carried out) and the extent to which programs across the region minimize political manipulation. While some programs, like those mentioned earlier, are designed and carried out so as to minimize manipulation, many others, like Bolivia's *Bono Juancito Pinto*, or Ecuador's *Bono Solidario*, are not. Even for some generally well regarded programs, there are indications of a mixed picture with respect to political manipulation. So, for example, De la O (2014) rates Colombia's *Familias en Accion* program very highly on measures of both design and implementation, a positive picture that is reinforced elsewhere (Attanasio et al., 2005). However, in a recent article, Camacho and Conover (2011) present evidence of political manipulation of the timing of household interviews and also show that the release of information on thresholds for inclusion in the program to local officials was followed by marked changes in enrollment patterns. All of this is to suggest that, in many countries, targeted social programs are implemented without an effective nationally driven effort to minimize clientelism.

While a centrally driven effort to reduce clientelism in social policy may have the best chances for success, understanding alternate paths away from clientelism in the absence of a top-down effort is equally important. When either political will or technical capacity to minimize clientelism is lacking at the national level, it is crucial to ask whether local factors nonetheless sometimes reduce reliance on clientelism. Though with some changes very recently, Argentina has not followed a top-down technocratic approach to social policy over the past three decades. In fact, if anything, Argentina's policies are repeatedly cited as examples of political manipulation of social programs of various kinds, both in terms of the allocation of funds across subnational governments and in the distribution of benefits to individuals (see, among others, Lodola [2005], Weitz-Shapiro [2006], and Gruenberg and Pereyra [2009]). Studying Argentina thus allows us to explore when and how greater accountability can be achieved in the *absence* of any central government effort to impede clientelism in the administration of social programs.

4.2 ARGENTINE SOCIAL POLICY AND THE PNSA

Compared to its Latin American counterparts, the Argentine state was among the earliest adopters of provisions for social welfare and the most generous and comprehensive in its coverage. The earliest pensions – to judges, federal civil servants, and public school teachers – were granted in the late 1800s (Mesa-Lago, 1978). Coverage slowly expanded over the early part of the twentieth century, although it continued to be aimed at a few privileged occupational groups (Haggard and Kaufman, 2008). It was not until Juan Perón's rise to power – first as Minister of Labor for the military government that took power in 1943, and then as the popularly elected president in 1946 – that the Argentine welfare state expanded dramatically to incorporate a substantial portion of the economically active population. Even at its most expansive, however, many citizens were still left outside of the welfare state's protections. In 1970, for example, 68% of the economically active population, but only 55% of the total population, was covered by social security (Mesa-Lago, 1978, 180). In spite of its limits, the growth of the welfare state in Argentina had important political implications. The expansion of benefits and the incorporation of urban workers into the welfare state were crucial for Juan Perón's consolidation of public support and remained key to the Peronist party's electoral strategy and identity in ensuing decades. However, these social welfare benefits were not targeted at the most poor, and those implementing social policies did not enjoy much discretion over the distribution of benefits at the individual level.[6]

Argentina's experience with large-scale noncontributory transfer programs began soon after the return of democracy in 1983, which followed harsh military rule from 1976 to 1983 and coincided with an economic crisis. In the new democracy, the existence of malnutrition and hunger was framed as yet another violation of human rights wrought by the military regime, and one that was particularly shocking in a country known for its abundance of "wheat and beef." In 1984, Congress passed legislation establishing a major food distribution plan, the *Programa Alimentario Nacional* (National Food Program), or PAN ("bread" in Spanish).[7] Although it had broader aims, the bulk of program funds and effort went to the regular provision of boxes of foodstuffs to "vulnerable" citizens and those in "extreme poverty." The identification of recipients was left mostly to the discretion of field coordinators, rather than governed by any clear criteria (Midre, 1992, 353). Both characteristics of the PAN – its emphasis on the direct provision of food and the vagueness of criteria for inclusion – were carried over to the PAN's

---

[6] I do not mean to suggest that there was no individualized distribution of social assistance by the state or affiliated actors in Argentina under Perón or afterwards. The Fundación Eva Perón, under the direction of Perón's wife, Eva Duarte Perón, famously engaged in the individualized delivery of social assistance (see Plotkin, 2002, Chapter 7, for a detailed discussion). Although this sort of distribution may have generated loyalty or gratitude from recipients, it was not enmeshed in ongoing individualized relationships, and it did not involve the possibility of monitoring and risk of punishment that characterize clientelism as described here.

[7] See Midre (1992) for a discussion of the debate leading up to the establishment of the PAN and a summary of its major characteristics. Note that the PAN was not the first program that distributed food on a large scale to some part of the Argentine population. As early as 1948 the Office of Maternity and Infancy, under the Ministry of Health, began the distribution of powdered whole milk to pregnant women and children younger than the age of two. On this and for a review of the history of food aid in Argentina, see Britos et al. (2003). The PAN was, however, the first major food distribution to target a wide swath of the poor at the *household* level, rather than focusing only on pregnant women or young or school-age children.

successor programs and persisted through the period under study in this book.

Other large-scale social safety net programs in Argentina emerged in the mid-1990s, conceived initially in response to the economic downturn that followed the 1994 Mexican peso crisis. In addition to food programs, the other major type of program implemented took the form of "workfare": regular cash transfers to unemployed individuals in exchange for their labor on community projects (see see Lodola [2005], Weitz-Shapiro [2006], and Giraudy [2007] for more details). As for food programs, in spite of its conception as an "emergency" program designed to last two years, the PAN persisted under the same name through the end of the Alfonsín administration in 1989. It was replaced by a series of other programs in the 1990s, which, although operating under different names, retained the same basic characteristics of the PAN (Britos et al., 2003).

The economic crisis surrounding the devaluation of the Argentine peso in January 2002 led to rocketing unemployment and sharply increased demand for social safety net programs in the country. Both food distribution programs and cash transfer programs were greatly expanded under the interim administration of President Eduardo Duhalde (2002–2003) and the presidencies of Néstor Kirchner (2003–2007) and Cristina Kirchner (2007–present). A major cash transfer program, the *Plan Jefes/Jefas de Hogar*, began to distribute a monthly payment to unemployed heads of households in 2002.[8] The distribution of food aid was also greatly expanded in this period, first under the *Programa de Emergencia Alimentaria*, in 2002, which then became the *Programa Nacional de Seguridad Alimentaria* (PNSA) in 2003. The implementation of the PNSA is the focus of the empirical analysis in this chapter and the next. In the conclusion, I touch on more recent changes to the model of social welfare provision in Argentina and consider whether these might be moving Argentina toward a different, less discretionary, model of social welfare provision.

4.2.1 PNSA

The *Programa Nacional de Seguridad Alimentaria* (National Food Security Program), or PNSA, is a large umbrella program that includes a number

---

[8] It was later divided into two successor programs. The *Plan Familias* provided an ongoing cash benefit to mothers with children in exchange for their compliance with certain health and education standards for those children. Beneficiaries who were believed to have better labor market prospects were channeled into an alternate program, the *Seguro de Capacitación y Empleo*, which provided a cash benefit and job training for a limited time period. For a concise summary, see Cruces et al. (2007). In late 2009, with the advent of a new conditional cash transfer program to families with school-age children outside of the traditional safety net (the Universal Child Benefit, or AUH in Spanish), eligible beneficiaries of all these preexisting programs were transferred to the AUH.

of food-related subprograms, including self-production of food (community farms) and *comedores* (soup kitchens). It is much larger in scope than those food programs that preceded it; as of 2008, it reached slightly more than 1.8 million Argentine households, of about 18% of the population (Argentina, Ministry of Social Developments, 2009).[9] I focus on the component that, at the time of my research, funded the direct, regular distribution to families of large boxes or bags of food stuffs (*módulos* or *bolsones alimentarios*) to households across the country.[10] Provincial guidelines for one of the provinces under study suggest that a package might include the following items: a kilogram each of flour, *yerba* (a local tea), sugar, and rice, half a kilogram of corn flour, tomato paste, and three different types of dried pasta, as well as a liter of oil and milk. Such a benefit is likely to be extremely important to a family suffering from food insecurity.

The PNSA shares a number of characteristics with previous Argentine food distribution programs, including the looseness of eligibility criteria and its decentralized structure, which make the program particularly amenable to clientelism. These same characteristics also allow me to compare the behavior of similarly situated politicians who face different demographic and competitive environments, thus making the program very well suited, from a methodological standpoint, for a study of the local determinants of clientelism. First, it is a nationally funded program whose broad parameters are the same across all municipalities; all towns and cities in Argentina have this program, and its basic content and structure are established by the national government. At the same time, local politicians enjoy significant discretion over program implementation.[11] In the law that established the program, municipalities are specifically given a number of responsibilities, including registering beneficiaries, administering funds, and establishing mechanisms for the distribution of the food within their municipalities (Argentine Congress, 2002). The PNSA is thus an ideal vehicle through which to test the theory developed here, as municipalities cannot change the overall structure of the program, but the decisions made by local politicians have a profound impact on how program-funded

---

9 The PNSA is not an "exclusionary" program – beneficiaries can also be recipients of other social welfare benefits, and most likely many are. The PNSA does not maintain a centralized list of beneficiaries, making it impossible to measure the overlap exactly. There are also many other smaller provincial and even municipal safety net programs, as well.

10 Since the time of my research, the program has largely shifted from the direct distribution of foodstuffs to the distribution of vouchers and debit cards. I discuss the possible implications of this switch for clientelism in Chapter 7.

11 The program is decentralized in its structure: the federal government signs agreements with each of the provinces, in which the two levels of government detail how the program will be administered in that province. These agreements establish the targeted population in each province; with only minimal variation across provinces, it is targeted at poor families with children younger than the age of fourteen, pregnant women, and the elderly. These national–provincial agreements also establish the program's budget and the criteria for distribution of funds across towns and cities within the province.

food is distributed within their jurisdictions. These decisions are unlikely to be merely an artifact of variation in administrative capacity, as municipal responsibilities within the PNSA are not technically complex.[12] Compared to local economic development or health care programs, for example, implementing the PNSA according to program criteria requires little specialized knowledge. At the same time, there is limited oversight of the program by central or provincial governments, and monitoring of how beneficiary lists are created or how food is distributed is far from rigorous.[13] In the case of the province of Córdoba, the wealthiest of the three provinces in which I carried out field work, at the time of my research, the evidence cities were required to provide to the provincial Ministry of Solidarity as proof of their compliance with broad program regulations consisted of photos of recipients picking up their food packages (Author interview, May 2006).[14] In Río Negro as of May 2006, the Ministry of Social Welfare compiled sheets with the signatures of all recipients, but had no way of monitoring the validity of those signatures. Given this lax enforcement of formal program rules, politicians who seek to use clientelism in the selection of beneficiaries for the PNSA are unlikely to be constrained from doing so by central government monitoring.[15]

Furthermore, the PNSA's beneficiary list is locally controlled and is "open" in the sense that families can be added and removed.[16] Indeed, evidence from the survey I conducted (discussed in more detail in the sections that follow) demonstrates that beneficiary list revisions occur frequently. Empirically, out of 127 cases for which I have information, 78 cities report revising the list once every 45 days (or more frequently – many claimed that the beneficiary list was being "permanently" or "constantly" revised), 41 report revising it more than once a year though less often than once every 45 days, and only 8

---

[12] The administration of targeted social assistance is much more complex in contexts with more extensive reporting and targeting requirements, but these are both lacking in the Argentine case.

[13] Most monitoring that I learned about seeks to ensure that the purchase of the food is done through competitive bidding rather than focusing on beneficiary selection or methods of distribution.

[14] Municipalities are also required to submit receipts demonstrating that the funds dedicated to the program were indeed used to purchase food, but this does not provide any information on beneficiary selection or methods of distribution.

[15] By choosing a program where oversight is lax or absent, I am necessarily unable to understand the extent to which monitoring by higher levels of government might improve city service provision or prevent the use of clientelism. There is some evidence from Brazil (Tendler, 2000) and Indonesia (Olken, 2007) that such monitoring can effectively limit clientelism and corruption.

[16] This is in contrast to the more widely studied *Jefes de Hogar* program, an unemployment subsidy program that was also created as a result of the 2001 economic crisis in Argentina. Beneficiary lists for that program were created between April and May 2002 and although beneficiaries could be dropped from the program, no additions were permitted after the initial enrollment period.

report revising once a year or less (and most of those in fact once a year).[17] In sum, focusing on the PNSA allows us to limit any potential variation in the defining characteristics of the policy, while the type of administration of the PNSA that we observe in a given city is likely to reflect the mayor's preferences and hence the incentives created by the local political and social conditions that he faces. Before I elaborate on my measure of clientelism in the PNSA, I discuss the challenges inherent in any attempt to measure clientelism.

4.3 OVERCOMING THE DIFFICULTY OF MEASUREMENT

Throughout this book, I define clientelism as the individualized, contingent exchange of goods or services in return for political support. It is a phenomenon that is perhaps possible to identify fully only by learning how citizens and politicians understand the interactions in which they engage over a long period of time. As Kitschelt (2000, 850, emphasis added) explains, the difference between clientelism and other modes of distribution is not in the ends that policies serve, but it is instead "*procedural*, in terms of the modes of exchange between constituencies and politicians."[18] This makes measurement difficult, and, and Hicken (2011, 304) highlights, researchers rely on "a stunning variety of (sometimes crude) proxies" for the phenomenon. In particular, scholars have resorted to three main approaches in their attempts to measure and understand clientelism – the direct observation of a single research site or small group of cases, the reliance on indirect measures for a large sample of cases, and the use of mass surveys. Though each has its advantages, all three approaches pose a challenge for any attempt to understand the correlates of clientelism across space. I discuss each in turn.

4.3.1 Existing Measures of Clientelism

Opting for the direct observation of the interactions between politicians (and their agents) and voters, scholars working in the tradition of ethnographic research have demonstrated with great richness how clientelism and related phenomena operate in settings as diverse as Argentina (Auyero, 2000b, Lázaro, 2003, Szwarcberg, 2008), Brazil (Gay, 1994, Nichter, 2009), Egypt (Singerman, 1995), India (Krishna, 2007), and Taiwan (Wang and Kurzman,

---

[17] I coded the frequency of beneficiary list revision on the basis of questions in a survey of a key informant in each municipality. The survey is described in greater detail in the appendix to this chapter. For this indicator, I asked questions about the most recent and next anticipated revision of the list. Where respondents replied that lists were revised at every distribution, I code this as being revised every 45 days, since distributions are scheduled to take place this frequently.

[18] In a recent review article, Hicken (2011, 294) makes a similar point, stating that the "terms" by which a good is offered, rather than the substance of the good itself, define clientelism.

2007), among others. Although this type of research illuminates *how* clientelism works, the intense amount of field work this type of research requires makes replicating such studies for a large number of locations difficult. As a consequence, such work is rarely conducted in settings where linkages between voters and politicians are not characterized by clientelism. Research on clientelism that relies on the direct observation of the interactions between politicians and voters therefore offers limited leverage for understanding what factors shape the incentives of politicians who can choose between clientelism and other strategies of distribution, nor does it shed much light on why some politicians choose *not* to use clientelism.

The collection of data across many units, although it allows for tests of competing hypotheses via statistical analysis, faces a different difficulty. In contrast to the proliferation of measures and assessments of cross-national corruption, for example (by Transparency International, the World Bank, and private firms), cross-national measures of clientelism are very limited. The paucity of readily available data on the topic forces authors to rely on rough proxies for clientelism, such as corruption or the rule of law (Keefer, 2007, Manzetti and Wilson, 2007), that may be related, but are analytically distinct. As far as I am aware, there is only one existing attempt to assemble a cross-national measure of clientelism, which relies on expert assessments of party practices in a large sample of countries (Kitschelt et al., 2009). Though a laudable attempt to compile cross-national data, expert assessments are themselves likely to be constrained by the limited reliable information available on clientelism within countries. They are also likely to disproportionately reflect practices in the large cities where academics and journalists tend to concentrate.

Even within-country studies that assemble quantitative measures of clientelism face serious constraints and many scholars circumvent the difficulty of directly measuring clientelism by instead comparing spending on different types of goods and services. So, for example, Magaloni et al. (2007) categorize spending data for a major Mexican antipoverty program implemented throughout the 1990s according to the nature of the goods provided. They consider any expenditures on excludable goods, such as individual scholarships, to be evidence of clientelism, which they contrast with expenditures on public goods, such as digging wells and building hospitals. Their approach is fairly typical of a body of work that uses spending data to examine variation in government responsiveness and patronage: these studies generally treat data on personnel spending as indicative of clientelism or poor government performance, while using spending on public goods or capital projects as evidence of good governance.[19]

---

[19] See for example Gordin (2002), Fundación Grupo Innova (2003), Calvo and Murillo (2004), Chhibber and Nooruddin (2004), Faguet (2004), Brusco et al. (2005), and Remmer

The ease of collection makes these attractive measures, but they are nonetheless problematic. Esping-Anderson's critique of the use of spending data in studies of the welfare state – that "[e]xpenditures are epiphenomenal to the theoretical substance" – is equally applicable to the literature on the evaluation of government performance and clientelism (Esping-Anderson, 1990, 19). It is difficult to assert that government spending on a particular type of good or service is sufficient to create the "contingent direct exchange" (Kitschelt and Wilkinson, 2007a) that separates clientelism from more programmatic policy implementation. Clientelism, as discussed here and elsewhere, is a *mode* of distribution and does not fit neatly into conventional distinctions between private and public goods. Analyzing the amount of spending on a particular good, or even looking at policy outcomes in a particular area, masks how such funds are used and how policy is implemented.

Consider, for example, government-funded food stamps. Food stamps are clearly private goods by any common definition of the term: assuming a fixed budget, one family's receipt of the good means that another family cannot receive it, and beneficiaries consume the benefit without sharing it with others. Yet, without knowing how a food stamp program is administered, it is impossible to say whether it is indeed distributed using a clientelist logic. Are recipients chosen on the basis of need alone, or do they believe that their continued receipt of benefits is contingent on their political behavior? If need governs distribution on an ongoing basis, then, although a private good is being distributed, some public end is also served. In contrast, if the continued receipt of these benefits is contingent on the recipient's political behavior, the benefit is not only private, but clientelist practices are in place. In fact, this book demonstrates that the very same government-funded food distribution program can be administered in strikingly different ways across space.

At the other extreme, devoting funds to a public good – such as the construction of a road or a hospital – does not necessarily preclude clientelism. The process required to create almost any public good embeds many private goods within it, some of which may be distributed via the contingent direct exchange that is a hallmark of clientelism. Temporary jobs created to construct large infrastructure projects may be doled out on the basis of political behavior, and the location of these "public goods" may be chosen as part of a quid pro quo with certain groups of constituents in pork-barrel type exchanges. Wilkinson (2006) describes how these problems, among others, afflict much of India's infrastructure spending, and in fact, in his research he treats spending on road construction as an indicator of clientelism rather than of the creation of public goods. The line dividing private from public goods is easily blurred. Although using information on funding for different goods as a proxy for clientelism allows for the comparison of outcomes across space, we run the risk

---

(2007). Other work on government performance has relied on outcome measures, such as the provision of water and electricity (Chhibber and Nooruddin, 2004, Cleary, 2007).

of making many wrong inferences if we assume a one-to-one correspondence between private goods and clientelism.

Finally, a third approach to the study of clientelism relies on citizen surveys. Carried out in locations including Argentina (Brusco et al., 2004), Brazil (Weber Abramo, 2004), Mexico (Lawson, 2009), and Nicaragua (Gonzalez-Ocantos et al., 2012), these studies offer substantial insight into the characteristics of those whose votes are "bought." However, even a large survey of individuals typically reaches only a limited number of geographic units and is not typically designed to assess differences in clientelism across space.

In this chapter, I propose a new measure of clientelism. I aim to maintain the richness of qualitative work and its focus on how policy is implemented. At the same time, I have collected this measure for a sufficiently large number of units such that I am able to document variation in the use of clientelism and to test hypotheses about the correlates of that variation while controlling for possible confounding factors.

4.3.2 Conceptualizing Clientelism: Personalized Decision Making

Chapter 2 describes the range of behaviors that politicians can employ to help make clientelism "work": these include concentrating decision making, politicizing bureaucrats, allowing unpredictable access, and having irregular distribution. It would be nearly impossible to observe these directly with any accuracy in a large sample of cities. Nonetheless, a survey of government practices in the administration of a particular social welfare policy allows us to do far better than we could do with aggregate measures such as spending on personnel or even spatial measures such as the location of program beneficiaries.

Although I cannot observe clientelism directly, I develop a proxy for clientelism that relies on evaluating whether the mayor is *personally* involved in the selection of program beneficiaries for the PNSA in a sample of more than 120 municipalities across 3 Argentine provinces.[20] The lack of central oversight of this important food program means that a mayor's choices with respect to clientelism are likely to fully reflect his preferences. In addition, a focus on a single program should increase the reliability of responses in the elite survey used to collect the measure. As detailed in Chapter 2, field work indicated that personal mayoral involvement in decision making allows mayors to become the public face of social welfare benefits. It is not uncommon for mayors in such municipalities to devote significant time to receiving and acting on individual requests for social assistance. This personalization of decision making has a number of consequences for how voters understand the benefits that they receive. First, even though benefits are funded by the national

---

[20] The appendix includes more details about the sample.

government, the mayor's personal involvement in beneficiary selection allows him to claim credit for the benefits he distributes. Second, because mayoral involvement concentrates decision making in the hands of very few people, it also lends substantial unpredictability to the process. Although clientelist mayors spend significant time receiving requests from constituents, other duties and tasks frequently intrude. As a result, where mayors are personally involved in beneficiary lists, constituents typically spend a significant amount of time waiting to make their requests, usually in the company of many others with similar requests, which heightens the sense of scarcity surrounding these benefits. Mayoral involvement is also an attractive proxy for clientelism because it indicates that a mayor is in a position to personally punish voters for their political behavior, one of the key requirements of clientelist exchange.

An original survey was used to collect much of the data of interest.[21] I focus on smaller municipalities (the mean population in the sample is 14,000), which allows me to examine cases where clientelism will be manifest in the personal involvement of mayors in clientelist exchange, rather than by reliance on large networks of brokers, as documented in more populous Argentine municipalities by Auyero (2000b) and Levitsky (2003).[22] The survey included a number of measures of mayoral intervention into the workings of the PNSA. The questions I analyze here focus on the mayor's role in drawing up or altering the list of program beneficiaries. Although interviewees were not informed that the main focus of the research was clientelism, and the questions were embedded in a larger survey, there may be some incentives for the interviewee to dissemble information to avoid the appearance of "unprofessional" practices to an outside interviewer. At times interviewees did answer these questions by emphasizing that the mayor only made "suggestions" to the beneficiary list or contributed to the list only "occasionally," which suggests some desire to hide information about mayoral involvement in program implementation.[23] In another attempt to deal with this potential problem, I asked four separate questions about mayoral involvement in list making, which I then combined into a single indicator variable, as I explain below.

The survey asked separately about the creation of the beneficiary list and additions to and subtractions from that list. In each case, the head was asked whether the mayor (along with a number of other actors) was "consulted" or otherwise "participated" in creating the list of beneficiaries, and then later whether the mayor definitively decided on the makeup of that list.[24] Each set

---

[21] The data appendix to this chapter details how the survey was conducted.

[22] See also Stokes et al. (2013) for a theory and evidence of the role of brokers in clientelism. Note that, according to the 2011 census, about 58% of the Argentine population lived in cities with populations less than 100,000.

[23] Regardless of the use of qualifiers, all mentions of mayoral participation in drawing up the beneficiary list were coded the same.

[24] The exact question wording is reported in the appendix to this chapter. In a few cases, the respondent did not mention the mayor when asked about who "participated" in making the

of questions (on the making of the list and on additions to/subtractions from the list) was posed separately, with a number of questions in between. Asking these questions repeatedly then serves to reduce the effects of any respondent attempt to hide this information from the interviewer. With that in mind, I use a blanket measure that takes a value of 1 if the interviewee claimed that the mayor suggested names either in the making of the list or in making changes to the list – a variable I call *mayor list*, which is the main outcome variable I examine in the empirical analysis that follows. Of the 126 cities for which I have data, the mayor was somehow involved in list-making in 84 of these (67% of the sample).[25] In other words, I find evidence that mayors in about two-thirds of the municipalities in the sample rely on clientelism. We thus have a specific measure of clientelism in each municipality in the sample that, overall, is in line with qualitative and journalistic work that points to the widespread nature of clientelism in Argentina.

4.3.3 The Validity of Measurement

The measure of clientelism proposed here is of course not a perfect one. There are two main objections that might be raised: first, it might be the case that the measure proposed does not capture clientelism, but something else. Second, it might be argued that a measure that represents the use of clientelism in the PNSA does not necessarily give us information about the use of clientelism more broadly.[26] I address both concerns below.

Beginning with the first, although there are alternative interpretations of the meaning of mayoral involvement in beneficiary selection within the PNSA, these are less plausible in the empirical setting examined here. It might be argued that individual mayoral involvement in beneficiary lists simply reflects municipality size, as mayors may be more likely to be involved in any decision in smaller localities. To some extent, the empirical design controls for this possibility by limiting the study to municipalities with less than 100,000 residents. Most municipalities in the sample are far smaller than this, and thus of a size where individual mayoral involvement should be feasible – and yet it is not observed in one-third of the sample. In addition, I include municipality size in the regression analysis reported in the next chapter and find that even when accounting for differences in population, mayoral intervention is

---

list, but then responded that the mayor was responsible for making the final decision about who would be included. In all these cases, I code the mayor as having participated in list-making.

[25] This breaks down into the following groups: twenty-seven cities where the respondent replied only that the mayor was involved in creating the list, eleven cases where she reported mayoral involvement only in making changes to the list, and forty-six cases where the head responded that the mayor was involved in both making the list and in making changes to it.

[26] For an articulation of this concern more generally with respect to the literature on distributive politics, see Posner and Kramon (2013).

associated with the theoretical variables of interest in the expected direction.[27] Alternately, it might be argued that politician involvement in decision making is an indicator of good governance and oversight, rather than clientelism. As described in Chapter 2, in-depth observation during field work suggested that mayoral involvement in beneficiary selection for the PNSA was used not to ensure appropriate targeting of beneficiaries, but rather to claim personal and political credit for a nationally funded program.[28]

The intuition that personalized decision making is a sign of clientelism, not good government, is corroborated by the fact that other indicators of the politicization of PNSA implementation, both also collected in the original survey described earlier, are positively correlated with personalized mayoral decision making. A mayor's physical presence at the actual distribution of the boxes of food is another practice that facilitates personal credit claiming and might signal the ability to withdraw benefits that is a hallmark of clientelist practice. This is a relatively rare practice, occurring in only 16% of the total cases (20 municipalities out of 126 total). The distribution of this activity follows a clear pattern: where the mayor was involved in making the beneficiary list for the PNSA, he was also present at food distribution 23% of the time, whereas the mayor personally attended food distribution in only 2% of those municipalities where he did not participate in list-making.[29] On the other hand, the involvement of social workers (presumably less likely to be political actors) in drawing up beneficiary lists, though relatively widespread, was significantly more common in nonclientelist municipalities. Where mayors were not personally involved in list-making, social workers were involved in developing and editing the list of beneficiaries in 79% of these cases, whereas this figure falls to only 43% in municipalities coded as clientelist.[30] Both of these patterns support the claim that personal mayoral involvement in the PNSA is a good proxy for clientelism within the context of that program.

To address the second concern in the same vein, we can examine whether measures of the politicization of social policy more generally, not only within the PNSA, are also correlated with the measure I propose here. For example, appointing a relative to head a town's social welfare office should facilitate a mayor's efforts to individually claim credit for benefits he distributes. Cases

---

[27] The same is true if we replicate the main analyses in Chapter 5 using only the smaller municipalities in the sample.

[28] A third possibility might be that mayoral involvement is simply an indicator of the normal credit-claiming that takes place in the course of politics, rather than clientelism per se. To some extent, this is refuted by the correlations with other measures discussed here. As I discuss in the next chapter, so-called normal credit-claiming also suggests clear empirical patterns in the data that are inconsistent with the results presented there.

[29] This difference is statistically significant ($p < .03$).

[30] This difference is statistically significant ($p < .01$) Note also that the mere involvement of social workers does not guarantee the absence of clientelism, as illustrated by the example of the conflict between the mayor and social workers in the municipality of Devoto related in the introduction.

where the mayor and bureaucrat who headed the social welfare office were related were rare, occurring in only 12% of cases for which I could collect data.[31] However, these were overwhelmingly concentrated in municipalities where the mayor was personally involved in the PNSA beneficiary list. In these municipalities, the head of social welfare and the mayor are related in 17% of the cases, whereas the head of the social welfare office is related to the mayor in only 3% of other cases.[32] Similar patterns present themselves in the case of two other possible indicators of the politicization of social policy. Also in a small number of cases, it was reported the the head of the social welfare office had previously been an elected member of the town council. Such direct political involvement would likely facilitate the direct political use of social policy. In municipalities I code as using clientelism, the head of the social welfare office has this occupational past 16% of the time, whereas this is true only 7% of the time in municipalities I code as not relying on clientelism.[33] Finally, I also have information about who headed a local joint municipal–community council charged with overseeing social policy more generally. To the extent such a body might act as a check on the politicization of social policy, this is presumably less likely when the mayor himself is at the helm. I find that the mayor headed such councils in 23% of the municipalities I code as clientelist, but only 10% of councils in other municipalities.[34] These correlations are again consistent with the picture presented in Chapter 2, which demonstrated qualitatively the set of behaviors that politicians frequently use across the range of their interactions with citizens to make clientelism work within the PNSA and more broadly.

In spite of the consistency of these indicators, it is of course impossible to know with certainty whether the behavior I code in the administration of the PNSA indeed carries over to all realms of government administration. However, once we take into account the extreme challenges to measuring clientelism in a valid way across space, the measure proposed here has clear appeal. Importantly, it is the first effort, to my knowledge, that develops a measure of clientelism across space that relies on an assessment of *how* policy is implemented, rather than on funds spent. In doing so, it provides a model of the type of information about policy implementation that could be used to develop similar measures in other contexts.

---

[31] This question was not answered in five of the municipalities where the survey was otherwise completed.

[32] This difference is statistically significant ($p < .03$).

[33] This difference is significant at the $p < .14$ level. Though this does not reach traditional levels of statistical significance, this information was collected inconsistently across the municipalities and so the data is less reliable than for the rest of the survey. For municipalities where I did not collect relevant information, I assume that the head bureaucrat had not previously been a member of the town council.

[34] This is significant at the $p < .08$ level.

It is also worth noting that the nature of the PNSA makes it a particularly apt, and in some senses difficult, test for a theory of clientelism in local politics. This book aims to understand the conditions under which local incumbents will face incentives to be accountable to voters. Highly centralized, well-enforced programs may in fact lessen reliance on clientelism, but they do not necessarily give us any insight into the incentives faced by local officials or reveal how local incumbents might act if unfettered from national level restraints. The decentralized nature of the PNSA allows for an examination of local incentives. In addition, the fact that the PNSA is explicitly targeted at the poor and hands out benefits that are unlikely to be of interest to nonpoor residents makes it a difficult test for the theory proposed here, which relies on middle-class distaste for clientelism. Given its very limited potential to affect middle class interests, we can imagine that nonpoor voters might ignore the administration of such a program entirely. If my theoretical predictions hold up in an examination of such a program, we should expect to see them stand up to other programs of more direct interest to the middle class, as well.

4.4 BIVARIATE RELATIONSHIPS

The theory developed in the previous chapter suggests that the interaction between political competition and poverty should affect an incumbent politician's incentives to use clientelism. In that chapter, I also explore the possibility of a role for partisanship – either as a level or interaction effect. In the next chapter, I report the results of various multivariate analyses that test my hypotheses in full, including the role of partisanship, and I also evaluate alternative explanations. Here, I present some simple bivariate relationships to examine whether there is initial evidence for my main hypothesis: that political competition and poverty jointly explain incentives for clientelism. I explain my measures of both poverty and competition, along with other variables, in more detail in the next chapter. To summarize briefly, competition is measured by the size of the opposition in the local town council, and I measure poverty using the most common measure in Argentina, the NBI ("necesidades básicas insatisfechas"), which measures the share of the municipal population with unsatisfied basic needs. The outcome variable, designed to capture the use of clientelism, is assessed using information collected on mayoral involvement in beneficiary selection for the PNSA, as already described.

Large Opposition

I begin with the case where political competition is high, and hence politician effort to win votes should be commensurately intense. As I argued in the previous chapter, when competition is high, we should expect to observe divergent behavior based on voter poverty. An increasing opposition should decrease the incentives for clientelism only in those cities with substantial

TABLE 4.1. *High Opposition:*
Relationship between Poverty and
Clientelism

		Poverty		
		Low	High	Total
Mayor List	No	25	4	29
		(52%)	(20%)	
	Yes	23	16	39
		(48%)	(80%)	
	Total	48	20	68

Source: Author-conducted survey.

numbers of middle-class residents. In contrast, clientelism should be an attractive political strategy when competition is high and voters are mostly poor.

Table 4.1 presents information on clientelism only for those municipalities where the size of the total legislative opposition is above the mean level for the sample.[35] It then compares the rate of mayoral involvement in list-making between those municipalities with low levels of poverty (below the mean rate of poverty for the entire sample) and those with relatively higher levels of poverty. It shows, consistent with the theory, a marked difference in clientelism in high- versus low-poverty municipalities. Where competition is high, the mayor intervenes in the beneficiary list in 80% of the high-poverty municipalities, whereas such intervention is far less frequent in the less poor municipalities, occurring only in about half of them. A chi-squared test indicates that this difference is statistically significant at the .02 level.

Limited Opposition

In a setting where political competition is low, the propensity to employ clientelism should not depend on the share of a city's residents who are poor. Though the theory makes no clear predictions about the likelihood of

---

35 Alternately, rather than divide the municipalities into two groups based on the mean share of seats held by the opposition in the sample, we could define high levels of opposition based on the difference in the absolute number of seats held by the mayor's party and opposition parties. If we do this, labeling a municipality as having a "large" opposition when the seats held by the mayor minus the seats held by the opposition is 1 or less (this value will be negative in cities where the opposition is a majority), the results from two by two tables constructed like those presented here are even more striking. Defined this way, the share of low and high poverty municipalities that use clientelism is almost identical when the opposition is limited in size, whereas there is an almost 30 percentage point difference in the use of clientelism between high- and low-poverty municipalities when the opposition is large.

TABLE 4.2. *Low Opposition: Relationship between Poverty and Clientelism*

		Poverty		
		Low	High	Total
Mayor List	No	6	7	13
		(25%)	(21%)	
	Yes	18	27	45
		(75%)	(80%)	
	Total	24	34	58

Source: Author-conducted survey.

clientelism in these cases, we might expect that a mayor's personal taste for clientelism, the non-vote – related costs or benefits of the practice, and possibly partisanship, could affect its incidence.

The results presented in Table 4.2 are consistent with the hypothesis that poverty is not an important determinant of clientelism where legislative opposition is low. The table examines only those cities where the size of the total legislative opposition is below the mean level in the sample. It then compares the rate of mayoral involvement in list-making between low- and high-poverty municipalities. Although about 60% of the "low-opposition" cities are poor, a substantial number of less poor cities experience low levels of opposition, as well. As the table demonstrates, in a setting with limited opposition, the share of municipalities where the mayor intervenes in list-making is quite similar across cities regardless of poverty level; although clientelism appears to be slightly more likely when poverty is high, a chi-squared test indicates that these differences are not statistically significant. This supports the hypothesis that, in a limited opposition context, the incentives to use clientelism do not vary with poverty levels.[36] It is also consistent with the assessment that clientelism serves as a "default" behavior in many Argentine municipalities, and that local incumbents depart from the practice only when the incentives to do so are particularly strong.

This chapter began by documenting the rise of new forms of social policy in Argentina and Latin America over the past few decades. The efficient, technocratic administration of a few exemplary social safety net programs in recent years has led these programs to be portrayed as a magic bullet for

---

[36] If it were instead the case that clientelism was much more common in high- versus low-poverty municipalities, even in the absence of competition, this would suggest that we do not need to take into account the interaction between competition and poverty in order to explain clientelism. However, the evidence presented here and in the next chapter strongly supports the claim that poverty matters in interaction with competition, rather than alone.

reducing poverty and simultaneously increasing accountability and responsiveness. Though compelling, this narrative neglects the many cases where social safety nets have been implemented in a very different manner. Argentina falls into this latter group, and it thus presents an interesting case for examining whether and when some local politicians might eschew clientelism even in the absence of any national-level mandate to do so. The theory developed in Chapter 3 presents an alternate path to accountability in these cases: a path that depends on the combination of high competition and a large nonpoor population. To test this theory, this chapter develops a unique measure of clientelism that reflects the nature of the interaction between citizens and politicians and does so for a large number of cases. Initial tests demonstrate that incumbent reliance on clientelism is at its lowest in municipalities where competition is high and poverty is low. Though these results are consistent with the theory, there are many possible confounding factors for which we cannot control in a simple bivariate table. The next chapter moves to a more thorough test of the theory and alternative hypotheses.

4.5 APPENDIX

The survey used to collect data on personalized mayoral decision making was conducted in person in each province by researchers trained by the author, between May and September 2006. The following criteria were used to select municipalities within each province. In Río Negro and Salta, all municipalities with populations greater than 2,000 as of the 2001 census were included (27 and 50, respectively).[37] In Córdoba, which has a much larger number of municipalities, the sample includes all municipalities with populations greater than 20,000, and a random sample of those with populations between 2,000 and 20,000 (55 in total). Towns with fewer than 2,000 residents do not have the legal status as municipalities in either Córdoba or Río Negro, so I restrict my analysis to towns of at least that size in all three provinces. I exclude the provincial capitals of Salta and Córdoba from the analysis owing to their substantially larger populations, which would make comparison difficult.[38] Although not a random sample of Argentine municipalities, the towns and cities selected for analysis are extremely diverse and represent a range of political and economic realities of the country. Of the 132 municipalities selected for analysis, I was able to complete the survey in all but 5 of these.

In the vast majority of cases, I first personally contacted the head of the social welfare office in each municipality via phone, explaining the project and informing her that a research assistant would follow up to arrange a particular

---

[37] There are actually 51 municipalities that meet this criteria in Salta, but one was inadvertently omitted from the original sample.

[38] For the same reason, I also exclude Córdoba's second-largest city from the sample.

day for the interview.[39] One researcher then traveled to each municipality and conducted the survey with the relevant official, asking a series of specific questions about the implementation of the PNSA, as well as some more general questions about the head of social welfare's background and contacts with the mayor. In a few towns, the head of the social welfare area was not available, so in those cases the interview was with another person who worked in the office and was knowledgeable about the administration of the PNSA. In cities where the head of social welfare was less familiar with the day-to-day workings of the program, she often asked another person to sit in on the interview to help answer detailed questions about program administration.

4.5.1 Question Wording

Making the List
Can you tell me if any of the following people recommended any families to be included in the list of beneficiaries [for the PNSA] or in some other way participated in the making of that list?

Changes to the List
Can you tell me if any of the following people is consulted or participates in decisions about adding to or taking anyone off (*dar de alta/baja a los beneficiarios*) the beneficiary list?

For both questions, respondents were then read the following names and asked to say yes or no to each one: the mayor, members of the local legislature, members of the local "consultative council" [an organization municipalities are supposed to establish to monitor social welfare policies, although not all have one], the head of social welfare, employees in the social welfare area, or others.

---

[39] Some municipal governments, particularly in rural areas of Salta, do not have phone service via landlines. In these cases, I either spoke to the mayor on his personal cell phone or, in the event that was impossible, left messages with and/or sent a fax to the local public telephone center.

5

Clientelism across Municipalities in Argentina's National Food Security Program

As detailed in the previous chapter, perhaps the most significant challenge in testing any theory of clientelism lies in measuring it. In spite of clientelism's apparent reach and importance, the difficulty of collecting data on the phenomenon on any large scale means that we actually know very little about how widespread it is. In that chapter, I explained a new measure of clientelism that seeks to faithfully capture how an important government policy is implemented while also allowing for comparison across a substantial number of geographic units. Using an original elite survey of municipal bureaucrats across a large number of cities in Argentina, I assessed personalized mayoral intervention in the implementation of a large food program in that country. The simple cross-tabulations presented in the previous chapter showed, consistent with expectations, that the use of clientelism appears to diverge between high- and low-poverty municipalities when political competition is high. In contrast, where competition is low, mayors rely on clientelism at similar rates, regardless of constituent poverty.

In this chapter, I turn to a more complete test of the full theory, with its emphasis on the interaction between competition and poverty, as well as the role of partisanship, in shaping incumbent incentives for clientelism. The results of statistical analysis are consistent with theoretical expectations. While neither increasing competition nor decreasing poverty *alone* is associated with a reduced likelihood of clientelism, the combination of these two conditions is associated with a lower likelihood of observing clientelism. This chapter also examines the interplay of partisanship with this dynamic. I test whether an incumbent's partisan affiliation might shape the likelihood of clientelism through either a supply-side or demand-side effect and find much stronger evidence in support of the latter hypothesis.[1] Partisanship does not appear

---

[1] As noted in Chapter 3, in an empirical test, these two mechanisms correspond broadly to an intercept versus slope effect.

to affect the baseline likelihood of relying on clientelism. However, the costs of clientelism prompt non-Peronist politicians to opt out of clientelism at high rates as soon as competition increases and poverty begins to decline. In contrast, Peronist politicians opt out of clientelism only when competition increases and poverty falls quite substantially. This suggests that the Peronist party continues to be a constraint on reducing clientelism in Argentina. I also include a close examination of alternative explanations, with particular attention to the possible role of civil society in curbing clientelism. Using a variety of measures, I find little evidence in support of these explanations.

5.1 MEASURING THE CORRELATES OF CLIENTELISM

I rely on an original survey of municipal bureaucrats to assess whether Argentine mayors included in my sample were personally involved in assembling the list of beneficiaries for a large food distribution program, the PNSA. I use that personalized intervention as an indicator of clientelism, and I find evidence of clientelism in about two-thirds of the 126 municipalities for which I have data. To examine the correlates of that variation, I detail how I measure the main explanatory variables that are used in the regression analysis that follows. The discussion of variables used to test alternative explanations comes later in the chapter.

Poverty
The theory predicts that, conditional on high competition, the incentives for clientelist behavior should decline as poverty declines, and increase as poverty goes up. I use the most widely available measure of poverty in Argentina, the proportion of households in each municipality with NBI ("necesidades básicas insatisfechas"), or unsatisfied basic needs.[2] A household is considered to have unsatisfied basic needs if it meets at least one of five characteristics that are considered indicators of poverty in Argentina, such as lack of indoor plumbing or more than three people per room.[3] As Gasparini (2004) has pointed out, the NBI measures primarily structural characteristics that on balance are not responsive to changes in a household's economic situation or its capacity to consume. Especially in periods of economic downturn or in circumstances

---

[2] Note that the use of household, rather than population data, is appropriate, because the food program I look at is targeted at households rather than individuals. Also, individual-level data is unavailable for Córdoba.

[3] These data are collected by Argentina's census agency, INDEC. A household is considered to have NBI if it has at least one of the following five characteristics: density of more than three people per room, precarious physical condition of housing, lacks indoor plumbing, includes children between the ages of six and twelve who do not attend school, or has more than four members per employed member and where the head of the household has less than a third grade education.

where prices increase without a corresponding increase in wages, we can be quite sure that this measure underestimates the share of households that have difficulty achieving subsistence. Nonetheless, the NBI is highly correlated with an alternate measure of poverty that relies in part on an estimate of household income.[4] Thus, although the NBI is less than ideal as an absolute measure of poverty, it should be a reliable measure of relative differences in poverty levels across cities.

Political Opposition

As I argue in Chapter 3, increased political competition should increase politician effort. However, because of the electoral tradeoff clientelism entails, that increased effort should have divergent effects on clientelism conditional on voter poverty: high competition and high poverty should be associated with clientelism, whereas high competition and low poverty should not be.

As noted earlier in this book, the conceptualization and measurement of competition varies widely in the literature. In many respects, the best way to conceptualize the variable underlying the diverse measures in the literature is as politician security in office. An incumbent politician's perceived security in office can be affected by many factors, including national or regional political trends and individual-level character traits, such as self-confidence. It is also likely to be affected systematically by the the degree and strength of political competition a politician faces. Depending on the circumstances of any given election cycle, a politician may feel confident that he will be reelected by a comfortable margin or instead believe that his future political prospects are under threat.

Ideally, we would have available a direct measure of each mayor's perceived security in office, which would likely depend on both observable outputs of previous political competition as well as unobservable information about

---

4 The alternate measure of poverty, available for Salta and Río Negro, is the *índice de privación material de los hogares* (IPMH), or index of household material deprivation. It uses a combination of structural characteristics similar to the NBI and an estimate of the household's subsistence capacity using information on household members' education, access to pensions, and the number of individuals living in the household. The Argentine census does not include questions on income. Differences between the NBI and IPMH data are substantial. For example, using the NBI data, the mean share of poor households in a municipality in Salta is 38%, with a minimum of 22% of poor households and a maximum of 69%. In contrast, using the alternate poverty measure, the share of poor households in Salta's municipalities ranges from 56% to 98%, with a mean of 80% of households in a given city reported as poor. Although very different in absolute terms, these measures are very highly correlated; for Río Negro and Salta, the NBI and the IPMH have a correlation coefficient of about .9. The "Encuesta Permanente de Hogares" is another commonly used source of data on poverty in Argentina, but it is available only for twenty-eight large urban areas and as such is of little use here.

changes in the political situation since the last election and variables idiosyncratic to each individual. In the absence of such a direct measure, I instead capture politician security in office using the size of the opposition presence in the local town council.[5] Opposition in a local council is likely to be correlated with a politician's perceived security in office for two reasons. First, the size of the legislative opposition should be negatively correlated with a politician's support in the population. This is obviously true if executive and legislative branch politicians are elected on the same list, as in a parliamentary system, but is also likely to be the case in any legislature where representatives are elected via party lists, as in the case in Argentina's municipalities.[6]

Second, in addition to serving as a signal of levels of incumbent support in the previous election, a legislative opposition is likely to actively seek to undermine an executive's hold on power. Opposition members of a legislature will generally seek to criticize the executive's decisions and present themselves as a viable governing alternative, and their ability to do so convincingly should be increasing in the size of the opposition. Though likely a more common strategy in national legislative bodies than in subnational ones, opposition members of Argentine town councils do have some tools available to them to complicate an executive politician's pursuit of his goals. The town of La Merced, in the province of Salta, is one of the municipalities in my sample where the mayor's party did not enjoy a majority in the legislature. There, a top aide to the mayor complained about the difficulties this caused, lamenting that "they [the opposition] put obstacles in the municipal regulations . . . you always have to be accountable (*rendir cuentas*)" (Author interview, August 2007). Furthermore, in the small and medium size towns I examine here, local town councilors frequently devote part or all of their salaries to political activities. In interviews, town council members in a number of cities explained

5   The most obvious alternative to relying on local council composition to assess a politician's security in office would be to use vote returns. Theoretically, this measure is somewhat problematic, because vote returns capture only a mayor's popularity among voters and does not account for how votes are translated into seats, and it thus may not reflect the ability of opposition members of a town council to further threaten that security through its actions. In addition, data on election returns for mayoral contests are missing for about 25% of the sample examined here and do not always indicate when multiple lists ran the same candidate for mayor, so the results are best treated as estimates of mayoral support, rather than firm figures. Nonetheless, if we replicate the results from column 1 and 2 in Table 5.2 using data on the total opposition vote share in the previous mayoral contest as a proxy for electoral competition for those areas in which data is available, the results are very similar to those displayed in that table. If instead we use a measure of the vote share received by the single largest opposition only, the coefficients on our variables of interest are smaller and not statistically significant.

6   Electoral systems at the municipal level in Argentina vary somewhat across provinces, as I discuss in more detail later, but in all the cases I examine here (and to my knowledge, in all Argentine provinces), the members of the local town and city councils are elected via closed lists. Of course, it is not always the case that executive and legislative popularity move together, but in general, a larger opposition presence in the legislature should indicate lower levels of incumbent popularity.

that they treated their compensation as a tool for political work; they use their salaries as councilors to give assistance to citizens on an individualized basis and/or to support organized partisan activities.[7] The larger the size of the opposition, the greater the pressure it is likely able to exert in the legislature and the greater the resources it can devote to non-legislative strategies to undermine the incumbent. A local council opposition, then, not only signals a politician's past electoral support (in the same way that vote returns do), but its behavior as an opposition is likely to affect a mayor's security in office.[8] As such, the larger the opposition, the less secure an incumbent is likely to feel in his prospects for reelection.

For the municipalities examined here, the relevant legislative body is the "Concejo Deliberante" (CD), which I refer to interchangeably as the local legislature or town council. All Argentine municipalities have these councils, which range in size depending on provincial regulations and population. In the sample of municipalities analyzed here, these councils range in size from three to twelve members, with the median council made up of seven members.[9] I measure the opposition's strength in the council by simply calculating the share of seats in the body held by members of any opposition party (individuals from all parties other than the mayor's party or parties explicitly allied with the mayor's party). The variable, *total opposition*, ranges from 0 to 1, with both the mean and the median at about .43.[10] I also consider the possibility

---

7   In the Argentine context, differences in the professionalization of local councilors and national legislators are likely not as pronounced as elsewhere. As Jones et al. (2002) document, most national legislators spend only a single term in Congress as part of a broader political career, and they therefore do not develop the highly specialized skills associated with legislators in countries like the United States.

8   The distinction between vote returns and opposition presence in the council is especially relevant here because the small number of seats in each council weakens the votes-seats correspondence. In a larger legislative body, vote share and opposition presence in the legislature have the potential to be more closely matched.

9   Information on the composition of the bodies was collected through publicly available provincial documents, supplemented with direct communication with municipalities when that information was missing or ambiguous.

10 Differences in electoral systems across provinces in part explain this wide variation in opposition strength. In Córdoba, mayors and members of local legislatures are elected on the same list in elections held every four years, and the provincial constitution states that the mayor is elected via plurality rule, and the list of councilors that the mayor heads is required to receive at least a bare majority in the local council. In Río Negro, the vast majority of councils serve four year terms and are elected on a separate ballot from the mayor, who is elected via plurality rule, although a few cities follow Córdoba's system. The data reflect the council's composition as a result of the 2003 elections. In Salta, the mayor and council are elected on separate ballots, and although the mayor serves a four-year term, council members serve for two years only. The data on council composition for Salta reflect the results of the 2005 elections for local councils. Cities from Salta make up the majority of cases in the dataset where members of the opposition make up more than half of the council. The survey of heads of social welfare in Salta was administered between August and September 2006, so using the council composition from the October 2005 election seems appropriate, as we should

that the size of the single largest opposition, rather than the total size of the opposition, is key to understanding mayoral incentives. It is possible that an incumbent might perceive a single, large, unified opposition as a greater threat to his security and reelection prospects than a larger but more fragmented opposition. The share of seats held by the single largest opposition in the local legislature ranges from 0 to .67 in the data, with a mean of about one-third. I present regression results using both measures of political competition, although, as I explain in Section 5.2, I focus on interpreting the results that use the total opposition size.

Partisanship

We can imagine two main pathways through which an incumbent mayor's partisan affiliation might affect the likelihood that he will rely on clientelism. As detailed in Chapter 3, I call the first a supply-side explanation: the rate at which mayors are willing, able, and interested in supplying clientelism may be correlated with their partisan identity. Differences in the availability of partisan-affiliated networks of political brokers, recruitment patterns, or even self-selection might explain these differences. If this supply-side explanation is correct, we should expect to see partisan differences in clientelism at all levels of competition. In contrast, what I call a demand-side explanation posits that the likelihood of relying on clientelism across parties depends in part on the attitudes of different groups of constituents toward different parties. In the case of clientelism, an incumbent will fear losing the political support of nonpoor voters only if he has a reasonable expectation of gaining some of that support in the first place. Thus, to the extent that nonpoor voters systematically differ in their willingness to support mayors based on their partisan affiliations, we might observe that mayoral sensitivity to the costs of clientelism varies across political parties. If this demand-side explanation is correct, partisan differences in clientelism should be especially acute when political competition is high.

Whether we adopt either a supply or demand perspective, in the Argentine context, it is clearly the *Partido Justicialista* (PJ), or Peronist party, which would be especially well-suited to employ clientelism. In terms of its ability to supply clientelism, the effectiveness of the PJ's extensive network of inter-mediaries (*punteros*) has been clearly documented (Auyero, 2000b, Levitsky, 2003). It has also been shown that the Peronist party has a larger broker network than any other Argentine party and that the PJ relies more heavily

expect the composition of the council at that time to shape the mayor's behavior. This is also consistent with other evidence that mayors in Salta do respond to changes in the compositions of the councils that they face. So, for example, the mayor installed a new head of social welfare after the October 2005 elections in thirteen out of the forty-seven cities for which I have data in Salta. In contrast, during that same period in Córdoba, the head was replaced in only three out of the fifty-two cities for which I have data.

on practices closely linked to clientelism, like patronage, at the provincial level (Calvo and Murillo, 2004, 2010).[11] Demand-side factors also support the fit between the Peronist party and the practice of clientelism. Even in the absence of clear ideological differences, Argentine parties have historically had distinct class bases of political support. As Lupu and Stokes (2009) demonstrate, in the period since World War II, workers and the poor have been the Peronist party's core supporters, while the Radical party has represented more middle-class constituencies.[12] Nonetheless, it is worth noting that there may be regional exceptions to these national patterns, including in one of the provinces studied here, Río Negro, which is a traditional Radical party stronghold. In that province, for the twenty-seven municipalities for which I have data, as of 2007, seven had Peronist mayors, eighteen had UCR mayors, and two had third-party mayors.[13] In this province, municipalities with Peronist mayors had poverty rates that were only slightly higher than non-Peronist municipalities (20% versus 18%), and this difference is not statistically significant. This suggests that, at least within certain provinces, the Peronist party does not have a monopoly on successful appeals to the poor. About 53% of the municipalities in the sample had Peronist mayors, and in the regressions below, I include either an indicator variable for this affiliation or an interaction term between PJ affiliation and other variables to test the supply and demand-side theories of partisanship, respectively.

Additional Controls: The Ease of Using Clientelism

Beyond the core predictions of the theory, other factors may affect the ease with which politicians can resort to clientelism. Although it is impossible to

[11] Though Calvo and Murillo (2013) note that the Radical party continues to enjoy a broker network that is surprisingly large, especially in light of its recent electoral travails.

[12] See also Mora y Araujo and Llorente (1980). I focus here on the difference between the Peronist party and other competitors which, for most of the past century, has meant the UCR. At the time of the resignation of Radical party president Fernando de la Rúa, in December 2001, six governors (out of twenty-three) and the mayor of Buenos Aires were affiliated with the Radical party. Nonetheless, since that time, the UCR has struggled to compete electorally, even in those districts where it was historically dominant. As of this writing, the PJ is increasingly hegemonic, with internal party divisions more salient than interparty competition, and new political parties are attempting to capture middle-class support. Though important in national elections, these new parties have had a more limited impact on municipal politics, especially in the country's interior. Of the municipalities in which I completed my survey, at the time of the survey, sixty-eight had PJ mayors, thirty-nine had UCR mayors, and nineteen mayors were from other parties – most of these from a long-standing ideologically conservative provincial party in Salta.

[13] Again, the electoral success of the UCR has weakened since that time. In 2011, the Peronist party won the governorship of Río Negro for the first time since the return to democracy in 1983. (The newly elected governor was killed in a domestic dispute only days after assuming office, ironically leaving his lieutenant governor, from another party, at the helm of the province.)

account for differences in personal taste for clientelism, a politician's propensity to engage in the practice may also be affected by systematic differences in politician access to certain resources, in the form of funds or in preexisting networks of supporters and organizers. A mayor from a party with a long history of access to power might more readily resort to clientelism. That history may provide him with greater opportunities to cultivate the type of dense social networks and extensive ties to voters or to networks of political brokers that facilitate the monitoring that forms an integral part of clientelism. The existence of such ties might be a product of an individual's personal history in office or that of his party. I consider three possible measures that might proxy for the strength of these ties: whether or not the sitting mayor was reelected (*reelected*), whether his party has held the mayor's seat continuously since Argentina's 1983 return to democracy (*mayor party dominates*), and, alternately, whether the mayor's party has held the mayor's seat for all or all but one of the administrations since the return to democracy (*mayor party dominates* [2]). On a related point, mayors who share the same partisanship with the governor might also experience reduced costs of clientelism, perhaps because the governor's control over party and/or public monies allows him to provide extra funds or staff to co-partisans, which might free more resources for the monitoring of clientelist agreements. I therefore also examine an indicator variable that takes on the value of one for mayors who are of the same party as the governor (*governor party*).

Population size may also affect the costs of clientelism. The type of monitoring that clientelism requires may be easier in smaller towns and cities, where direct social ties between politicians and voters are more likely. In fact, Brusco et al. (2004) do find that vote buying in Argentina was more commonly reported by individuals residing in smaller towns than in large cities. The population of the municipalities included in this study ranges from 2,026 to 93,101. The mean is about 14,000 inhabitants, while the median is 8,300. I use the log of population in the regression analysis to account for these differences.

Table 5.1 presents summary statistics for all the variables discussed here and notes the expected sign on all predictor variables. The main variables of theoretical interest are the measures of the size of the legislative opposition, municipal poverty, and the interaction between these two. Where the political opposition is extremely limited in size, we do not expect a correlation between poverty and the incidence of clientelism. For this reason, the coefficient on the variable measuring poverty should be at or near zero and is not expected to be statistically significant. In contrast, where poverty is extremely low, increasing levels of opposition should decrease a mayor's incentives to rely on clientelism, and as such, the coefficient on the opposition variable should be negative and significant. As the size of the opposition increases, I predict that poverty is increasingly likely to be important in the mayor's decision making, with the incentives for clientelism increasing in the share of the population that is poor. So, the coefficient on the interaction term between these two key variables is

TABLE 5.1. *Summary Statistics: Municipal Clientelism*

Variable	Mean	Std. Dev.	N	Expectation
Mayor list	0.67	0.47	126	
Poverty	0.23	0.14	132	0
Total opposition	0.42	0.17	132	(−)
Largest opposition	0.32	0.13	132	(−)
Poverty * Total opposition	0.1	0.1	132	(+)
Poverty * Largest opposition	0.07	0.06	132	(+)
PJ	0.53	0.50	132	(+)
Governor party	0.62	0.49	132	(+)
Reelected	0.55	0.5	133	(+)
Mayor party dominates	0.27	0.44	132	(+)
Mayor party dominates (2)	0.49	0.5	132	(+)
Population (ln)	9.07	0.97	132	(−)

expected to be positive and significant. In the first set of models, I explore the role of partisanship from a supply-side perspective only. For that reason, I include an indicator variable that takes on the value of one for municipalities with a Peronist mayor at the helm of local government. If Peronist mayors systematically "supply" more clientelism, we should expect this variable to have a positive coefficient.

The expected signs for the other variables are straightforward. As the non-vote related costs of clientelism increase, clientelism should be less appealing, and hence less likely. Three indicator variables are intended to measure these costs – taking on a value of 1 when the mayor and governor are from the same party, the mayor has been reelected, or the mayor's party has dominated the mayor's office in the past, respectively. Thus, higher values indicate a lower cost to (and a higher likelihood of) clientelism and the coefficients on these indicator variables are expected to be positive and significant. As a town or city grows in size, implementing clientelism should pose greater difficulties, and so the coefficient on the measure of population is expected to be negative. Finally, I incorporate indicator variables for two of the three provinces included in the analysis – Córdoba and Río Negro – omitting Salta as the left-out category. Although I have no strong theoretical priors on the expected signs of these coefficients, the popular press would likely predict Salta, as part of Argentina's poor Northwest, to have a greater use of clientelism, so we might expect the other two provincial indicator variables to be negative.

5.2 EXPLAINING CLIENTELISM IN THE PNSA

Table 5.2 presents the results of a series of logistic regressions where the outcome variable takes on the value of 1 if, at the time of my research in 2006–2007, the mayor was involved drawing up or altering the beneficiary list for the PNSA. The regression results reported in column 1 measure the opposition using total opposition size, whereas column 2 relies on a measure of the size of the single largest opposition. The results from the two regressions are quite similar and are largely consistent with theoretical expectations with respect to the role of political competition and social class, as discussed in more detail later. The model reported in column 1 does a somewhat better job predicting cases correctly, and I focus on interpreting the results presented there.[14]

A more crucial comparison is with column 3, which highlights the importance of including the interaction term between opposition size and poverty for the results reported here. Column 3 shows the results of the same regression reported in column 1, with the sole difference that the interaction term between poverty and legislative opposition is omitted. This serves as a test of some existing explanations of clientelism and governance more generally.[15] As reviewed in the introduction and Chapter 3, many of these theories posit a monotonic relationship between poverty or political competition on the one hand and clientelism (or other types of poor performance) on the other. The results of this regression do not support these explanations. In the absence of any interaction term, we would conclude that neither poverty nor opposition presence is associated with an increased propensity to use clientelism. In contrast, the results reported in the first two columns in Table 5.2 demonstrate that opposition size is indeed correlated with the likelihood that a mayor will use clientelism, and that this correlation varies with the level of poverty in any given municipality. Thus, the interaction term is critical for recognizing

---

[14] All the models improve on random guessing. Two-thirds of the municipalities in the sample use clientelism, and so randomly guessing that all municipalities use clientelism would leave us with an error rate of 33%. In contrast, the models reported in columns 1, 2, and 3 have error rates of 28%, 30%, and 32%, respectively. (All of these figures treat a predicted probability of .5 or higher as predicting clientelism.) The model reported in column 1 then improves the percent correctly predicted by 5 percentage points, or about 17% over the original error rate of 33%.

[15] It also helps serve as a test of the validity of my measure of mayoral intervention as a proxy for clientelism. If mayoral intervention measured normal credit claiming, we could expect to observe one of three empirical patterns. First, given the salience of food programs, it might be the case that the vast majority of mayors in poor municipalities would intervene in list-making, whereas mayors in middle-class municipalities would not. Alternately, we could posit that most mayors in competitive municipalities would engage in credit-claiming in their pursuit of votes, while mayors in noncompetitive municipalities would not bother. The results in column 3 support neither of these hypotheses. A third possibility might be that most mayors in poor municipalities engage in credit-claiming and only mayors in middle-class communities who face high competition would bother to engage in it. Results presented in columns 1 and 2 also speak against this possibility. Instead, they show that most mayors in low competition municipalities intervene in decision making, while those mayors in middle-class municipalities who face high competition are the most likely to opt *out* of intervening in decision making. This further supports the use of mayoral intervention as a proxy for clientelism rather than "normal" credit-claiming.

TABLE 5.2. *Mayoral Intervention: Regression Results*

	Total opp	Largest opp	No interaction
	(1)	(2)	(3)
Population (ln)	−.43*	−.49**	−.49**
	(.25)	(.24)	(.24)
Poverty	−5.53	−1.84	5.33
	(5.07)	(4.79)	(4.12)
Total opposition	−9.28**	—	1.03
	(3.67)		(1.49)
Largest opposition	—	−7.02*	—
		(4.10)	
Poverty*Total opposition	37.89***	—	—
	(11.88)		
Poverty*Largest opposition	—	37.43**	—
		(14.88)	
PJ	.55	.61	.55
	(.46)	(.46)	(.44)
Mayor party dominates	1.14	.99	.71
	(.72)	(.71)	(.63)
Cordoba	1.92	1.91	.97
	(1.29)	(1.14)	
Rio Negro	.99	.83	.16
	(1.04)	(1.03)	(.92)
Percent correctly predicted	72	70	68
Percent reduction in error	17	10	5
Obs.	126	126	126

Results are from logistic regressions where the dependent variable equals one if the mayor is involved in drawing up the beneficiary list, and zero otherwise. *, **, *** indicate significance at the .1, .05, and .01 levels.

the role that political competition and poverty play in shaping incentives for clientelism in the implementation of government policy.

For the purpose of interpretation, I focus on the results presented in column 1. The coefficients on the main variables of interest are consistent with the theoretical expectations in both direction and statistical significance. The coefficient on the legislative opposition variable is negative, indicating that, where poverty is low, increasing levels of opposition presence decrease the probability of mayoral intervention. In contrast, the coefficient on the interaction term is positive, supporting the argument that, as poverty increases, increasing opposition size is associated with a higher probability of mayoral intervention. The results thus support the claim that high political competition does not have a uniform effect on clientelism. Instead, incentives to use clientelism when competition is high are correlated with voter poverty.

With respect to the role of partisanship, the inclusion of an indicator variable for Peronist mayors allows for a test of the supply-side hypothesis that Peronist mayors are systematically more willing and able to rely on clientelism, regardless of whether competition is high or low. Although the coefficient on this variable is positive, in the expected direction, it is not statistically significant.[16] As I illustrate below, mayoral membership in the Peronist party is substantively associated with a modest increase in the likelihood of clientelism. These results lend only limited support to the hypothesis that Peronist politicians are willing to supply greater amounts of clientelism across all levels of competition.

Given the nonlinearities in the predictions inherent in logistic regression, the substantive significance of the coefficients, and especially the interaction term, is best illustrated with a graph. For the purpose of illustration, Figure 5.1 shows the predicted probability that a mayor will be involved in drawing up lists of beneficiaries in two typical municipalities. The top graph shows the predicted probability that the mayor of a city of average size, affiliated with the Peronist party, but where the party has not continuously held the office of mayor since 1983, will intervene in the making or alteration of the beneficiary list for the PNSA as legislative opposition ranges from its minimum to its maximum.[17] The bottom graph shows the predicted probability of clientelism in a typical municipality with the same characteristics – except with a non-Peronist mayor. Consistent with the results discussed earlier, the predicted probabilities of clientelism are somewhat higher in the Peronist case. However, these differences are slight: it is clear that the most important substantive effect is driven by the interaction between poverty and competition.

The three lines in each graph show how the link between legislative opposition and personalized decision making varies with constituency poverty. In both graphs, the solid line represents the predicted probability of mayoral intervention for a municipality with the median level of poverty in the sample. The top and bottom dashed lines estimate that probability for a municipality with poverty set to its 75% value and 25% value in the sample.[18] Although both graphs appear to suggest that mayoral intervention will be slightly less likely in poor municipalities at very low levels of opposition, simulations

---

[16] The Peronist party is more likely than other parties to have won all elections since 1983, and the coefficients on the PJ and "mayor party dominates" variables are jointly significant at the .1 level. Nonetheless, even if we omit the indicator variable for mayor party dominance, the Peronist party indicator still does not reach conventional levels of statistical significance.

[17] The figure is drawn using coefficients taken from the regression results in column 1 of Table 5.2.

[18] The median, 25% and 75% rates of household poverty are 18%, 11%, and 32%, respectively. As noted previously, these figures likely underestimate actual poverty levels (Gasparini, 2004).

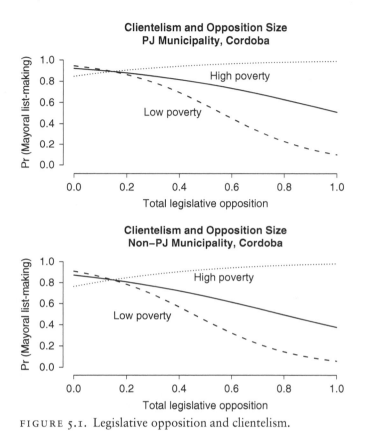

FIGURE 5.1. Legislative opposition and clientelism.

(discussed later) demonstrate that these differences are statistically insignificant. As opposition size increases from that point, the predicted probability of mayoral decision making increasingly diverges based on poverty rates. As the opposition's share of seats in the local council increases, so does the probability that the mayor will intervene in the PNSA beneficiary list in the typical high-poverty city, whereas it declines quite sharply in the typical low-poverty municipality.[19]

To give a sense of the uncertainty surrounding these estimates, I conduct 1000 simulations of the difference in the expected probability of mayoral intervention in a high- versus low-poverty Peronist municipality over the whole

---

[19] In only seven observations of the 126 included in the regression analysis does the opposition make up more than 70% of the legislature. If we exclude these extremely high opposition municipalities and repeat the analysis in Table 5.2, the coefficients are very similar to those reported there.

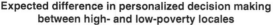

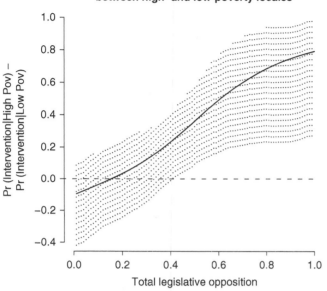

FIGURE 5.2. Simulations.

range of values of legislative opposition.[20] Figure 5.2 presents the results. The horizontal axis measures the share of the town council held by the legislative opposition, while the vertical axis shows the estimated predicted difference in the probability of mayoral list-making between a high- and low-poverty municipality. The solid line depicts the mean difference in these probabilities for each corresponding value of legislative opposition, while the dotted lines indicate 95% confidence intervals drawn from the simulations. The dashed line at zero indicates the baseline where there is no difference in the predicted probability of personalized decision making between cities with these different levels of poverty. Positive values indicate that the model predicts that we are more likely to observe mayoral intervention in a city where poverty is at its 75% value in the sample than in a city with a poverty level equal to its 25% value in the sample. Conversely, negative values indicate that the model predicts that personalized decision making is more likely in relatively better off municipalities.

[20] The simulations were done using the sim function in the arm package, developed by Gelman and Hill (2007) for the statistical package R. For each of 100 values of legislative opposition, I simulate 1,000 times the difference in the predicted probability of clientelism as poverty shifts between its 75% and 25% values in the sample. The mean difference and 95% confidence intervals are taken from these simulations.

As the figure makes clear, there is substantial uncertainty about the relationship between poverty and mayoral intervention where legislative opposition is minimal. The estimated difference of about zero and the confidence intervals that include zero suggest that, as hypothesized, poverty does not affect the incentives to use clientelism when opposition is low. Where competition is low, personalized decision making in the PNSA is predicted to be extremely likely, a result that is consistent with the literature's description of the pervasiveness of clientelism in Argentina as a whole. As the size of the legislative opposition increases, however, the picture changes. The predicted probability of personal intervention in the PNSA increasingly diverges between two otherwise similar cities with poverty at the 75% and 25% levels of our sample. Once the legislative opposition surpasses around 40%, a mayor in a high-poverty city is expected to be significantly more likely than his counterpart in a competitive but lower poverty city to engage in this clientelist practice. The estimated size of this difference in the propensity to use clientelism continues to increase as the opposition increases. As levels of political opposition increase, knowing a city's poverty rate becomes an increasingly reliable tool to predict whether the mayor of that city will engage in personalized decision making.

Among the other variables of interest, only municipal population is statistically significant and in the expected direction. Clientelist practices appear to be less likely in larger cities, which is consistent with findings reported by Brusco et al. (2004) on Argentina. In the data, an increase in the size of a municipality from the mean (a population of about 8,000) to one standard deviation above the mean (equivalent to a population of about 23,000) is associated with a 7 percentage point decrease in the average predicted probability that a mayor will use clientelism.[21]

Turning to the variables intended to measure the ease with which a politician can employ clientelism, the regression results reported in Table 5.2 include an indicator variable for whether the mayor's party has held the position continuously since 1983.[22] Although never statistically significant, the coefficient on this variable is positive (the expected direction). In addition, if we omit

[21] I define the average predicted difference following Gelman and Hill (2007, 101–104). The authors consider a case in which u denotes the input variable of interest, v is a vector of all other variables, in this case held constant, and β is a vector of regression coefficients. Then they define the predictive difference in probabilities, δ, associated with a change in the value of u from its high to low value as follows:

$$\delta(u^{high}, u^{low}, v, \beta) = Pr(Y = 1|u^{high}, v, \beta) - Pr(Y = 1|u^{low}, v, \beta)$$

To calculate the average predictive difference, we simply calculate δ for each observation in the dataset, each time setting v equal to the values the other variables obtain for that particular observation, and then average over all values of δ.

[22] I also ran regressions including an indicator variable for whether the mayor shared a partisan affiliation with the governor, whether he was reelected, and whether his party had held office for all but one or all administrations since 1983. I do not include these in the results reported here because they were not consistently positive, were often small in magnitude, were not

the Peronist party indicator, the indicator variable for mayor party dominance reaches significance at the .08 level. The magnitude of the average predictive difference associated with a change from a situation where the mayor's party has not dominated the office since 1983 to one where it has is substantial: such a switch is associated with an 18 percentage point difference in the probability of mayoral intervention in the PNSA.[23]

Taken together, these results offer some evidence that the use of clientelism is related to the ease with which politicians can engage in it. Mayors with a long history of control over local government and those governing smaller municipalities are more likely to intervene directly in the beneficiary list for the PNSA. These characteristics move slowly over time and are unlikely to reflect the nature of political competition in any given administration. Nonetheless, even controlling for these factors, the likelihood of personalized decision making appears quite responsive to the interaction between voter poverty and competition. This suggests that the use of clientelism does not simply reflect certain immutable characteristics, but rather that politicians' decisions about whether to use clientelism reflect the practice's relative electoral costs and incumbents' perceived security in office at a given point in time.[24]

5.3 THE COSTS OF CLIENTELISM: VARIATION ACROSS PARTIES

The evidence examined thus far supports the claim that political competition and constituent demographics shape politician incentives to engage in clientelism, while offering only limited support for the partisanship hypothesis. This analysis, however, has only explored the possibility that partisan affiliation exercises a level effect, in which Peronist party identity might systematically increase the likelihood of observing clientelism across all levels of political competition. As detailed in Chapter 3, there are in fact two paths through which partisanship might shape the likelihood of observing clientelism. The first is a supply-side effect, which has already been tested. The second is a demand-side effect. That is, it might be the case that partisanship matters only when competition is high and triggers increased politician effort. When competition is high and constituents are mostly middle-class, I expect incumbent politicians to refrain from using clientelism because they fear losing middle-class support. However, it may be the case that politicians from some

statistically significant, and their inclusion did not affect the coefficients on the main variables of theoretical interest.

[23] In contrast, the average predictive difference in the probability of clientelism associated with a shift from a non-Peronist to a Peronist mayor is approximately 10 percentage points.

[24] These results can help to explain some puzzling empirical results presented by Brusco et al. (2006). Those authors find that, in at least some cases, particularistic spending does not benefit incumbent mayors and may even hurt them. They speculate that electoral costs to these practices might explain these results, and the theory and data analyzed here present a framework and evidence that shows how this could come about.

parties (in Argentina, the PJ) receive only limited support from nonpoor voters anyway, and hence that they have less to fear from the loss of such support. If this is true, the link between high competition, low poverty, and the rejection of clientelism will be stronger among non-Peronist, as opposed to Peronist, mayors.

An additional empirical test is required to evaluate this possibility. In addition to the interaction term between poverty and competition included in the original model, an expanded model interacts this term, and its two constituent terms, with an indicator variable that takes on the value of 1 for mayors with Peronist party identification. The results of this analysis are presented in Table 5.3. The first column presents the main analysis presented and discussed in Table 5.2. The second column presents the results with the additional interaction variables included.

The combination of multiple interaction terms, including a three-way inter-action, with a logistic regression complicates any attempt to directly interpret the results reported in the table. Instead, the results are best summarized graphically. Figure 5.3 presents two graphs that are quite similar in form to those in Figure 5.1. As was the case there, the horizontal axis indicates the size of the total legislative opposition. Each curve in the figure indicates, for a "typical" municipality at a given level of poverty, how the expected probability of personalized decision making varies as a town's legislative opposition changes in size. In both figures, the dotted line sets poverty to its 75% value in the sample, the solid line indicates that poverty is set to the median in the sample, and the dashed lines indicate poverty is set to its 25% value in the sample. The crucial difference between Figure 5.3 and Figure 5.1 is that in this one, reflecting the decision to include a three-way interaction term, we allow the shapes of the curves to vary between Peronist and non-Peronist municipalities. The top graph depicts these predicted probabilities for a typical Peronist municipality in the province of Cordoba, while the bottom half depicts predicted probabilities for a typical non-Peronist municipality in the same province. Although both graphs are consistent with the theory of the costs of clientelism, there are important differences between them. Most notably, the model results suggest that the costs of clientelism "kick in" at a much lower threshold for non-Peronist mayors; in contrast, a much higher threshold must be met for Peronist mayors to opt out of clientelism. The graphical presentation of the results helps illustrate that point.

The top curve in each panel in the figure depicts the predicted probability of personalized decision making for a typical high-poverty municipality (set to 75% of its value in the sample) as opposition size runs from 0 to 1.[25] For the

---

[25]   Although the x-axis runs from 0 to 1 in both graphs, for the purpose of visual comparability, the highest level of opposition observed in a Peronist municipality in .66. In both cases, the bulk of the data is concentrated between opposition levels of .2 and .7. If we replicate the analysis excluding cases where the opposition exceeds two-thirds, results are very similar to

TABLE 5.3. *Mayoral Intervention and Partisanship:*
Regression Results

	Total opp	PJ interact
	(1)	(2)
Population (ln)	−.43*	−.45*
	(.25)	(.24)
Poverty	−5.53	−20.27
	(5.07)	(13.77)
Total opposition	−9.28**	−19.23**
	(3.67)	(8.86)
Poverty*Total opposition	37.89***	67.81**
	(11.88)	(32.22)
PJ	.55	−6.62
	(.46)	(4.34)
PJ*Poverty	—	19.68
		(14.28)
PJ*Total opposition	—	15.91
		(10.48)
PJ*Poverty*Total opp	—	−40.82
		(34.74)
Mayor party dominates	1.14	1.01
	(.72)	(.85)
Cordoba	1.92	1.72
	(1.29)	(1.28)
Rio Negro	.99	.71
	(1.04)	(1.06)
Obs.	126	126

Results are from logistic regressions where the dependent variable
equals one if the mayor is involved in drawing up the beneficiary list,
and zero otherwise. *, **, *** indicate significance at the .1, .05, and
.01 levels.

highest levels of poverty, the two panels look remarkably similar. The model
predicts clientelism to be quite likely when poverty is high, especially once we
go beyond the lowest levels of opposition.[26]

The differences between Peronist and non-Peronist municipalities become
more pronounced once we move to the curves that depict expected behavior at
lower levels of poverty. To focus attention on these differences, Figure 5.4

those portrayed here, although the downward slope for the low poverty condition with a PJ
mayor is steeper than that depicted here, and thus somewhat more similar to the predicted
curve for a non-Peronist mayor.

[26] Although the slight upward slope of this curve may seem surprising, it may simply be due to
the fact that there are so few observations at the lowest levels of council opposition.

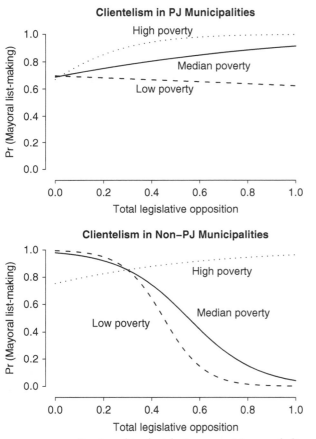

FIGURE 5.3. Partisanship, legislative opposition, and clientelism (I).

reproduces in a single graph the bottom two curves from both graphs in Figure 5.3. The black lines show the expected relationship between opposition size and poverty in Peronist municipalities, while the gray curves depict this same expected relationship for non-Peronist municipalities. I begin with the dashed curves, which depict how the expected probability of clientelism varies in a low-poverty municipality as legislative opposition increases. Note that, although the model predicts clientelism will be more likely in non-Peronist municipalities when competition is very low, this situation reverses when competition exceeds about 39%, and the expected probability of clientelism becomes markedly less likely in non-Peronist municipalities.[27] For the typical non-Peronist, low-poverty municipality (depicted in gray), the dashed curve has a clear, inverted-S shape that shows the following: as the size of the

---

[27] The large majority of the data fall in this range.

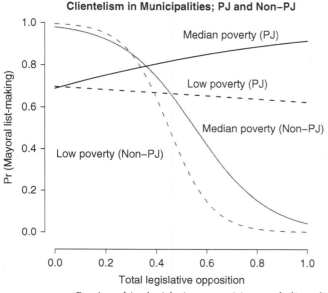

FIGURE 5.4. Partisanship, legislative opposition, and clientelism (II).

legislative opposition increases, the expected probability of clientelism quickly and sharply declines. The black dashed curve, which depicts the expected probability of clientelism in a low-poverty, Peronist municipality looks quite different. It is, as the theory predicts, downward sloping: increased competition decreases the expected likelihood of observing clientelism when poverty is low, even in a Peronist municipality. However, the relative flatness of the slope indicates that the predicted decline in clientelism for a Peronist municipality is far more limited than that the model predicts for a non-PJ municipality.[28] In spite of the differences in the two graphs, it is worth noting that the difference in the expected likelihood of clientelism between high- and low-poverty municipalities is statistically significant in *both* cases. For both Peronist and non-Peronist mayors, once legislative opposition size exceeds about 40%, clientelism is statistically significantly more likely in high as opposed to low-poverty municipalities.[29]

---

[28] Note that the curve for the Peronist municipality does become more steep if we set poverty to a lower level. However, even at the 10% level of poverty in the sample, the corresponding decline in expected clientelism is more limited in the Peronist as compared to the non-Peronist case, and the Peronist curve does not take on the clear S-shape of its non-Peronist counterpart.

[29] I estimate these differences using simulations in the same manner described for Figure 5.2. Not surprisingly, the figure for non-Peronist municipalities looks very similar to Figure 5.2. In contrast, the figure for Peronist municipalities shows a much flatter, though still upward sloping curve. Confidence intervals around this difference illustrate that in the case of the PJ, that difference narrowly achieves statistical significance at the 95% level when competition exceeds about 40%.

Nonetheless, there are important substantive differences in the patterns across parties. In this respect, perhaps most telling is the contrast in the slope of the solid lines for these two partisan groupings. The solid lines depict how the expected probability of mayoral intervention changes as competition increases for a municipality with a median level of poverty in the sample. Once again, the black line indicates the expected probability of clientelism in Peronist municipalities, while the gray line indicates the expected probability in non-Peronist municipalities. For non-Peronist municipalities, the predicted effects of increasing competition at median levels of poverty look much like the predicted effects at low levels of poverty. The model predicts that, even at median levels of poverty, increasing competition would lead non-PJ politicians to shift away from clientelism in large numbers. The expected relationship between political competition and clientelism in a typical Peronist municipality with median poverty (depicted by the solid black line) presents a stark contrast. For these cases, the predicted behavior of a mayor in a municipality with a median level of poverty "looks" much like that of a mayor in a municipality with a high level of poverty. In other words, it does not appear that the costs of clientelism, combined with high competition, begin to trigger an exodus away from clientelism in Peronist municipalities at this level of poverty. In Peronist municipalities, the model predicts that poverty must fall further before the costs of clientelism dynamic kicks in and mayors begin to turn away from clientelism.

The results presented here and in Section 5.2 together offer a test of the two possible mechanisms through which partisanship might affect incumbent incentives for clientelism. The results of regressions that include a Peronist party indicator variable (presented in Table 5.2) provide little support for the supply-side dynamic outlined in Chapter 3. Looking at all levels of competition together, there is no statistically significant relationship between partisanship and the predicted likelihood that a mayor will rely on clientelism. In contrast, the results displayed in Table 5.3 do support a demand-side story. It appears that, in the presence of high competition and a large middle-class, non-Peronist mayors eschew clientelism at higher rates than do Peronist mayors. This is consistent with the claim that Peronist mayors enjoy only limited support from nonpoor voters, and hence that these mayors have less to fear from the audience costs that accompany clientelism.[30] Chapter 6 offers individual level evidence that corroborates this claim. The results presented here support the key theoretical claim that the combination of high competition and a large nonpoor constituency leads incumbents to reject clientelism, while they also demonstrate that the strength of this effect varies across parties.

---

[30]   The results are broadly consistent with the findings of Calvo and Murillo (2004), who show that Radical party governors are not rewarded for patronage spending, although I focus on audience effects, rather than budget constraints and differential skill profiles, as the underlying mechanism.

5.4 CIVIL SOCIETY AND STATISM: ALTERNATIVE EXPLANATIONS

The theory developed in this book builds directly on two schools of thought on the determinants of the quality of governance and accountability: those that emphasize political competition and poverty, respectively, as important explanatory factors. As noted in the introduction, other scholars have pointed to political institutions, the state's role in the economy, and civil society as explanations for variation in the quality of governance. The subnational empirical approach taken in this book means that institutions are constant across the municipal cases. This section tests the two remaining alternative explanations mentioned previously and finds very little evidence that either civil society (operationalized with a variety of measures) or the state's role in the economy help to explain incumbent reliance on clientelism.[31] Before turning to the empirical tests, I outline the logic behind these alternative explanations in greater detail.

Beginning with the state role in the economy, a number of authors argue that the more resources a government has under its control – or what Kitschelt and Wilkinson (2007a) call the "public control of the political economy," the more likely it will be to manipulate those resources for overtly political ends. On clientelism in particular, Chandra (2004) characterizes what she calls a "patronage democracy" as one in which a large public sector is combined with individual discretion over the distribution of state resources and services. The combination of these two factors produce what she describes as an "overwhelming preoccupation with politics on the part of both elites and voters seeking both material and psychic goods," which she illustrates with respect to the Indian case (Chandra, 2007). In a similar vein, Medina and Stokes (2002) develop an argument that illustrates how a politician's control over risk-free economic resources facilitates clientelism, although in their model, that control can come from either state or nonstate resources. Further evidence for the relevance of state control over the economy can be gathered from its downfall: Kitschelt (2007) and Scheiner (2007) both argue that the decline of that control has precipitated the decline of patronage politics in some advanced economies. Nor need this dynamic be limited to democracy: within the context of the PRI's electoral authoritarian regime in Mexico, Greene (2007) points to state control of the economy as crucial for sustaining practices such as patronage and vote-buying. In short, these theories argue that state control over the economy can increase the appeal and viability of the individualized, contingent exchange of goods and services for political support. This connection between state control over the economy and clientelism has parallels to a broader literature that

---

[31] Data limitations mean that my test of a hypothesis focused on the state's role in the economy is much more limited, and hence with respect to that hypothesis, results should be treated with some caution.

links a large state role in the economy to a variety of deviations from good governance, most notably through corruption and bribe-taking (de Soto, 1989, Goel and Nelson, 1998, Fisman and Gatti, 2002).[32]

In some sense building on a similar intuition to that which links a large state role in the economy to clientelism, a separate body of work argues that a robust *nonstate* civil society improves governance and accountability. Definitions of civil society, as well as the postulated mechanism that links it to governance, vary somewhat in the literature. Peruzzotti and Smulovitz (2006), writing on Latin America, focus mostly on organizations explicitly aimed at holding governments accountable, like "civic associations, NGOs, social movements, and media organizations" (Peruzzotti and Smulovitz, 2006, 10). They make a strong argument for the effectiveness of what they call "social accountability" and highlight the extent to which such organizations can improve accountability by making denunciations in cases of wrongdoing and activating legal claims. Other work specifically on the media also demonstrates how local media can play an important role in disseminating proven information of incumbent wrong-doing, with the result that incumbents are more likely to be punished electorally (Ferraz and Finan, 2008).

Another approach in the literature, which includes work on Mexico (Cleary, 2007, 2010), Italy (Putnam, 1994), and China (Tsai, 2007), offers more expansive definitions of civil society and includes under this umbrella informal and formal groups and organizations of citizens, even when they are not specifically aimed at achieving accountability. Putnam (1994, 15), for example, describes the "civic community" that improves government performance as characterized by an "active, public-spirited citizenry, by egalitarian public relations, by a social fabric of trust and cooperation." Scholars in this second category tend to focus on the role of symbolic and moral sanctions as the main mechanism through which civil society can improve accountability. Tsai (2007), for example, argues that if citizens and leaders share moral criteria, and if citizens can learn about and disseminate information about politician behavior, the existence of encompassing local solidary groups can create incentives for local leaders to provide public goods, even in a nondemocratic context. In a similar vein, Cleary (2007) argues that in Mexican municipalities where most citizens actively participate in politics, residents are more able to enforce social norms that elected officials "should act as faithful public servants" (285).

The paucity of municipal-level data in Argentina poses a challenge for measurement of either the state role in the economy or civil society. With respect to the former, we would ideally like to be able to measure the role of government in the local economy, for example, by measuring the share

---

[32] Note that evidence on the link between government size and corruption is mixed; Montinola and Jackman (2002), for example, do not find evidence of this. I return to a broader theoretical discussion of the link between corruption and state size in Chapter 7.

of local employment in the public sector. Unfortunately, such measures are not available at the municipal level in Argentina. Instead, I rely on a measure collected in my own survey: the number of PNSA beneficiaries over the total number of households in the municipality.[33] This simplified measure obviously does not allow for a full test of the theory. However, it does allow for a test of the basic intuition that underlies the theory – that the greater the fiscal share of a publicly funded program, the more amenable and attractive it will be for clientelism.

With respect to civil society, I compile an original dataset that includes a number of measures, including the number of radio stations, Rotary or Lions clubs, and Catholic churches located within each municipality, along with the number of Catholic priests residing there.[34] Following the logic outlined earlier, incumbents may be more likely to eschew clientelism when local media, including radio, exists that can hold them to account.[35] The other indicators capture the type of moral pressure that Cleary and Tsai point to, and so we might expect their impact to be weighted by their influence in their community.[36] For that reason, I report these data as the ratio per 10,000 residents.[37] Table 5.4 reports summary statistics for all of the variables described here.

Results

Table 5.5 presents the results. Column 1 reports the results of column 1 from Table 5.2 – that is, the main results reported earlier in this chapter without the additional partisan interaction term.[38] Column 2 presents these main results with the addition of the measure of the number of program beneficiaries per

[33] Results are unchanged if we instead use the number of PNSA beneficiaries over the number of poor households only. I choose a per household, rather than per population measure, because the PNSA itself is targeted at the household level.

[34] I thank Jazmin Sierra for her persistent efforts in collecting data on the Catholic church and on Rotary and Lions clubs. Unfortunately, the decentralized nature of Evangelical churches make it impossible to collect similar data.

[35] In some cases, a single local media outlet might be controlled by the incumbent himself, as Boas and Hidalgo (2011) discuss for the case of Brazil. For that reason, I replicate the regressions reported below with alternate operationalizations of this variable – for example, separating municipalities with two or more radio stations from all others. In all cases, the results reported below are unchanged.

[36] Note that Cleary (2007), in his study of municipal government performance in Mexico, uses alternative measures of civil society, including municipal education levels and voter turnout. These are, as he acknowledges, quite imperfect, and I believe the measures I employ here better capture the underlying concept. Nonetheless, results presented below can be replicated with Cleary's measures and remain unchanged.

[37] Winters (2013) uses a similar measure of mosques per capita to operationalize civil society at the local level in Indonesia.

[38] Including those additional interaction terms does not change the results, but it does substantially complicate the table, so I rely on these more simple results here.

TABLE 5.4. *Summary Statistics: Alternative Hypotheses*

Variable	Mean	Std. Dev.	Min.	Max.
Beneficiaries per household	0.32	0.191	0.049	1.189
Churches per 10,000	1.324	1.216	0	4.764
Priests per 10,000	1.179	1.613	0	12.735
Rotary/Lions per 10,000	0.247	0.611	0	4.318
Radio stations	1.962	2.987	0	14
N		132		

TABLE 5.5. *Alternative Hypotheses: Regression Results*

	(1)	(2)	(3)	(4)
Population	−.43*	−.41	−39	−.64*
	(.25)	(.27)	(.37)	(.33)
Poverty	−5.53	−5.62	−5.51	−7.63
	(5.07)	(5.12)	(5.07)	(5.33)
Total opposition	−9.28**	−9.18**	−9.24**	−9.81***
	(3.67)	(3.74)	(3.69)	(3.77)
Poverty * opposition	37.89***	37.64***	37.69***	40.48***
	(11.88)	(12.03)	(11.99)	(12.37)
PJ	.55	.54	.55	.60
	(.46)	(.46)	(.46)	(.48)
Mayor party dominates	1.14	1.14	1.14	1.21*
	(.72)	(.72)	(.72)	(.73)
Salta	−1.92	−1.92	−1.91	−1.94
	(1.29)	(1.29)	(1.29)	(1.30)
Rio Negro	−.92	−.89	−.92	−.96
	(.68)	(.72)	(.68)	(.69)
Beneficiaries per household	—	.28	—	—
		(2.03)		
Radios	—	—	−.01	—
			(.12)	
Churches per household	—	—	—	−.31
				(.24)
Civic orgs per household	—	—	—	−.25
				(.36)
Obs.	126	126	126	126

Results are from logistic regressions where the dependent variable equals one if the mayor is involved in drawing up the beneficiary list, and zero otherwise. *, **, *** indicate significance at the .1, .05, and .01 levels.

municipal household. As discussed previously, this serves as a rough proxy for the importance of state programs in the local economy. Columns 3 and 4 are intended to test the civil society hypothesis, with the inclusion of the measure of the number of radio stations (column 3) and Rotary/Lions clubs and Catholic churches per capita (column 4). Overall, it is quite clear that the results of these analyses do not lend support to either alternate hypothesis. With a single exception, these results are not altered by the inclusion of a range of different variants of any of these variables – for example, counting instead the number of priests per capita, or distinguishing municipalities with two or more radio stations from all others.[39]

In the case of the state role in the economy, the quite imperfect nature of our data mean that these results should by no means be understood as a definitive rejection of this hypothesis within the sphere of local government. Our more complete measures of civil society afford more confidence in the results presented with respect to that hypothesis, at least in the empirical setting examined here. Although contrary to some findings from the civil society literature, the results presented here are consistent with alternate voices, even from the policy community, that raise questions about the likelihood that civil society, particularly at the subnational level, will have the capacity to serve as a check on government behavior.[40] Alternately, it may be the case that civil society matters less where robust political competition is possible. It is worth noting that two prominent examples of a positive role for civil society on municipal governance are drawn from settings with limits on competition – either nondemocratic, as in the case of China, or in a setting where reelection is prohibited (Mexico). The scope conditions under which we should expect civil society to enhance local accountability (or not) are certainly worthy of further investigation.

5.5 THE DIRECTION OF CAUSALITY

Before concluding, I turn to the question of the direction of causality. Both theoretically and empirically, this book treats political competition as a factor that is independent of clientelism and that can explain a politician's incentives to use the practice. At the same time, the book also treats clientelism as a political tool that likely affects the competitiveness of an election, at least at the margins. The desire to win elections is part of what motivates a politician to employ clientelism.

---

39 The sole exception is in the case of churches. When we compare municipalities with at least one church against all others, the presence of at least a single church is significantly negatively associated with the likelihood of clientelism. This variable itself is highly correlated with population size, and the effect does not show up if we measure merely the total number of Catholic churches within a municipality. Nonetheless, even when significant, it does not substantially alter the values or statistical significance of our main variables of interest.

40 See Linder (2012).

As noted in Chapter 3, the empirical setting of this project, with its focus on municipal politics, helps assuage to some extent concerns about reverse causation. Voting behavior in municipal elections is likely to reflect a mix of local and national concerns, thus ensuring that the competitiveness of local elections is at least in part exogenous to local politics. The cross-sectional and observational nature of the data collected for this project make it impossible to disentangle fully the effects of political competition on clientelism and the reverse. Nonetheless, a number of patterns observed in the data are consistent with the claim that political competition affects incentives for clientelism, and they are inconsistent with the claim that clientelism wholly determines levels of local political competition.

I begin by considering the most straightforward alternative story. An approach that treated clientelism as the main driver of political competition, rather than the reverse, would likely presume that clientelism would decrease competition. If this were true, we would expect that, over time, clientelist municipalities would experience decreasing levels of political competition and that an equilibrium would emerge in which municipalities where clientelism was practiced would experience low levels of competition.[41] At an extreme, it is possible to imagine that the use of clientelism at some early point fundamentally suppresses political competition in the town in which it is employed. If this were to be the case, then clientelism might persist purely due to path dependence, while being in no way responsive to the contemporary state of political competition. The data collected for this book are not consistent with this pattern. Among nonclientelist municipalities included in the sample, the mean town council opposition size is 43%. Among clientelist municipalities, the opposition comprises on average 41% of the town council. Although the decrease in competition in clientelism municipalities is in the expected direction, this is an extremely small substantive difference, and it is not statistically significant.

A more nuanced alternative might suggest that the practice of clientelism would suppress competition only in predominantly poor municipalities. Again, if this were the case, we would expect that mayors in this type of locality would use clientelism to systematically suppress competition. To explore this possibility, I divide the sampled municipalities into two groups, separating high from low poverty municipalities.[42] Among the poorer municipalities in the sample, the typical council opposition is actually larger in clientelist municipalities that in nonclientelist locales. Among poor, clientelist municipalities, the average opposition share is 42% whereas it is 37% among

---

[41] Municipal elections in Argentina resumed with the return of national democracy in 1983, giving plenty of time for such an equilibrium to emerge, even allowing some time for learning.
[42] The median level of poverty, using the NBI, is 18%.

poor, nonclientelist municipalities.[43] Once again, this is inconsistent with the claim that clientelism inexorably decreases competition. It instead suggests that politicians use clientelism in response to the exigencies of political competition.

Finally, given the importance of partisanship in the Argentine context, we might suppose that clientelism is capable of systematically suppressing competition only in poor, Peronist-dominated municipalities. Although the number of observations here is small, an examination of the data is once again not consistent with that alternate story. Among poor, Peronist municipalities, the average size of the legislative opposition is actually higher in municipalities that employ clientelism.[44]

The practice of clientelism and political competition undoubtedly affect one another. However, this need not mean that clientelism is so powerful that it is capable of "locking in" low levels of competition on a long-term basis, especially subnationally. The data analyzed here are not consistent with this story. Instead, the balance of evidence is consistent with the claim that incumbent decisions about whether to employ clientelism respond to political competition and constituent demographics, though they are also constrained by partisanship.

5.6 CONCLUSIONS: THE MIXED CONSEQUENCES OF COMPETITION AND THE HIGH BAR SET BY POVERTY

The theory developed in Chapter 3 takes the discussion of clientelism away from an exclusive focus on the poor recipients of government goods and examines the possible effects of clientelism on the voting habits of middle-class constituents, as well. As a result, it departs from existing predictions about the relationship between political competition and clientelism. Rather than expecting competition to have a uniform effect on politician incentives to employ clientelism, I predict that only the combination of high competition and low poverty will create incentives for politicians to opt out of clientelism. High poverty and high competition are expected to be quite compatible with clientelism. Finally, at low levels of competition, I do not expect poverty to be an important predictor of a politician's decision about whether to opt out of clientelism. These expectations are lent further nuance by a consideration of the ways in which partisanship might shape interest in, or opportunities for, clientelism, through either a demand or supply-side effect.

I have tested these predictions using an original dataset developed for this project, which provides a measure of the way in which government policy

---

[43] Given the relatively small sample size, this difference is not statistically significant. By this criterion, fifty of the "poor" municipalities use clientelism, while fifteen do not.

[44] Of the forty poor, Peronist municipalities, the average level of competition in the thirty-five where we observe clientelism is 40%, whereas it is 27% in the five where we do not observe clientelism.

is implemented. By focusing on the workings of a single important social welfare program in Argentina, I am able to generate a fairly direct measure of clientelism and therefore conduct a reliable test of the theory. With respect to the interaction between poverty and competition, the results are consistent with expectations. The interaction between these two variables, rather than either alone, appears to explain deviations from clientelism.

Although the theory does not make predictions about the incidence of clientelism in the absence of political competition, evidence from the Argentine context shows that it is widespread. When voters are mostly poor, the results presented here show no clear path away from this practice. Little in the Argentine context, whether partisanship or political competition, appears to create incentives for high-quality governance in the presence of high poverty.

However, as poverty decreases, an opportunity to move away from clientelism appears to present itself to at least some mayors. High competition tends to decrease the incidence of clientelism when poverty declines, and the scope for opportunities to depart from clientelism is mediated by partisanship. For non-Peronist mayors, relatively small demographic shifts away from poverty appear to make politicians sensitive to the costs of clientelism. For Peronist mayors, in contrast, poverty must sink quite low before this same mechanism is associated with a shift in behavior. While consistent with much work on Argentina that points to the centrality of the Peronist party for explanations of clientelism, my results suggest a different explanation of why Peronism matters. I do not find evidence that Peronist incumbents are systematically more prone to employ clientelism in all circumstances, but rather than they are less sensitive to the electoral *costs* of the practice. Middle-class reluctance to support the PJ in any circumstances limits the extent to which Peronist mayors can be punished by nonpoor voters. This conclusion is further buttressed by individual level data examined in the next chapter.

This chapter has also explored other common explanations of clientelism, including civil society, the state role in the economy, and competition or poverty alone, and finds little support for these hypotheses in the data. It highlights that, in the absence of a nationally driven, top-down effort to minimize clientelism in social policy, there may nonetheless be conditions under which local incumbents eschew clientelism because of their own electoral incentives. At the same time, the chapter demonstrates that these are a rather narrow set of conditions. The results thus draw attention to the serious difficulty of establishing good governance practices in contexts where clientelism is deeply embedded. In the next chapter, I return to the mechanism that I argue drives any possible departures from clientelism – the costs of that practice for middle-class support. I use the results of a large citizen survey and a survey experiment to support the claim that nonpoor voters will reject politicians who engage in clientelism.

6

Survey and Experimental Evidence
for the Costs of Clientelism

In this book, I argue for the importance of bringing the nonpoor into the analysis of political clientelism. While poor voters are most frequently the targets of clientelist exchange, they are not the only voters whose behavior may be affected by these exchanges. The core assumption around which the theory is built is that nonpoor voters dislike clientelism and are willing to withdraw political support from politicians who rely on it. Nonpoor voters might reject clientelism for one of two reasons. First, they might reject the practice out of a moral or normative disdain for the exchange of goods or services for political support. Second, they might reject clientelism out of self-interest. Clientelism does not occur in a vacuum. Most nonpoor voters rely on a variety of government services and administrative capabilities; the time and effort dedicated to making clientelism work may decrease the quality of government service provision more broadly. If either of these two mechanisms hold, nonpoor voters who are not a party to clientelist exchange might withdraw support from a politician who relies on it. In this chapter, I test that claim using original analyses of two separate public opinion surveys in Argentina: a large in-person survey of a representative sample of the Argentine population, and an original telephone survey experiment of somewhat better-off voters.[1] Results from both surveys provide compelling evidence that Argentine citizens who are not poor react negatively to information about clientelism and related practices. In addition, the original survey experiment allows me to test the demand-side argument on the relationship between partisanship and clientelism. Within the survey framework, I find that nonpoor voters withdraw support for Radical party mayors who rely on clientelism at a faster rate than they do for Peronist mayors. These results thus provide individual-level evidence consistent with the municipal-level results presented in Chapter 5.

---

[1] Data from the in-person survey was generously shared by Ernesto Calvo and María Victoria Murillo. Strictly speaking, that survey is representative of the Argentine population residing outside of Patagonia; I provide more details about both surveys later.

6.1 EXISTING RESEARCH, NEW QUESTIONS

The large literature on clientelism has focused almost exclusively on the relationship between politicians and their (mostly poor) clients. Using both ethnographic approaches and public opinion surveys, scholars have provided ample evidence of who is targeted in clientelist exchange and the behavioral (and to some extent attitudinal) implications of clientelism for those who are party to it.[2]

In contrast, the possibility that clientelism could have attitudinal or behavioral consequences for nonclients has attracted very little research. Gonzalez Ocantos et al. (2014) and Bratton (2008) are two important exceptions, both of whom explore these questions in the context of public opinion surveys. Gonzalez Ocantos et al. (2014) carry out surveys in a number of Latin American countries in which they describe a hypothetical scenario wherein a citizen exchanges his vote for a monetary payment from a politician. The survey then asks respondents to evaluate the acceptability of the citizen's (not the politician's) behavior. The authors find that, on the whole, higher education is correlated with attaching greater stigma to the act of selling one's vote. While these results are, broadly speaking, consistent with my own expectations, there is an important difference in the outcome Gonzalez Ocantos et al. (2014) analyze and that of interest here. In order to test the "costs of clientelism" hypothesis, we need to learn how citizens view and evaluate the behavior of the *politician* engaged in such an exchange. The stigma attached to the two participating sides of clientelist exchange may be distinct; we can certainly imagine, for example, that some voters may condemn clientelist politicians yet be understanding of citizen vote sellers.[3] Furthermore, by asking about stigma, the authors elicit responses that predominantly reflect the moral, rather than self-interested, dimension of evaluations of clientelism. In a similar attempt to measure citizen attitudes toward clientelism, Bratton (2008) describes the results of a related question from the 2007 Afrobarometer survey carried out in Nigeria. In that case, the survey included questions about whether the behavior of the vote-buyer (the politician), as well as the vote-seller (the citizen) was acceptable or should be punished. The Nigerian context is quite different than the one examined here, especially in light of the fact that Nigerian respondents were far more concerned about outright violence than

---

2 See work by Auyero (2000b), Bratton (2008), Faughnan and Zechmeister (2011), Nichter (2008), and Stokes (2005), among others.

3 Indeed, some of their reported results from an experimental component that varies characteristics of the citizen selling his vote highlight the ways in which attitudes toward the two sides of clientelist exchange might differ. Gonzalez Ocantos et al. (2014) find, for example, that the stigma attached to the citizen selling his vote decreases when he is described as poor. In contrast, we would likely expect politicians to suffer greater stigma when they target poor, as opposed to well-off, voters via clientelism.

vote-buying or related practices (Bratton, 2008). Nonetheless, the results are broadly consistent with the expectations of audience costs. Bratton finds that higher social class respondents are more likely to condemn both sides involved in clientelist exchange.[4] In sum, the results from both Gonzalez Ocantos et al. (2014) and Bratton (2008) offer some evidence that is consistent with my claim that nonpoor voters are likely to punish politicians for clientelism.[5] Nonetheless, they also point to the need for the more direct work on this question that this chapter provides.

Carrying out that direct work poses some challenges. An individual's attitudes and behavioral response toward a politician who employs clientelism are, like the phenomenon in general, difficult to study empirically. The pitfalls of measurement have been amply noted in the survey literature that focuses on citizens who exchange their votes. There, the social stigma attached to clientelism may make citizens reluctant to admit their participation in clientelist exchange. In that context, the introduction of the use of list experiments by Gonzalez-Ocantos et al. (2012) has been an important innovation, and it demonstrates that traditional survey instruments underestimate the true extent of citizen participation in clientelist-type exchanges.[6] Asking nonrecipients about their attitudes toward clientelism is a less fraught task, as these respondents are not themselves engaged in an exchange that is stigmatized or illegal. Nonetheless, normative pressures to answer in a certain way may still exist; in this case, respondents may feel pressure to give the more socially acceptable answer that they disapprove of clientelism, even if they do not. In addition, using public opinion data to examine the behavioral consequences of clientelism for nonclients brings with it some unique challenges of its own. Notably, unlike clientelist exchange, which is expected to become a focal point for the voting behavior of clients, the existence of clientelism is likely to be only one of many issues other voters take into account. Asking a citizen directly to assess the impact of information about clientelism on her vote, for example, may prove a cognitively difficult task that could yield quite unreliable results.

Here, I employ data from two different surveys, both carried out in Argentina, that have different advantages and disadvantages with respect to the challenges of measuring the behavioral effects of clientelism on nonclients. The first data analysis I present comes from a survey that included information

---

4 He also finds that overall levels of condemnation of politicians are about 10 percentage points higher than levels of condemnation of citizens. In both cases, differences in condemnation across the lowest and highest social classes are statistically significant, and of moderate size: about 10 percentage points.

5 Perhaps most similar to my effort is the ongoing work of Kramon (2011) in Kenya; I discuss it in the conclusion to this chapter.

6 Other strategies to learn about clientelism have included asking about the behavior of a respondent's neighbors, rather than herself directly. See Stokes (2005). As she points out, the stigma attached to admitting participation in clientelism might be due as much to the fact that it identifies the respondent as poor as to the censure attached to the act itself.

about politician behavior that is generally treated as an indicator of clientelism, although it does not refer to exchange as such. It includes a question about respondent attitudes toward that behavior, rather than behavioral consequences. In spite of these drawbacks, it has a major advantage in that it includes large samples of both poor and nonpoor respondents, and thus it allows us to examine differences in attitudes across social class. The second data analysis is of an original survey experiment specifically designed to test the costs of clientelism hypothesis. Respondents are overwhelmingly nonpoor, which limits our ability to make comparisons across groups. Nonetheless, this survey includes a vignette that more fully captures the phenomenon of clientelism and asks respondents about their likely behavioral response to it. The experimental setup has two additional advantages. It allows us to embed information about clientelism in a relatively unobtrusive manner and also to explore how the effects of information about clientelism vary with the partisanship of an incumbent. As we shall see, results from both surveys support the claim that there are audience costs to clientelism among the nonpoor. Furthermore, results from the second survey are consistent with municipal-level results from Chapter 5 and show that Peronist mayors are less likely to suffer electoral punishment for clientelism than Radical party mayors. This is largely because Peronist party mayors enjoy only limited support from nonpoor voters in the first place.

6.2 DIFFERENTIAL ATTITUDES ACROSS SOCIAL CLASS: SURVEY EVIDENCE

The analysis I present first uses data from a large survey carried out by Ernesto Calvo and Victoria Murillo.[7] They conducted a large citizen survey with almost 2,800 respondents who were interviewed in person.[8] The in-person nature of the survey offers a crucial advantage in the Argentine context: it allows for a sample that is representative of the population along class lines and includes ample numbers of poor respondents. As such, the survey permits us to compare the responses of a large sample of the poor and the nonpoor. Though the survey's primary aim was not to measure the attitudinal or behavioral response of nonclients toward clientelism, it included a question that can be treated as a proxy for such attitudes. The large survey also included questions about attitudes toward redistribution in general, allowing for controls for those attitudes in regression analysis.

---

7   See Calvo and Murillo (2013) for more details. The survey was carried out in Argentina and Chile. To streamline the presentation of the results, I focus on the results from Argentina only, but the results from Chile are very similar to those presented here.

8   The survey was representative of Argentine residents in cities with populations over 10,000 outside of the sparsely populated Patagonian region.

The crucial question I analyze here asked respondents the following: "In your opinion, how appropriate is it that political parties distribute clothing, food, and money?"[9] Although the survey did not specify the target of these goods or the way in which they were distributed, the Argentine press commonly decries the distribution of these types of goods to poor voters as a form of clientelism. In past election cycles, for example, newspapers have characterized as clientelism the distribution of money, bags of food, and other material goods (including bathroom fixtures and roofing materials) in the run-up to gubernatorial elections in a number of provinces.[10] I treat attitudes toward this distribution as a proxy for attitudes toward clientelism in the analysis below. Those surveyed were asked to respond on a ten point scale, with an answer of 1 indicating "not at all appropriate," and an answer of 10 indicating their belief that such a practice is completely appropriate. Responses reflect a population split in their views of the practice. The modal response was that such distribution is "not at all" appropriate, with about 47% of respondents giving that answer, while the remaining 53% of respondents replied that this distribution is at least "a little" appropriate. Those answers were spread more or less uniformly across the remaining categories, with the number "5" being the second most frequent response, reflecting the opinion of about 12% of those surveyed.[11] For the purposes of analysis, I divide this into a 0–1 variable that takes on a value of one for respondents who describe the practice of distributing small items as at least a little bit acceptable. This separates out the group of respondents who completely reject the practice from all others. It is this former group for whom we should believe that clientelism is most likely to affect voting behavior, which is our underlying outcome of interest.[12]

If the costs of clientelism hypothesis is correct, nonpoor respondents should be the most likely to hold this view and to say that the distribution of small handouts by parties is not at all appropriate.[13] Social class is measured using

---

9   In the original Spanish: "En su opinión, cuán adecuado es que los partidos políticos provean ropa, comida, dinero?"

10   See, for example, Lladós (2007), Petersen (2011), and Ybarra (2011). This final article, focused on Misiones, notes a somewhat lower rate of distribution than normal and attributes this to the fact that the governor did not face strong competition for reelection. Misiones is a poor province, and so this is consistent with my own expectation that, in the presence of poverty, strong competition intensifies rather than diminishes incentives for clientelism.

11   Responses to the other categories are not entirely uniform, with more responses concentrated on the lower end of the scale.

12   If we instead use the 10-category outcome variable in the analysis presented in Table 6.1, the coefficient on the social class variable remains negative and significant in columns 1, 3, and 4, and it is still negative, though no longer significant, in column 2.

13   As noted in Chapter 3, it is possible that poor citizens might dislike clientelism even if they comply with clientelist exchange. Because this survey asked only about attitudes toward clientelism, to the extent this is the case, this could attenuate any relationship between social class and attitudes. The raw data do illustrate that a relatively large minority of even the

a common Argentine survey measure, the NES (*nivel económico social,* or socioeconomic status) that takes into account household goods as well as the education and occupation of the head of the household. Depending on the specification, I either use the full range of possible values of social class or create a dichotomous variable that separates poor from nonpoor respondents. For the former, the lowest social class ("E") takes on a value of 1, while the highest social class included in the sample ("C1") takes on a value of 6.[14] For the latter, I separate the 34% of respondents in the two lowest social categories (E and D2) from the remainder of respondents, whom I refer to as the "nonpoor." In both cases, higher values indicate higher social class. As a value of 1 on the outcome variable indicates at least some acceptance of the political practice of distributing food, clothing, and money, we should expect a negative relationship between social class (in either coding scheme) and the outcome variable.

In addition to looking at the main relationship of interest, all of the results presented here also control for other demographic characteristics that might be associated with attitudes toward distribution: age, gender, and education. Gonzalez Ocantos et al. (2014) find that the more educated, older people, and women all attach higher levels of stigma to citizen participants in vote-buying, so we might also expect them to view the related practice by political parties as less acceptable.[15] Although we are interested in the relationship between social class and attitudes toward clientelism, it is possible that responses to the prompt might reflect attitudes toward redistribution per se, in addition to attitudes toward clientelism as a *method* of redistribution. Though the question did not explicitly mention redistribution to the poor, the goods mentioned – food, clothing, and (presumably small amounts of) money – are likely to be predominantly of interest to the poor. Thus, in some regressions, I include as additional controls responses to two questions that might proxy for attitudes toward redistribution. The first asked respondents whether, to reduce poverty, the government should "give money to the poor and raise taxes," or "promote investment and leave tax rates as they are." I code those who favored the first option as favoring government redistribution.[16] The second asked respondents whether they believed that the government or individuals

---

poorest Argentines say that they find the distribution of small goods totally unacceptable (34% in the lowest social category). Even with these rates of disapproval among low social class respondents, results displayed below are also clearly consistent with the hypothesis that the likelihood of disapproval increases with social class.

[14] The Argentine NES runs from A to E, with group C having three subgroups, and group D having two subgroups. The group jointly referred to as ABC1 is considered the highest social class (Mora y Araujo, 2002). None of this survey's respondents fell into group A or B, which represent only a very small share of the Argentine population.

[15] In the case of women, results reported by Gonzalez Ocantos et al. (2014) do not reach conventional levels of statistical significance.

[16] Only 6% of respondents chose this option, and almost 10% of respondents replied "neither" or failed to answer. I have coded those respondents as missing; if we instead code them as not

TABLE 6.1. *Approval of Party Distribution: Regression Results*

	(1)	(2)	(3)	(4)
Social class (6 cat)	−.19***	−.16**	—	—
	(.07)	(.07)		
Nonpoor (0–1)	—	—	−.47***	−.34***
			(.11)	(.12)
Age	−.28***	−26***	−27***	−.26***
	(.05)	(.05)	(.05)	(.05)
Female	.05	.05	.05	.06
	(.08)	(.10)	(.09)	(.10)
Education	−.07	−.06	−11**	−.11*
	(.06)	(.07)	(.05)	(.06)
Favors Redistribution	—	.70**	—	.70**
		(.29)		(.29)
Favors Govt Role	—	.26	—	.25
		(.17)		(.16)
Obs.	2660	2052	2660	2052
Locality dummies?	Y	Y	Y	Y

Results are from logistic regressions where the dependent variable equals one if the respondent finds the distribution of small goods by parties at least a little acceptable, and zero otherwise. *, **, *** indicate significance at the .1, .05 and .01 levels. All regressions take into account the sampling method and include indicator variables for twenty-nine out of the thirty municipalities sampled, although coefficients are not reported here.

should be responsible for individuals' economic well-being. I code those who responded "the government" as preferring a larger government role in society, and this may also be a proxy for redistributive preferences.[17]

Table 6.1 presents the empirical results. Column 1 reports results using the full social class variable, whereas column 3 reports results using the dichotomous measure of social class; columns 2 and 4 repeat these results with the addition of the variables that proxy for attitudes toward redistribution. To begin with the control variables, I find, consistent with Gonzalez Ocantos et al. (2014), that both older and (in some specifications) more educated respondents are significantly less likely to approve of parties' distributive behavior. Gender has no significant effect on attitudes. With respect to redistribution, the results are also consistent with expectations. A belief in government redistribution is

favoring redistribution, the coefficients on social class continue to be negative and significant and are in fact larger than those reported here.

[17] About 80% of respondents answered this question as directed, and they were evenly split among the two replies. The remaining 20% of respondents either answered "both" or refused to answer. In my analyses, I have coded those respondents as missing, but if we instead code them as not favoring redistribution, the coefficients on social class again continue to be negative and significant and are larger than those reported here.

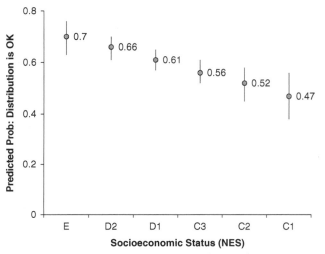

FIGURE 6.1. Socioeconomic status and attitudes toward clientelism.

strongly and significantly correlated with an accepting attitude toward party distribution of small goods. The broader measure of attitudes toward government's role in society is positively, though not significantly, correlated with our outcome.

With respect to the main hypothesis, the results show quite clearly that higher social class is associated with a lower likelihood of believing that the distribution of small benefits by political parties is at least somewhat acceptable. To give a sense of the substantive effect, Figure 6.1 presents the results of simulations that show how attitudes toward the distribution of small items by political parties change with social class. Socioeconomic status runs along the horizontal axis from the lowest category (E) to the highest included in the sample (C1).[18] For each category of social class, I use the results from column 1 in Table 6.1 to graph the predicted probability, along with 95% confidence interval, that an otherwise typical respondent in this group would find it at least a little acceptable for parties to distribute food, clothing, and money.[19] As the graph makes clear, as social class increases, there is a decline in the likelihood of viewing such exchanges as acceptable; the predicted likelihood of giving that response drops from 70% in the lowest socioeconomic status group to 47% among those who fall into the C1 group.[20]

---

[18] Recall that no respondents fell into the "AB" category of social class.
[19] This "typical" respondent is a woman between the age of thirty and forty-two with completed high school education who resides in the suburbs surrounding Buenos Aires.
[20] Confidence intervals were estimated using the Clarify program in Stata (King et al., 2000). I run the simulations on a version of the regression reported in column 1 with weights and twenty-nine locality dummies, but without robust standard errors.

In sum, the results from this survey show quite clearly that increased socioeconomic status is associated with a decreased likelihood of responding that the distribution of small benefits by parties is an acceptable practice. Although these results are certainly consistent with the existence of audience costs of clientelism, the Calvo and Murillo data have some limitations in fully establishing that such costs exist. As noted previously, the scenario posed to respondents is often equated with clientelism in the press and popular discourse, but it does not explicitly mention any type of exchange between parties and voters. In addition, it asks respondents about attitudes toward the distribution of these individualized goods, rather than trying to measure the behavioral consequences of that distribution. Finally, the survey does not include information about the party doing the distribution, so it does not allow us to test the demand-side theory of how partisanship shapes incentives for clientelism.

6.3 ELECTORAL COSTS AMONG THE MIDDLE CLASS: EXPERIMENTAL EVIDENCE

To more fully establish the existence of audience costs to clientelism, I analyze a second dataset from an original public opinion survey with an embedded experiment designed to examine whether the nonpoor are likely to withdraw electoral support from incumbents who rely on clientelism. The conclusion from the Calvo–Murillo data is reinforced and expanded by this analysis. The key part of the survey experiment is a vignette in which the respondent hears a description about a hypothetical incumbent mayor running for reelection. As with all experiments, there is a control and treatment group, and respondents are randomly assigned to hear only one version of the vignette.[21] In the control group, respondents learn about the mayor's party, along with some other basic information about the race for mayor. Respondents in the treatment group hear the same information, along with one additional piece of information. They learn that the mayor "distributes food assistance programs to poor people in exchange for promises to vote for him."[22] In addition, the mayor's political party affiliation is also varied at random, so that approximately half of the respondents in both the control and treatment groups learn that the mayor is a member of the Peronist (or Radical) party.[23] Afterward, they are asked how likely they are to vote for the mayor.

Experiments have been embedded in mass public opinion surveys in the United States for a number of decades now and are particularly common

[21] The design was slightly more complicated than this, as I detail in the text that follows.
[22] The exchange described in the scenario of course does not capture the long-term relationships within which clientelism is often embedded, but within the context of a brief public opinion survey, the scenario offers a fair amount of detail and reflects a key part of clientelism.
[23] I use the Radical party because of its historical status as one of Argentina's two major national political forces, in spite of the sharp decline in its fortunes over the past decade.

in research on sensitive topics.[24] Nonetheless, survey experiments are still a relatively recent research tool outside of the United States and other long-standing democracies.[25] Survey experiments offer the researcher a unique tool to make causal arguments about citizen attitudes. The technique crucial to survey experiments is the method crucial to experiments more generally – random assignment. By randomly assigning respondents to either the control or the treatment group, we can assure that respondents in the two groups are indistinguishable on observable and unobservable characteristics. Then, we can attribute any difference in responses to questions of interest to the dimension that differed between the two groups. Like any survey, a survey experiment can be somewhat artificial. Nonetheless, in many substantively important settings, a survey experiment will be the only feasible approach to isolate causal effects. It is implausible, for example, to imagine assigning some incumbents to use clientelism in governing and others not to.[26] Furthermore, the artificiality of an experiment allows the researcher to control the respondent's information environment and isolate the causal effect of a particular piece of information or other experimental treatment.

In the case examined here, we want to know how the support of nonpoor voters for a politician will vary with that politician's reliance on clientelism. As far as I am aware, no existing survey research, whether experimental or conventional, explicitly examines the relationship between clientelism and the likely voting behavior of those who are *not* targets of clientelist exchange. The technique of the survey experiment has significant appeal in this substantive domain. By randomly assigning respondents to hear about clientelism or not, we are able to learn about the effects of clientelism in a relatively unobtrusive manner. Although we cannot eliminate entirely the possibility of social desirability bias if we are to ask about clientelism at all, by including that information in a vignette with other information about the incumbent, we likely lessen any bias. Including other information can help to insulate

---

[24] See Sniderman and Grob (1996) and Gaines et al. (2007) for good summaries of the state of survey experiment research in political science and sociology.

[25] The use of survey experiments (as well as field experiments) in new democracies and competitive authoritarian regimes is growing; see, for example, research on partisanship in Eastern Europe and Russia (Brader and Tucker, 2008) and on deliberative democracy in Africa (Humphreys et al., 2006). The 2006 Mexican Panel Survey also included a number of experiments, described briefly in Mexican Panel Survey (n.d.). On the growing use and advantages of survey and field experiments in political science, see Druckman et al. (2006) and McDermott (2002).

[26] Random assignment to clientelism is not entirely impossible. For example, Wantchekon (2003) uses a field experiment to explore the effects of "public policy" and what he calls "clientelist" appeals on voter support for an incumbent party in Benin. In that experiment, political parties agreed to vary campaign strategies at random only within districts they were confident of winning. It is also worth noting that his definition of clientelism falls closer to what Kitschelt (2000) calls pork-barrel politics; it would be harder to manipulate clientelism as defined here, especially because it is commonly embedded in ongoing relationships.

the respondent from the fear that the interviewer might interpret support for an incumbent who is described as employing clientelism as support for the practice of clientelism itself.[27] The use of a survey experiment also allows us to test the demand-side theory of partisanship and clientelism, that stipulates that the nonpoor react differently to clientelism depending on the party of the mayor involved, in a relatively unobtrusive manner. Each respondent learns only about either a PJ or UCR mayor but is not asked to compare them directly. The experimental setup allows us to compare results across groups to evaluate the effect of learning information about clientelism on intended voting for both Peronist and Radical party incumbents.

The survey was administered to 617 respondents reached across eight Argentine metropolitan areas in September 2007, just prior to the October presidential and congressional elections.[28] Data were collected using a telephone survey that dialed landlines only, which has important implications for the demographic makeup of those sampled. Telephone coverage is far from universal in Argentina, and this is particularly true among lower-income sectors of the population.[29] Perhaps most telling is the very small portion of respondents to the survey experiment who report that they are recipients of social welfare program benefits targeted at the poor. Two recent, nationally representative surveys conducted via in-person interviews found that 21% and 22% of all respondents, respectively, reported that they or someone in their family was the beneficiary of such a program. In contrast, in the telephone survey analyzed here, only 7% of respondents answered such a query in the

---

[27] It is also worth noting that if social desirability bias is sufficiently strong to shape answers to survey questions, it might also reflect a sufficiently deeply held belief that could translate into voting behavior. In that sense, even if negative responses to vignettes that include information about clientelism in part reflect social desirability bias, they might nonetheless be useful for predicting behavior. I thank Robert Kaufman for discussion on this point.

[28] In some provinces local elections also took place in October. Because of concerns about phone penetration in more remote areas, the survey was conducted in eight medium to large metropolitan areas. Although centered around cities much larger than those included in the sample studied in earlier chapters, many of these metropolitan areas encompass smaller municipalities of the type included there. See also Druckman and Kam (2011) for a discussion of how the use of nonrepresentative samples in survey experiments can nonetheless yield valid results (they focus on student samples). The appendix contains more complete details about sampling and data collection for this survey.

[29] Telephone land line penetration in Argentina is relatively low, although recent national surveys, all conducted in-person, suggest different levels of phone penetration. In a large 2007 survey run by the United Nations (the Survey on the Perception of Social Programs, or *Encuesta sobre la Percepción de los Planes Sociales* (EPPS)), 50% of respondents report having landlines. In the 2008 and 2010 LAPOP surveys, between two-thirds and 70% of respondents report having landlines. Data also support the claim that households without landlines are concentrated among the poor. According to the Argentine national statistics institute (INDEC), in 2001, among poor households (those with NBI), 71% did not have a landline *or* a cellphone (INDEC, 2003). Given the relative expense of the two, we can presume that the overwhelming majority of NBI households did not have a landline.

affirmative.[30] Given the underrepresentation of the poor, especially social program beneficiaries, in the sample, I treat the whole sample as being composed of nonpoor respondents for the purposes of the analysis carried out here.[31]

The vignette heard by respondents assigned to the control group (approximately one-third of the total respondents) gave the following information about a hypothetical upcoming election:[32]

Control

Imagine that you live in a city where the mayor is running for reelection next month. The opposition candidate is a member of the city council. The mayor is a member of the Justicialist [*or*, Radical] party. Imagine that you hear on the radio that the election will be very close.

Another third of the respondents heard a very similar vignette, although they received one additional piece of information, intended to simulate the type of information a nonpoor voter might receive about clientelist practices in the municipality where she lives. This vignette was as follows.

Treatment: Clientelism

Imagine that you live in a city where the mayor is running for reelection next month. The opposition candidate is a member of the city council. The mayor is a member of

---

[30] The 21% and 22% figures come from the 2007 EPPS (see previous footnote) and the 2010 LAPOP survey, respectively. The marked underrepresentation of social program beneficiaries in a telephone survey fits with anecdotal evidence from fieldwork. An interview with the bureaucrat in charge of overseeing the PNSA in the city of Viedma, in the province of Río Negro, is particularly telling in this respect. She informed me that if a recipient called her office to find out the date of the next food distribution, she would treat this as a sign that the person was sufficiently well off that she probably did not need the program's assistance.

[31] To the extent that responses of the poor differ from those of the nonpoor, the inclusion of some poor respondents in the sample should bias our estimates of the effects of the clientelism treatment on responses toward zero. Indeed, if we replicate the regressions reported in Tables 6.2 and 6.3 but exclude social program beneficiaries, the negative coefficients on the clientelism treatment variable are larger than those reported here. Another alternative would be to analyze respondents in the two lowest social classes separately from the remainder of respondents. If we do this, we find, not surprisingly, that exposure to information about clientelism significantly depresses support for the incumbent among the higher social class respondents. Responses from citizens in the two lowest social classes shift in the direction we would expect. Although the estimated response to clientelism is still negative for this group, it is much smaller in size and is not statistically significant. See Weitz-Shapiro (2012) for more details. Note that the survey prompt was designed to provide respondents with the type of information a middle class voter might receive about clientelism, and as a result, it is less likely to accurately capture the reaction of poor voters to information about clientelism.

[32] An earlier version of the survey included more details about both candidates, but in the pretests this proved to be too long for many respondents to remember; a number of respondents in the pre-test asked for the information to be repeated. As a consequence, I proceeded with this more direct version.

the Justicialist [*or*, Radical] party. Imagine that you hear on the radio that the election will be very close. **They also say that the mayor distributes food assistance programs to poor people in exchange for promises to vote for him.**

Finally, the remainder of the respondents (slightly more than one-third) heard a different vignette in which they learned that the hypothetical mayor was alleged to have engaged in corrupt behavior; I do not analyze responses to that prompt here, though I include controls for those respondents who heard this prompt in the analyses presented below.[33]

6.3.1 Clientelism and Vote Intention

As noted previously, the survey was designed to test whether nonpoor voters, who are unlikely to be targets of clientelist exchange, react negatively to information about the use of clientelist tactics by an incumbent politician. The main outcome variable of interest is the survey respondent's reported likelihood of voting for the incumbent described in the vignette. After hearing the vignette – either the control or treatment – the respondent was asked the following question: "How likely is it that you will vote for the mayor?" Respondents were offered the following choices: not at all likely, a little likely, fairly likely, and very likely.[34] In this section, I present the analysis (both bivariate and regression results) pooling across mayoral partisanship, before exploring the influence of mayoral partisanship in the following section.

Responses to the question about vote intention reveal the lingering effects of the severe anti-incumbent mood that emerged in Argentina's 2001–2002 economic and political crisis. Of the 192 respondents in the control group, 38% of them said they would be "not at all likely" to vote for the incumbent mayor, and an additional 31% of them said they would be "only a little likely" to do so. In contrast, only 19% of respondents in the control group responded that they would be "fairly likely" to support the mayor, leaving a remaining 12% of respondents who said they would be "very likely" to vote for the mayor. As I show below, the distribution of responses among individuals in the treatment group is skewed even more markedly toward the bottom end of this distribution.

Bivariate Results

A major advantage of a randomized survey experiment is that, with a large enough sample of respondents, randomization ensures that the the control and treatment groups are, on average, indistinguishable on both observable

---

33 In the corruption treatment, the phrase about food distribution was replaced with this alternative: "They also say that the mayor took a bribe in exchange for giving an important public contract to a friend of his."

34 In Spanish: nada probable, poco probable, bastante probable, muy probable.

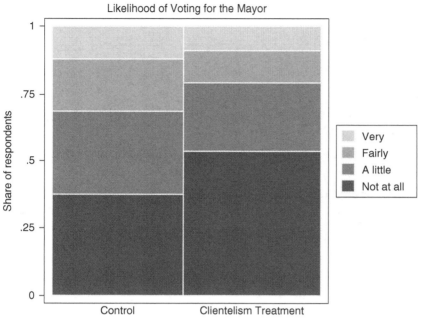

FIGURE 6.2. Clientelism and vote intention: Raw data.

and unobservable characteristics. This, in turn, means that simple statistical tests will give reliable estimates of the effects of the treatment on the outcome of interest.[35] Using simple graphs, I first illustrate that hearing information about clientelism depresses incumbent support among respondents. In the next section, I replicate these results using regression analysis, which allows me to control for confounding covariates.

Figure 6.2 compares vote intention across the control and clientelism treatment group. It shows the share of respondents who, after hearing either vignette, said they were not at all, a little, fairly, or very likely to vote for the incumbent. As the figure shows, respondents who receive information about clientelism respond quite differently to the question on vote intention from those who do not hear such information. Whereas 37% of the latter group say that they are not at all likely to vote for the mayor in this hypothetical contest, that figure jumps substantially for those in the clientelism treatment group. A clear majority of respondents in the treatment group (53%) say that they are not at all likely to vote for the hypothetical mayor. The percentages displayed in each column are based on a total of 394 respondents; 192 in the control

---

35 A balance check indicated that those in the clientelism treatment group were somewhat less educated than their counterparts in the control group, but were otherwise indistinguishable on pretreatment characteristics. See the appendix to this chapter for details on balance between the control and treatment groups.

TABLE 6.2. *Vote Intention: Regression Results*

	4 category	2 category
	(1)	(2)
Clientelism treatment	−.68** (.29)	−.71** (.32)
Corruption treatment	−1.48*** (.26)	−1.45*** (.29)
Age	−.26*** (.04)	−.26*** (.06)
Education	.24 (.20)	.29 (.21)
Male	−.09 (.19)	−.07 (.20)
Partisan	−007 (.15)	−13 (.14)
Vote Kirchner	.59** (.23)	.67** (.27)
Party match	.69*** (.13)	.55*** (.21)
N	597	597

Results in column 1 are from an ordered logistic regression where higher values indicate a greater likelihood of voting for the incumbent. Results in column 2 are from a logistic regression where the outcome variable takes on the value of 1 if the respondent is at least "a little" likely to vote for the incumbent. All regressions include indicator variables for seven of the eight metropolitan areas sampled. Standard errors are clustered by metropolitan area.
*, **, *** indicate significance at the .1, .05, and .01 levels.

group and the remainder who received the information about clientelism.[36] A chi-squared test indicates that we can reject the null hypothesis that vote intention is independent of the treatment at the .01 level.

Regression Analysis

Next, I examine the effects of information about clientelism on vote intention using regression analysis. Table 6.2 shows the results of two regressions that examine the effect of information about clientelism on the respondents' intended vote choice. Column 1 of that table shows the results of an ordered logistic regression where higher values indicate a greater likelihood of voting for the incumbent. In light of the results discussed earlier, where most of the change in responses occurred due to movements in and out of the "not at all" category, column 2 shows the results of a logistic regression where the outcome

---

[36] Recall that this is a subsample of the 617 respondents in total. Two hundred and ten respondents were in the corruption treatment group, not analyzed here.

variable takes on a value of 0 if the respondent is "not at all" likely to vote for the hypothetical incumbent described in the survey, and 1 otherwise.

The key variable of theoretical interest is whether the respondent was in the control group or one of the treatment groups. In addition, I include other variables that might affect a respondent's likelihood of supporting the incumbent in the hypothetical election that is described in the survey. These include typical controls like age, gender, and level of educational attainment, in addition to a number of more explicitly political variables.[37] The variable "party match" takes on the value of 1 if the respondent said she was "close" or "very close" to the party of the hypothetical incumbent she heard about in the vignette, and zero otherwise.[38] I also include an indicator variable that takes on the value of one for those respondents who considered themselves likely to vote for Cristina Kirchner in the October 2007 presidential elections (*Vote Kirchner*) and those respondents who considered themselves close to *any* party (*partisan*).[39] Finally, both regressions include indicator variables for seven of the eight metropolitan areas from which respondents were sampled, and standard errors are clustered by metropolitan area. For ease of interpretation I focus on discussing the results presented in column 2, which predicts the probability that a respondent will be at least a little likely to vote for the mayor, in contrast to being not at all likely to support that incumbent.[40]

The main variable of theoretical interest is the indicator variable for the clientelism treatment. Consistent with the hypothesis that nonpoor voters will react negatively to information about clientelism, the coefficient on this variable is negative and statistically significant. Figure 6.3 presents the results in graphical form. It shows the predicted probability of being at least "a

---

[37] The age variable takes on values from 1 to 5, corresponding to respondents who are 18–25, 26–35, 36–45, 46–55, and 56 and older. The education variable takes on values from 1 to 3, corresponding to individuals for whom the highest level of education completed is primary school or less, secondary school, and tertiary or university education.

[38] Note that all political questions were asked after the initial prompt, so responses may be affected by the treatment. Indeed, as detailed in the appendix, those in the corruption treatment group were less likely to say that they identified with the party of the mayor than those in the control group, although the clientelism treatment does not have a similar effect.

[39] Although eligible for reelection and enjoying high levels of public support, Néstor Kirchner, the sitting President, opted not to run for reelection in 2007, instead supporting his wife's bid for office. She ultimately won the election with about 45% of the vote; her next closest competitor garnered only 23% of the vote. After Néstor Kirchner's sudden death in 2010, Cristina Kirchner was resoundingly elected to a second term in office in 2011. For the purposes of the analysis, I treat individuals who failed to answer questions on partisanship as nonpartisans, and those who failed to answer the question on vote intention as not intending to vote for Cristina Kirchner in the then-upcoming election. Regression results are very similar if I instead code those individuals as missing.

[40] This model improves significantly our ability to predict interviewees' responses vis-a-vis random guessing. Simply guessing the modal category (in the case of the dichotomous outcome variable, one), would result in the correct prediction of 54% of the cases. In contrast, the model in column 2 correctly predicts the responses of about 68% of those surveyed.

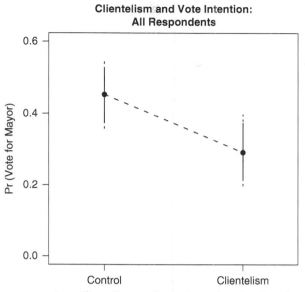

FIGURE 6.3. Clientelism and vote intention: Predicted probabilities.

little" likely to vote for the mayor for four different "typical" respondents. In each case, I use the specification in column 2 of Table 6.2 to run 1,000 simulations of the predicted probability that an average female respondent from the city of Mar del Plata will support the incumbent and then calculate the mean predicted probability and 90 and 95% confidence intervals around that prediction from the simulated probabilities.[41] The figure shows quite clearly the large negative effect that information about clientelism has on a respondent's intention to vote for the hypothetical incumbent mayor. The likelihood that this respondent will support the mayor is estimated to be 48% when the respondent hears the control vignette. In contrast, after hearing the clientelism treatment, the likelihood that an individual with otherwise identical characteristics will support the mayor drops to only 29%. Although there is a slight overlap in the 95% confidence intervals for these estimates, the 90% confidence intervals do not overlap.[42]

Examining the other coefficients in the regression, hearing the corruption treatment also led to a sharp decrease in vote intention for the mayor among

[41] The "typical" respondent is assumed to be a woman from the municipality of Mar del Plata with median age and education who is a supporter of some party, but who did not intend to vote for Kirchner and who did not identify with the party of the hypothetical mayor in the vignette that she received (that is, *party match* = 0).

[42] The 90% confidence interval for the control group runs from 38% to 53% likelihood of support, whereas the 90% confidence interval for the clientelism group ranges from 22% to 37% likelihood of support.

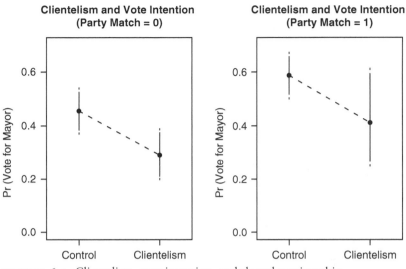

FIGURE 6.4. Clientelism, vote intention, and shared partisanship.

respondents. Of the political variables included in the model, respondents who reported they were likely to vote for Néstor Kirchner in the 2007 presidential election, as well as those who expressed an affinity for the party of the mayor named in the prompt, were more likely to express an intention of voting for the mayor. The former may reflect an underlying inclination of some respondents to support incumbents, both the incumbent presidential candidate, as well as a hypothetical incumbent mayor. As shared partisan identity is typically a strong predictor of voting behavior, the size and significance of this coefficient is not surprising.[43] Comparing the effects of the clientelism treatment on vote intention with the effects of shared partisanship can thus give us a sense of the relative importance of the treatment.

Figure 6.4 reproduces on the left hand side the graph from Figure 6.3. On the right-hand side, it replicates these same predicted probabilities for a typical individual who is otherwise identical to the respondent in the left-hand panel, but who in this case is a partisan of the party of the hypothetical mayor in the vignette she heard. Not surprisingly, an individual who claims she feels close or very close to a given party is more likely to also say she intends to vote for a mayor from that party. The figure shows this positive "bump" in support from

43 Note that in this context, respondents' reports of shared affinity might be in part a product of the survey itself. Within the context of the experiment, those in the corruption treatment group were actually less likely to identify with the party of the member in their vignette than those in the control group, suggesting that exposure to information about corruption could decrease party affinity (at least temporarily). The clientelism treatment did not have a similar effect. Results of the regression analyses reported here are very similar if we exclude the partisan variables from the analysis.

copartisans among respondents in both the control and clientelism treatment settings. The point estimate of the magnitude of this increase in the likelihood of supporting the incumbent is in the range of ten to fifteen percentage points. Shared partisanship increases a typical respondent's predicted likelihood of supporting the incumbent from about 46% to 59% in the control condition and from about 29% to 41% in the clientelism treatment.

In this survey, then, the effects of information about clientelism on vote intention are at least as large or larger in magnitude than the effects of copartisanship. Obviously, we need to exercise caution when extrapolating from survey responses to behavior. Nonetheless, these results further support the conclusion that nonpoor voters disapprove of clientelism and are likely to withdraw their political support from local incumbents who rely on it.

6.3.2 Robustness

Before turning to an examination of the mediating role of partisanship, I briefly discuss alternative interpretations of the survey experimental data. Throughout this chapter, I interpret the effect of the experimental treatment as capturing respondent reactions to information about clientelism. As compared to the control group, however, the clientelism treatment in fact includes information about redistribution – the mayor distributes food to poor people – as well as information about the *nature* of that distribution – it is conditioned on political behavior. This raises the possibility that respondents' stated vote intention reflects both preferences over redistribution as well as preferences over clientelism per se. The Calvo–Murillo data analyzed above does allow for explicit controls for attitudes toward redistribution, and the fact that the main results were robust to the inclusion of these controls is reassuring. The survey experiment did not include an alternate condition that included information about redistribution without information about clientelism, nor did it ask respondents directly about their attitudes toward redistribution. However, additional analyses of the data from the survey experiment, along with other survey evidence from Argentina, strongly suggest that attitudes toward clientelism, not redistribution, explain the negative reaction of nonpoor respondents to the experimental prompt.

Evidence from other surveys shows that Argentines, even the nonpoor, are on the whole highly supportive of redistributive policies. The 2010 LAPOP asked respondents how strongly they agreed with the statement that "[t]he Argentine state should implement firm policies to reduce income inequality between the rich and the poor."[44] On a seven-point scale, a clear majority – 57% – of respondents indicated the highest possible agreement, and 69%

---

44 In Spanish, "[e]l estado argentino debe implementar políticas *firmes* para reducir la desigualdad de ingresos entre ricos y pobres."

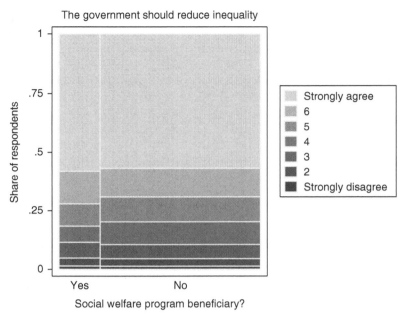

FIGURE 6.5. Redistributive preferences and social class.

of respondents fell into one of the top three categories.[45] Not only are Argentines very supportive of redistribution, but also that support is not particularly linked to social class. Figure 6.5 shows the results from that same survey, separating responses from beneficiaries of social programs (about 20% of respondents) from those of the rest of the sample. As the figure makes clear, responses are almost identical across the two groups. Similarly, the mean response to this question from top income earners is statistically indistinguishable from that of the majority of the population.[46] Given the widespread support for redistribution among Argentines, it seems most likely that the negative responses to the treatment in the survey experiment reflect a distaste for clientelism, rather than for redistribution.

In addition, evidence from the survey experiment analyzed here supports the claim that respondents reacted primarily to the information about clientelism in the prompt, rather than to the information about redistribution. In the

45 The 2008 results show even stronger support for redistribution. In that survey, 61% of respondents expressed the highest possible agreement with the statement, and 88% of respondents fell into the top three categories.
46 Out of eleven possible income ranges, I separate respondents who place their income in the lowest six categories (87% of all respondents) from the highest five categories. The mean response to the question on redistributive preferences is statistically indistinguishable across these two groups. Results are similar if we divide the data slightly differently, comparing the top 20% of respondents to all others.

absence of a direct question about redistributive preferences, I use respondents' closeness to two small political parties as a proxy for attitudes toward redistribution.[47] Argentina's two historically largest parties, the UCR and the PJ, have ambiguous ideological identities. In a separate part of the survey administered by Calvo and Murillo, these authors find that a substantial minority – 36% and 40% of respondents, respectively – are unable or unwilling to place the PJ and the UCR on a conventional left–right scale. Of those who do place these parties on such a scale, about half of respondents place them in either the center, center-left, or center-right.[48]

In contrast, recent years have seen the emergence of a number of smaller parties with clearer ideological profiles. At the time of the survey, in 2007, two of these parties – the ARI and the PRO – were particularly prominent.[49] ARI, known by its Spanish initials for the "Affirmation for an Egalitarian Republic," includes in the first article of its party platform a call for a just distribution of wealth (see www.ari.org.ar). The PRO, short for "Republican Proposal," emerged from an alliance of two center-right parties whose leaders advocated market-friendly policies and pointed to economic growth as the key to improving the distribution of income. Calvo and Murillo (2007) show that Argentine voters more readily identify these parties as being associated with the center-left (ARI) and the center-right/right (PRO).

To the extent that sympathizers with ARI and PRO at the time of the survey share the ideologies described above, we can use information about party preference to proxy for preferences over redistribution. If those surveyed focus on the redistributive component (rather than the clientelism component) of the experimental treatment, we would expect that PRO sympathizers in the clientelism treatment group would be especially unlikely to vote for the hypothetical incumbent, while ARI sympathizers would not be particularly sensitive to hearing the clientelism treatment and might even prefer the incumbent who is described as redistributive and clientelist.

In fact, however, the data do not fit this pattern at all. I compare the mean vote intention for the hypothetical mayor between the control and

---

47 If we could demonstrate that respondents who favor redistribution to the poor nonetheless withdraw support from the mayor described as implementing clientelist redistribution, this would strongly suggest that clientelist manipulation is responsible for the observed negative effects of the treatment.

48 According to Calvo and Murillo (2010), the modal category for each party is only about 20%. They contrast these results with the Chilean case, where respondents much more readily place the major parties on clearly differentiated positions on the left-right spectrum.

49 In the 2007 presidential election, a coalition with Elisa Carrió, the leader of ARI, as its candidate, came in second with 23% of the vote. In the 2011 presidential contest, however, the strongest candidate from the left was a former governor of the province of Santa Fé and a member of the Socialist party, Hermés Binner. Binner won almost 17% of the vote in the 2011 presidential election, whereas Carrió's candidacy garnered less than 2% of the vote in that election. Mauricio Macri, the businessman who heads the PRO, has been mayor of the city of Buenos Aires since 2007. The PRO did not present a candidate in the 2007 or 2011 presidential elections.

clientelism treatment groups for both PRO and ARI sympathizers.[50] Among PRO sympathizers, the clientelism treatment has basically no effect on vote intention.[51] Among ARI supporters, exposure to the clientelism treatment depresses support for the hypothetical mayor. Although this difference is not statistically significant, this drop in support for clientelist mayors among ARI sympathizers is the opposite of what we would expect to find if they were reacting primarily to the redistributive component of the prompt.[52] Although a respondent's party affiliation is obviously an imperfect proxy for redistributive preferences, these results contribute further evidence that attitudes toward clientelism, rather than redistribution, explain the results discussed here.

6.4 CLIENTELISM AND VOTE INTENTION: THE PARTISAN CONNECTION

Thus far, I have shown that nonpoor Argentines are less accepting of clientelist practices than their poor counterparts and that the nonpoor are willing to withdraw support from a local incumbent mayor if he engages in clientelism in office. This provides direct empirical evidence of the "costs of clientelism" and is also consistent with the municipal level results from Chapter 5, which showed that clientelism is less likely where the nonpoor population is large and competition is high. That cross-municipal analysis also tested two alternative hypotheses about how political parties affect departures from clientelism. Evidence presented there supports the hypothesis that demand-side, rather than supply-side, considerations help explain why the Peronist party relies on clientelism more heavily than non-Peronists. In low-competition settings, Peronist and non-Peronist mayors rely on clientelism at similar rates. However, when competition is high and poverty is low, non-Peronist mayors are more likely to depart from clientelism. The municipal results suggest that Peronist mayors might continue to use clientelism because they have little support to lose from nonpoor constituents in the first place. The random variation of the party of the mayor in the survey experiment prompt allows for a direct test of that mechanism.

Each survey vignette mentioned the partisan affiliation of the hypothetical incumbent mayor, identifying him as either a member of the Peronist or

---

50 A small number of respondents identified themselves as close to both the ARI and the PRO; I exclude these from the analysis. Note that given the relatively small size of each party's base, there are fifty-nine PRO sympathizers and fifty-five ARI sympathizers in the data.

51 On the four-point scale of vote intention, the mean value for both groups is about 2.1, and the very small difference is not statistically significant.

52 For ARI supporters, hearing information about clientelism drops incumbent support from about 55% of respondents being at least a little likely to support the mayor in the control group to 38% in the treatment group. The mean support on a four point scale drops from 1.8 to 1.6. Neither difference is statistically significant at conventional levels.

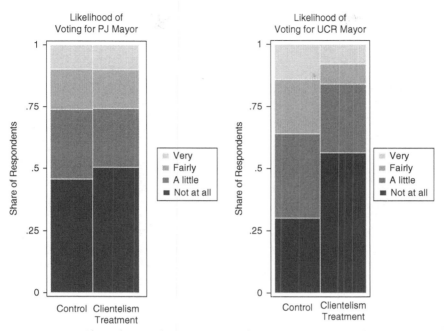

FIGURE 6.6. Clientelism and vote intention, by mayor party: Raw data.

Radical party. This identity was assigned at random, and 49% of respondents were informed the mayor was Peronist.[53] To explore how voter reactions to clientelism vary with mayoral partisanship, I first present the results graphically. Figure 6.6 displays respondents' answers to the question "how likely are you to vote for the mayor?" The right-hand side shows the results only for those respondents who heard about a mayor from the UCR. The results show the same pattern observed in Figure 6.2, although even more pronounced. Among those respondents in the control group, only 30% reported they would be "not at all" likely to vote for the mayor. In contrast, this increases to 56% among those respondents who were assigned to the group that learned that the Radical mayor had exchanged goods to poor people in return for promises to vote for him. The left-hand side of the figure shows how respondents who learned about a Peronist mayor responded to information about clientelism. The graph shows high baseline levels of reluctance to vote for a Peronist candidate for mayor. Of those in the control condition, 46% reported that they were "not at all" likely to vote for a Peronist incumbent mayor. There is, once again, an increase in the share of respondents who say they are not at all

53 Respondents in the Peronist and Radical mayor treatments were indistinguishable along a number of dimensions, including gender, education, socioeconomic status, and the proportion of respondents receiving social programs. Those in the Peronist group were slightly younger than those in Radical party treatment group (this difference is significant at the .06 level).

TABLE 6.3. *Vote Intention and Partisanship: Regression Results*

	No interaction	Interaction
	(1)	(2)
Clientelism	−.71**	−1.06***
	(.32)	(.34)
Clientelism *PJ	—	.69
		(.56)
Corruption	−1.45***	−1.93***
	(.29)	(.33)
Corruption * PJ	—	.96**
		(.48)
PJ treatment	—	−.76**
		(.36)
Age	−.26***	−.27***
	(.06)	(.06)
Education	.29	.29
	(.21)	(.21)
Male	−.07	−.07
	(.20)	(.19)
Partisan	−13	−15
	(.14)	(.11)
Kirchner	.67**	.65**
	(.27)	(.28)
Party match	.55***	.63***
	(.21)	(.22)
N	597	597

Results in both columns are from logistic regressions where the outcome variable takes on the value of 1 if the respondent is at least "a little" likely to vote for the incumbent. Both regressions include indicator variables for seven of the eight metropolitan areas sampled. Standard errors are clustered by metropolitan area. *, **, *** indicate significance at the .1, .05, and .01 levels.

likely to vote for the mayor in the clientelism condition. However, in contrast to the large penalty for Radical mayors who engage in clientelism, Peronist mayors who engage in clientelism appear to suffer only a small penalty: in the raw data, the share of respondents who are not at all likely to vote for the mayor increases to 51% in the clientelism condition.

The results of regression analysis confirm the conclusion that the nonpoor punish clientelism by Radical party mayors more harshly than they punish the practice by Peronist mayors. Table 6.3 shows the results of two logistic regressions where the outcome variable takes on a value of one if the respondent is at least "a little" likely to vote for the mayor. Column one replicates the results reported in Table 6.2 and does not include an interaction term. Column two reports the results of a regression that includes an indicator variable for

Peronist mayor affiliation and an interaction term between Peronist affiliation and the clientelism treatment indicator variable.[54]

The coefficients on the Peronist indicator variable and the interaction term suggest that partisanship matters in important respects. First, the negative coefficient on the indicator variable for Peronist mayors reinforces the finding that respondents in the control condition are less likely to support a Peronist mayor than a Radical mayor. This is consistent with the conventional understanding that the Peronist party relies heavily on support from the poor and working classes (Lupu and Stokes, 2009). These groups, as already noted, will be markedly underrepresented in a telephone survey. Second, the size and direction of the interaction terms suggests that party matters not only for the baseline evaluation of candidates, but also for whether and how respondents might change their attitudes when they receive information about clientelism. The coefficient on the indicator variable for the clientelism treatment is negative, which supports the claim that respondents are likely to punish this behavior. At the same time, the positive coefficient on the interaction term between the Peronist treatment and the clientelism treatment indicates that Peronist mayors will suffer less at the ballot box for clientelism than mayors affiliated with the Radical party.[55]

Figure 6.7 shows how voters respond to information about clientelism using the same format as in Figure 6.3.[56] Once again, the graph displays the estimated likelihood that a typical respondent would respond that she is at least a little likely to vote for the mayor.[57] Confidence intervals are drawn from simulations. The graph reinforces the initial conclusions from the raw data. Among these nonpoor respondents, Peronist mayors enjoy less support than Radical party mayors when no information about corruption or clientelism is shared.[58] The dotted lines depict visually the extent to which a mayor of each party loses support when he is described as clientelist. The steep slope for Radical party mayors shows that these mayors suffer a large penalty for relying on clientelism – with expected vote intention dropping from about 54% to

---

[54] To allow comparisons across the two treatment groups, I also include an interaction between the partisan treatment and the corruption treatment.

[55] The regression results point to the existence of a similar trend with respect to corruption. When described as corrupt, the hypothetical Radical party mayor suffers greater punishment as compared to an otherwise identical Peronist mayor.

[56] Recall that respondents were not asked to make direct comparisons. Instead, respondents were randomly assigned to one of the four groups shown in the graph (PJ-Control; PJ-Clientelism; UCR-Control; UCR-Clientelism). Random assignment allows us attribute differences in responses to the different information given to each group.

[57] I use the same typical respondent as in the earlier discussion – a female from Mar del Plata with median age and education who was not planning on voting for Kirchner in the 2007 presidential contest.

[58] Note that there is some overlap in the confidence intervals in the control condition, so although these differences are highly suggestive, they are not statistically significant.

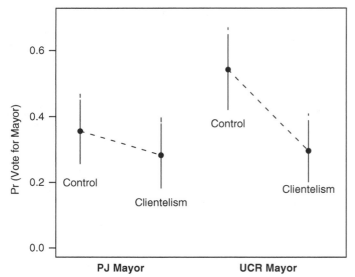

FIGURE 6.7. Clientelism and vote intention, by mayor party: Predicted probabilities.

29%.[59] In contrast, though the model predicts that the typical respondent will penalize a Peronist mayor for clientelism (the predicted probability of support drops from 36% to 28%), this difference is smaller in magnitude and not statistically significant.

6.5 CONCLUSION

This chapter uses evidence from two public opinion surveys to offer the, to my knowledge, first available mass survey evidence that examines behavior and attitudes toward clientelism by citizens who are *not* likely to be the targets of these exchanges. It demonstrates in a controlled setting the existence of a negative reaction among nonpoor voters to the individualized exchange of goods for political support by local politicians. The middle-class Argentines who were surveyed would have little or no interest in receiving benefits from a food distribution program of the type mentioned in the experimental treatment or mass survey. Nonetheless, a sizable share of these respondents hold negative attitudes toward the distribution of small goods and appear likely to change their voting behavior after learning about the politicized distribution of food benefits. This supports the argument that politicized exchanges, even when exclusively directed at poor constituents, cannot be understood by examining the links between politicians and that group of voters only. The punishment for clientelism is especially strong for Radical mayors, whereas Peronist mayors

59   This difference is significant at the .05 level.

suffer only a modest electoral cost for relying on clientelism. These results also help explain why Peronist mayors, as the previous chapter showed, shift away from clientelism only at a higher threshold of both competition and the middle class.

The combination of data from two surveys offers an unusually complete picture of the costs of clientelism among nonpoor Argentines. Although we do not have access to the same range of data for other cases, there is evidence that the audience costs of clientelism exist in other countries and other regions. The Calvo and Murillo survey described here was also conducted in Chile and reveals a similar trend. Even when controlling for attitudes toward redistribution, the nonpoor and those in higher socioeconomic status categories are less likely to describe as "acceptable" the distribution of small goods by parties. As noted earlier, results presented by Bratton (2008) suggest that clientelism or the related phenomenon of vote buying might also incur audience costs in lower-middle income countries like Nigeria. Perhaps the work most directly related to the survey experiment described here is research carried out by Kramon (2011). Working in Kenya, he embeds a mock radio broadcast with an experimental component into a public opinion survey. The embedded prompt is more subtle than that included here, and yet he finds quite similar effects. While information about vote buying in the treatment condition increases support from poorer respondents, he finds that same information reduces politician support from respondents with more assets. In fact, support for the named politician among wealthier respondents decreases by about 20 percentage points – strikingly similar to the effect I estimate here – as a result of the information about vote-buying. Taken together, these results from other contexts suggest a potentially large scope for the costs of clientelism argument. They point to the usefulness of collecting additional empirical data on the existence of audience costs for clientelism and related practices.

6.6 APPENDIX

6.6.1 Survey Experiment Methodology

The survey experiment was administered by MORI Argentina in August 2007. Respondents in eight large metropolitan areas were reached via phone calls to landlines. Numbers from public records of phone numbers were stratified by metropolitan area and then selected at random for dialing. Once a respondent was reached, he or she was randomly assigned to the control or one of the treatment groups. Until age and gender quotas were met, the person answering the phone was interviewed. Once quotas were filled, the surveyor asked whether a member of a group with an unfilled quota (e.g., a young man) lived

TABLE 6.4. *Examining Randomization*

Corruption Treatment	
Age	−.02
	(.07)
Education	−.24
	(.16)
Male	.05
	(.20)
Social Plan	−.27
	(.43)
Socioeconomic Status	.01
	(.06)
Clientelism Treatment	
Age	−.01
	(.07)
Education	-.28*
	(.16)
Male	−.11
	(.20)
Social Plan	.07
	(.40)
Socioeconomic Status	.05
	(.06)
(N)	612

Results are from a multinomial logistic regression where selection into the control group is the comparison category. *, **, *** indicate significance at the .1, .05 and .01 levels. Indicators for seven of the eight metropolitan areas in which the survey was conducted are included but not shown here.

in the household and sought to speak with that person. The firm conducted one callback before moving to a new phone number.

6.6.2 Balance

To examine whether randomization was successful, I run a multinomial logistic regression where the outcome variable indicates whether the respondent heard the control vignette, the clientelism treatment, or the corruption treatment. As predictor variables, I include a number of pretreatment characteristics, as well as indicator variables for seven of the eight metropolitan areas from which the survey was drawn.[60] The results displayed in Table 6.4

---

[60] None of the coefficients for the indicator variables for geographic location approach statistical significance and they are omitted from the table.

indicate that respondents in the clientelism treatment were somewhat less educated than those in the control group. With this exception, there are no other significant differences in the composition of the respondents across groups.[61]

---

[61] In an earlier analysis of this data (Weitz-Shapiro, 2008a), I also included as predictor variables a number of characteristics linked to partisan identity, which showed some additional significant differences between the control group and the corruption treatment group. Questions about partisanship were asked only *after* the prompt. The fact that those in the corruption treatment group were are less likely to identify with the party of the hypothetical mayor suggests that corruption information decreases expressed support for a given party. For this reason, I believe it is most appropriate to treat partisan variables as post-treatment variables, and so I do not include them here.

7

Moving Toward Accountability? Comparative Perspectives and Policy Implications

The third-wave transitions to democracy in Latin America were met with optimism that governments in the region would become more accountable to their citizens, as well as trepidation that these transitions might collapse in the face of military coups. In most of these countries, democracy's long endurance has allayed fears of the latter. Questions about the quality of these now not-so-young democracies, however, remain extremely relevant. Scholars, citizens, and other observers increasingly recognize that it is no straightforward task to make democracy work well, and that there may be significant variation in government performance even *within* a single country. In spite of this growing concern with the quality of subnational democracy, our understanding of why, within a democracy, some governments perform better than others remains incomplete.

In this book, I use the case of clientelism both to illustrate the breadth of variation in government quality and to test a theory of what explains improvements in local government performance. Clientelism undermines ties of accountability between citizens and politicians. It narrows the issue space about which clients make political decisions to the question of access to particularistic goods; in doing so, it insulates politicians from the need to be responsive to the full potential range of citizen preferences. Although the costs of clientelism to accountability are widely recognized, those costs may be unevenly distributed across a country's territory. This book speaks to situations where the national-level political will or capacity to improve local governance is missing, but where local conditions may nonetheless create incentives for some local politicians to move toward better governance on their own.

I argue that the existence of high levels of political competition in the presence of a large middle class (and especially in a hospitable partisan environment) creates the incentives for some local incumbents to depart from the practice of clientelism. Underlying this argument is the observation that clientelism, even though a practice that almost exclusively involves the participation of poor voters, can incur *audience costs* in political support from the nonpoor. Though not a party to clientelist exchange, the nonpoor might punish incumbents who rely on clientelism because of normative distaste for the practice or because clientelism serves as a signal of poor government performance in areas of more direct interest to the middle class. The costs of clientelism are most likely to affect politician behavior in the presence of high levels of political competition, which increases incumbent efforts to be reelected. They are also most likely to be relevant for politicians from parties that have a reasonable expectation of winning middle-class support in the first place.

This argument is new, but it builds on two long-standing schools of thought that emphasize either modernization or competition as the source of good government more broadly. Both are important contributing factors to the elimination of clientelism, but alone, neither will be sufficient to lead politicians to reject clientelism. High levels of political competition do increase incumbent effort. However, from the perspective of winning votes, eliminating clientelism may or may not be the most effective strategy. Clientelism increases support from the poor, even though it costs support from the nonpoor. The existence of a growing middle class creates electoral costs to clientelism, but in the absence of high competition, an incumbent may safely ignore those costs without risking his continuity in power. It is only the *combination* of competition and a large nonpoor population that provides an incumbent with both the incentives and political will to eschew clientelism.

Given the stigma attached to clientelism and its partially hidden nature, the task of measuring clientelism and citizen responses to it is a difficult one. Clientelism relies on personalized interactions between patrons and clients and is most accurately documented at the local level, and so I adopt a subnational comparative approach in this study. In Chapter 2, I draw on field work in small towns and cities in Argentina to illustrate how a mayor can communicate to citizens his discretion and control over valued benefits by individually claiming credit for goods and services and manufacturing a sense of scarcity around these goods. Building on that qualitative work, I then develop a unique measure of clientelism that is amenable to theory-testing through quantitative analysis. As explained in Chapter 4, this measure focuses on how mayors implement an important food distribution program in a large sample of Argentine municipalities. The results of statistical analysis presented in Chapter 5 support the claim that as mayors face increasingly high competition and increasingly prosperous constituents, they are more likely to opt out of clientelism. This effect exists for all parties, though it is weaker for the Peronist party, which does not count the middle class among its core voters. To further support my argument, Chapter 6 brings to bear individual-level evidence for the costs of clientelism. The analysis of a large public opinion survey and an original survey experiment show that the nonpoor find the targeted distribution of small goods by political parties less acceptable than do the poor, and that middle class Argentines are willing to withdraw support from incumbents who engage in clientelist practices. It also provides individual-level evidence consistent with municipal-level differences across parties: middle-class voters punish non-Peronist mayors more severely for clientelism than they do Peronist mayors. The combination of methods used here thus allows for an unusually detailed picture of how clientelism works, how the nonpoor perceive it, and the conditions under which incumbent mayors opt out of clientelism.

This book's focus on a possible subnational path away from clientelism and toward accountability has received relatively little attention from scholars or policymakers. The neglect of this scenario may be due to the fact that the type of success highlighted here is partial. The absence of any national-level effort to limit clientelism in social policy in Argentina means that shifts toward accountability are uneven across the country's territory. At the time of my research, clientelism was the dominant form of interaction in the municipalities studied here. Nonetheless, a focus on this subnational variation is important because it speaks to the large number of countries where the political will or technical capacity to improve governance in social policy from the top down does not exist. For such settings, this book provides a theory of the local-level conditions that increase the possibility of improved governance.

At the same time, this subnational focus can yield insights into a very different path toward accountability: a top-down one. In the realm of social policy, recent years have seen increasing policy and scholarly attention paid to a few very prominent programs. These programs, the Bolsa Familia in Brazil and Progresa/Oportunidades in Mexico, have been praised not only for their effects on poverty alleviation, but for eliminating local clientelism in their implementation, and for doing so uniformly across these countries. These are complex programs that bundle many innovations together, making it difficult to isolate precisely what matters for curbing clientelism. Admittedly, our study of the Argentine experience with social programs such as the PNSA does not provide a model policy that advisors from international organizations would likely want to advocate or emulate. Nonetheless, clientelism is inherently a local phenomenon, so insights from the subnational study of how clientelism works can help us to understand how and why other national initiatives have succeeded in improving accountability relationships. Drawing on the subnational examination of a case like Argentina can also shed light on other aspects of policy design from these exemplary programs that, though they may be desirable for other reasons, have limited consequences for accountability.

In the rest of this chapter, I turn from an examination of variation in subnational incentives to use clientelism in a permissive policy environment to an examination of an alternate policy environment: one that limits opportunities for clientelism. The success of programs in Brazil and Mexico in ending clientelism stems from the fact that they have eliminated local incumbents' ability to claim credit for the distribution of social benefits or to plausibly threaten the withdrawal of those benefits. The importance of a strong and large presence of the central state in curbing clientelism in these cases leads me to conclude with a call to revisit our understanding of the relationship between the size of the state and politician accountability to citizens.

7.1 FROM INCENTIVES TO OPPORTUNITIES: BRAZIL AND MEXICO

In addition to being the sites of two of the largest and most-studied targeted social safety net programs in place today, Brazil and Mexico provide an ideal comparison with Argentina. Like Argentina, both are federal countries with elected subnational officials with at least some potential influence over social policy. Although all three countries went through long periods in the twentieth century where power was, de facto, highly centralized, the relevance of subnational actors has increased in all three countries with democratization (which occurred in 1983 in Argentina, 1985 in Brazil, and 2000 in Mexico).[1] Perhaps as a consequence of their large territorial extent, there is a long history of internal diversity in terms of the practice of politics within all three countries. Especially relevant for this study, traditional relationships and individual control and discretion over public resources have been an important feature in each of these countries. Brazilian politics has traditionally been portrayed as riddled with individualized, clientelistic relationships and ties, both among politicians and between politicians and voters. Historically, local elites and power brokers – in the form of *coroneis* and *cabos eleitorais* – were able to use individualized exchange, economic pressure, or coercion to deliver the votes of their followers and economic dependents.[2] In Mexico, single party rule by the PRI (*Partido Revolucionario Institucional*) for most of the twentieth century was manifest subnationally through the control that local strongmen, or *caciques*, exercised over state resources in both rural and urban settings.[3] In light of these shared characteristics, it would have been difficult to predict such different outcomes with respect to clientelism and social policy across the three countries. Yet, in spite of an apparently long history of reliance on clientelism in the realm of social assistance, Brazil and Mexico seem to have broken out of this pattern while it continues to be dominant in Argentina. Before examining Brazil and Mexico's successes, I provide a bit more background on the history of social policy in these cases.

---

[1] Brazil and Mexico experienced gradual openings; I use the date of democratization most commonly used in the literature in each case.

[2] For more on these phenomena, see the descriptions in Leal (1977), Roniger (1987), and Hagopian (1996), among others.

[3] See Cornelius (1977) and the contributions in Knight and Pansters (2005), among others. See also Roniger (1987) for more on the historical importance of *coroneis* in Brazil and *caciques* in Mexico.

7.1.1 Historical Antecedents

Both the Brazilian and Mexican welfare states, like those in the region more broadly, have historically been both limited in scope and regressive in nature (Lindert et al., 2006). In Brazil, although the country has a long history of noncontributory benefits in the form of social security for some rural and informal sector workers, actual coverage of these sectors in the pension system remained quite low through the 1990s (Weyland, 2004). As elsewhere in the region, pensions and other benefits for formal sector workers, especially public employees, were relatively generous, while many citizens were left out of the system of social protection entirely.[4] In comparison to Argentina and Brazil, the twentieth century Mexican welfare state was more limited, though it did come into being earlier, and was more comprehensive, than that of most Central American (and some South American) countries.[5] The Mexican social welfare state also had its own particularities that resulted from the dominance of the government and the state apparatus by a single party through much of the century. For example, the concentration of social welfare benefits in urban centers helped prevent possible political dissent in its most likely location (Spalding, 1980, cited in Haggard and Kaufman [2008]). As elsewhere, there was a strong urban bias in social security benefits such as pensions; in Mexico, this urban bias was replicated in other benefits, such as generalized tortilla and bread subsidies, from which the poor benefited to a relatively limited degree.[6]

Changes to the prevailing model of social welfare provision began to emerge in both countries in the late 1980s and early 1990s. In Mexico, change began with the implementation of a new social program by President Carlos Salinas, in the wake of his victory in a hotly disputed (and likely fraudulent) electoral contest in 1988. The National Solidarity Program (PRONASOL, or the Programa Nacional de Solidaridad in Spanish) was designed to deliver benefits to the poorest individuals living in Mexico's poorest places – almost exclusively rural areas. PRONASOL was a large program that funded a variety of policies targeted both at individuals and infrastructure creation at the community level. PRONASOL received mixed evaluations from outside observers and was seen by many as a political tool used to buttress the reputation and political fortunes of the PRI and of Salinas himself, which had been badly damaged by the 1988 elections. There is substantial evidence that political criteria played an important role in the distribution of funds across the Mexican territory and in

---

4   Until 1998, the generous pension system for public employees was funded entirely out of the general budget (Lindert et al., 2006, 91), which heightened the unequal burden of financing.

5   Mexico is generally considered to fall into the middle of the spectrum of welfare state size and commitments (Lindert et al., 2006, Haggard and Kaufman, 2008).

6   Because tortilla consumption is so widespread, the poor captured only a small part of the benefit from the subsidy. See Levy and Rodríguez (2004) for a more detailed discussion. Cost savings from eliminating these subsidies helped to pay for the Progresa and Oportunidades programs that are described in this section.

the program's broader operation.[7] Many observers believe that the program was an important factor in the PRI's strong electoral showing in 1994. Even so, PRONASOL did shift the focus of the social welfare agenda to Mexico's poorest, rural communities.

In Brazil, a new model of social welfare provision had a more auspicious start with its emergence in 1995. In January of that year, two large municipalities (the capital city of Brasilia and Campinas, a large city in São Paulo state) each independently launched a large conditional cash transfer (CCT) program. Although the cities were governed by mayors from different parties, both programs had a similar structure: they delivered cash assistance to poor families with children in exchange for guarantees of school attendance.[8] By 2001, more than 200 municipalities had adopted similar programs (Villatoro [2004], cited in Sugiyama [2008]). In that year, the presidential administration of Fernando Henrique Cardoso (a member of Brazil's centrist PSDB, or Partido da Social Democracia Brasileira), launched the federal Bolsa Escola program, based on the existing municipal model.[9] In the remaining two years of his term (2001–2002), the Cardoso administration launched two related federal programs targeted at similar populations, including Bolsa Alimentação, a CCT in which conditionalities were based on compliance with health-related tasks.[10]

7.1.2 New Policies and the Decline of Clientelism

The large social welfare programs took shape in their current form in 1997 in Mexico and in 2003 in Brazil. In Mexico, Ernesto Zedillo succeeded Salinas as president and created the Education, Health and Nutrition Program, otherwise known as PROGRESA, using its Spanish acronym. Although a member of the PRI, Zedillo was seen as more sympathetic to technocratic approaches to policy. Using a model similar to that employed by the nascent conditional cash transfer programs in Brazilian municipalities, PROGRESA distributed a cash transfer and a separate scholarship for school expenses to families. In return, families were expected to comply with certain conditionalities. Children of school age needed to meet minimum attendance requirements, all family members were required to attend preventive health visits, and family members older than age fifteen were required to attend lectures on health and nutrition.

---

7 See, among others, Cornelius et al. (1994), Dresser (1994), Molinar and Weldon (1994), Magaloni (2006), and Haggard and Kaufman (2008).

8 This section draws heavily on the excellent review of CCT's in Brazil in Lindert et al. (2007) and Lindert and Vincensini (2010).

9 The government's first involvement in a CCT program actually dates to the 1996 implementation of the Program for the Eradication of Child Labor, although it was much smaller in scale.

10 The other program, the Auxilio Gas, was not conditional and was intended to replace a reduction in a cooking gas subsidy.

As the first large, nationwide implementation of a CCT, the program received significant attention in Mexico and in international policy circles.[11] The 2000 election of Vicente Fox, a member of the conservative PAN party, brought about the first electoral defeat of the PRI in more than seventy years. The decision to continue to fund PROGRESA after that change in party power was seen as evidence of its success and technocratic nature (Adato and Hoddinott, 2010; De la O, 2013). Under the Fox administration, the program became known as Oportunidades, though it retained most of its salient characteristics. It also expanded, first to semi-urban and then to fully urban areas (beginning in 2002), as well as to elderly people with no other means of support. By 2006, the program covered about 25% of the country's population and almost all of its extremely poor (Adato and Hoddinott, 2010, 68).

In Brazil, President Luis Inácio Lula da Silva, popularly known as Lula, took office in 2003. The first member of the Workers Party (PT) elected to Brazil's highest office, Lula grew up in poverty, and he made the eradication of hunger and the reduction of poverty a central theme of his campaign and a top priority of his time in office. In October 2003, Lula launched the Bolsa Familia program, which consolidated four existing programs targeted at the poor into a single umbrella program. As Lindert and Vincensini (2010) document, from 2004 to 2006, the program underwent a number of changes in its organization and structure as it scaled up and was subject to intense media scrutiny. It has continued to expand under the presidency of Lula's successor, Dilma Rousseff, also from the PT. With coverage of more than eleven million beneficiaries and a budget of more than five billion U.S. dollars, Bolsa Famillia is currently the largest existing conditional cash transfer program in the world. In its essence, Bolsa Familia's basic structure follows that of the very first municipal programs from the mid-1990s as well as Mexico's CCT: it gives beneficiaries cash transfers in exchange for compliance with health-related activities and meeting minimum required levels of school attendance.

In both Brazil and Mexico, observers were quite attune to the risk that these new programs would become coopted by local officials for clientelist exchange. Yet, in both cases, overwhelming evidence suggests that this type of manipulation has been exceedingly rare. In a piece detailing Mexico's experience with Progresa and Oportunidades, Yaschine and Orozco (2010, 69) summarize the interest in this question and the consensus view: "[a]lthough much attention was given to the potential political use of the program, no

---

[11] In addition to the features I focus on here, Progresa innovated by explicitly incorporating a randomized design to facilitate impact evaluation. After the initial selection of families to be included in the program, some were incorporated immediately, whereas others were incorporated after a period of a year. This experimental design has facilitated numerous evaluations of the program's impact on education (e.g., Morley and Coady [2003]), health (e.g., Rivera et al. [2004]), and even political participation (De la O, 2013).

evidence was found of any systematic political manipulation."[12] In Brazil, findings on the Bolsa Familia have been quite similar. Many World Bank assessments of the program point explicitly to the extent to which Bolsa Familia limits the risk of clientelism (e.g., Lindert et al. (2007, 72)). Even skeptics of the program's effectiveness do not assert that beneficiaries believe that their continued receipt of the program is dependent on their vote choice or other aspects of individual political behavior (see, e.g., Hall [2008]). The success of these programs in curbing clientelism seems to be recognized by voters, as well: De la O (2014) (for Mexico) and Zucco (2013) (for Brazil) provide evidence that these programs' reputations for being well-administered and largely free of clientelism reap political rewards for federal government officials.

From the perspective of policy design, the success of these programs in curbing clientelism apparently uniformly – in countries with diverse competition and social conditions at the local level – begs the question of *how* they have done this. Both Bolsa Familia and Progresa/Oportunidades are complex programs with many features that have been praised in policy circles, including the conditionality of benefits, the use of geographic targeting, the creation of forums for community participation, and the reliance on technocratic central government agencies. Insights from the subnational study of clientelism in Argentina can help shed light on which of these features are likely to be critical for curbing clientelism from the top down.

7.2 POLICY DESIGN: DIFFERENT PATHS TO REDUCING LOCAL DISCRETION

Clientelism is inherently a local phenomenon. Chapter 2 calls attention to the fact that, for clientelism to "work," voters must believe that politicians maintain control over the distribution and withdrawal of valued benefits. Local incumbents in Argentina encourage these beliefs by personally claiming credit for benefits they distribute and fostering a sense of scarcity around valued goods. In contrast, through policy design, both Bolsa Familia and Progresa/Oportunidades have successfully *severed* the link (both real and perceived) between those who exercise discretion over programs benefits and those who are most likely to have direct relationships with voters. In the case of Mexico, the program's extreme centralization is crucial. In the case of Brazil, a partially centralized design combined with widespread coverage

---

[12] This is a view corroborated by Fiszbein and Schady (2009), Adato and Hoddinott (2010), and Diaz-Cayeros et al. (2012), among others. Diaz-Cayeros et al. (2012) point to only two evaluations of Progresa (Rocha Menocal, 2001, Takahashi, 2006) that suggest a political calculus in its implementation. In both cases, however, they suggest that these results are likely to be the result of looking at the data at an inappropriate level of aggregation and failure to account for possible endogeneity.

and the apparent *failure* of conditionality – a lauded feature of these programs – appears to contribute to the program's success in curbing clientelism.

7.2.1 Centralization

Both Bolsa Família and Progresa/Oportunidades centralize crucial components of their programs.[13] In the case of Mexico, Oportunidades is run almost entirely out of an autonomous central government agency. Officials from this agency use an index of marginality to first select communities for inclusion and then, in a second step, national officials use household surveys to determine eligibility.[14] Program beneficiaries receive their cash benefits directly from national officials or through the use of debit cards.[15] Municipalities' role in selection is limited to naming a local representative to help national government bureaucrats with field work, and political party representatives (and their blood or "political" relatives to the fourth degree) are explicitly not eligible to be named to this role. Santiago Levy, the architect of Progresa, describes the decision to cut state and local officials out of the decision-making process as a choice designed explicitly to "limit the opportunities for political manipulation" (Levy, 2006, 98). The implications of centralization were well understood by local officials, too. Observing mayors at a national convention on local development in 2005, De la O (2014, 182) notes that many municipal presidents requested "an active role in the selection of recipients, full access to the list of program beneficiaries, and the power to purge this list at their discretion." As we have seen in the Argentine case, these are precisely the powers that facilitate clientelism.

Although Bolsa Família has important centralized components, Brazilian municipalities play a larger role in the implementation of this CCT than their Mexican counterparts. As in Mexico, the central government relies on poverty data to set quotas for the number of beneficiaries per municipality, but in Brazil, municipalities themselves are charged with carrying out the first step of identifying and registering potential beneficiaries by administering a standard household questionnaire.[16] Municipalities enter potential beneficiaries into a single, independently maintained database, known as the "Cadastro Único," and municipal entries are directly transmitted to the federal government's Ministry of Social Welfare (MDS), which then determines precisely which

---

[13] In this section, I rely heavily on excellent existing summaries of these programs, especially those carried out under the auspices of the World Bank and IFPRI. See especially Skoufias et al. (2001), Lindert et al. (2007), Fiszbein and Schady (2009), Adato and Hoddinott (2010), and Lindert and Vincensini (2010).

[14] The operational rules for the program can be found here: http://www.oportunidades.gob.mx.

[15] See Niño-Zarazúa (2010).

[16] Note that, because of municipal autonomy granted by the Brazilian constitution, the federal government signs an agreement with each municipality in order to ensure consistent implementation.

households/families will be incorporated into Bolsa Familia. Almost universally, these benefits are delivered through special electronic benefit cards that can be redeemed at designated locales, including banks, lottery sales points, and other stores.[17] The payments themselves are made directly by the Caixa Económica Federal, a large government-owned bank that maintains an extensive presence throughout the country.

In spite of their differences, both programs share the important characteristic that the ultimate decision-making power over beneficiary selection *and* disbursement of program benefits (such as cash or refilling electronic debit cards) is retained by *national* officials.[18] The centralization of these two crucial stages means that the two most obvious junctures at which local officials could try to create a clientelist bargain – when citizens are signed up for and then actually receive a benefit – are disrupted.[19] It is also important to note that both programs share a similarity in that they centralize decision making to a well-insulated, highly technocratic bureaucratic body that is not seen as subject to political influence. Brazil and Mexico's success does not mean that simply any centralized program design will necessarily eliminate clientelism. We can certainly imagine a scenario wherein centralized decision making creates opportunities for federal bureaucrats or legislators to intervene on behalf of copartisans, favored constituents, family members, and so on. This was the case with Mexico's PRONASOL program under President Salinas, for example, where federal bureaucrats charged with administering PRONASOL in the states often used the program to achieve clearly political aims (Kaufman and Trejo, 1997). In the case of Progresa/Oportunidades and Bolsa Familia, in contrast, the agencies responsible for implementation are seen as both technically competent and politically neutral.

Not only are both programs centralized, but the fact of central control is widely publicized and understood by voters.[20] In the Brazilian case, the massive scale of publicity surrounding the program is undoubtedly crucial for generating high levels of public awareness of how the program works and who distributes benefits.[21] Although Bolsa Familia is jointly administered by the municipal and federal governments, it is overwhelmingly identified

---

[17] Most beneficiaries (about 65%) redeem their benefits at lottery sales points, with an additional 30% using ATM machines (Lindert et al., 2007, 52–53).

[18] See Fenwick (2009) for a similar argument that centralization limited the potential for abuse of Bolsa Familia by state-level political machines.

[19] In the Brazilian case, the selection of potential beneficiaries occurs at the local level. However, the fact that local officials do not decide who enters the program undermines any attempt by these officials to claim credit for it. Lack of conditionality enforcement and near-universal coverage also undermine clientelism in this case, as detailed below.

[20] In her discussion of successful public health reforms in the state of Ceará, in Brazil, Tendler (1997) also notes the importance of widely advertised state control over a new outreach program in circumventing possible municipal interference.

[21] Initially, the Mexican government did not employ a mass public information campaign, in part because it did not want to heighten expectations while the program's future was still

with the national government, and in particular, with the administration of President Lula (2003–2010). Lula's Workers' Party affiliation, his long advocacy on poverty issues, and his personal story undoubtedly contribute to this perception (Hall, 2006), and the program's centralized payments structure, its active media efforts, and initiatives like the existence of national hot lines to report problems strengthen this link. Recent data demonstrate the extent to which Lula "owned" this issue in the public arena. According to a 2010 panel survey, large majorities of the population attributed responsibility for Bolsa Familia to then-President Lula, rather than to any other political actor. This was true of 84% of respondents by election time (Ames et al. [2013], cited in Zucco [2013, 5]). In contrast, there is little or no evidence that other politicians, including national legislators and state and municipal officials, exercise any issue ownership over the program. Local politicians appear to recognize the futility of such attempts; Fried (2012) recounts interviews with municipal politicians who claimed that there was no point in attempting to manipulate program benefits, as the president would nonetheless receive credit for the program. Similarly, Zucco (2013) finds that while the incumbent party's presidential candidate gains electorally from the implementation of Bolsa Familia, this support does not trickle down to other candidates from the same party.[22]

In the case of Mexico, De la O (2014) shows that Mexican citizens are well aware of the federal nature of Oportunidades, and in fact that program beneficiaries are better informed than other citizens. This may be due in part to the wording that is included in all printed program materials that explicitly states that the receipt of program benefits is not at all contingent on political behavior.[23] The degree to which the central government claims credit for the program is also reflected in the frustration of political brokers in Mexico. A quote from a PRI broker in the Mexican state of Tabasco, from an interview reported in De la O (2014, 181), is particularly revealing: "[w]hat the Oportunidades staff doesn't get is that they have to let us decide who enters and exits the program; otherwise, we can't punish people who didn't vote for us. And we know who didn't; we know because we know the people,

uncertain (Levy, 2006, 110). Public information about the program did expand beginning in 2006.

[22] Interestingly, he finds that this holds true for the 2002 election, as well, when the PSDB presidential candidate gained electorally from the Bolsa Escola program, even though it was smaller in scope and received less publicity than Bolsa Familia.

[23] This is the text itself, as cited by Levy (2006, 107): "We remind you that your participation in Oportunidades and receipt of benefits are in no way subject to affiliation with any specific political party or to voting for any specific candidate running for public office. No candidate is authorized to grant or withhold benefits under the program. Eligible beneficiary families will receive support if they show up for their doctors visits and health education talks and if their children attend school regularly. Any person, organization, or public servant that makes undue use of program resources will be reported to the competent authority and prosecuted under applicable legislation."

where they work and what party they are loyal to. With the inflexibility of the program we can't include our people and take out the ones that are not with us."

7.2.2 Failed Conditionalities and Broad Coverage

In both Brazil and Mexico, widespread awareness of central control over program administration makes it difficult for local incumbents to actually exercise discretion – or to convince voters that they might exercise discretion – over the distribution of valued program benefits. Brazil's Bolsa Familia program incorporates a larger role for municipalities, and as such, it might be more susceptible to the manipulation of benefits by local officials. To some extent, this risk of manipulation is minimized by additional layers of central control, made up of both carrots and sticks. Brazil's Ministry of Social Development cross checks names on the centrally controlled beneficiary list with other government records, including those that contain data on formal employment, social security receipt, obituaries, and elected officials.[24] The government also offers financial rewards to municipalities that meet certain guidelines in administering social policy and properly updating the Cadastro Unico.

Apart from these efforts, it is worth calling attention to two additional features of how the Bolsa Familia program is administered that make it difficult to use the program in clientelist exchange. They are the *weakness* of enforcement of conditionality and the near universal coverage of the targeted population. Beginning with the latter, universal coverage makes any threat of potential future withdrawal of benefits less plausible to voters.[25] As one observer of the Bolsa Familia program writes, coverage of the targeted population is so comprehensive that "mayors find it hard to exclude any income-eligible household, reducing their leeway for discretion" (McGuire, 2011, 14).

A similar argument can be made with respect to the *weak* enforcement of conditionalities. This is a more controversial statement, as the "conditional" nature of conditional cash transfers is these program's most well-known and salient innovation. Precisely because they link benefits to schooling and health requirements, CCT's have been defended on economic grounds as an investment in human development and thus a long-term strategy to reduce poverty. Conditionalities may also increase the palatability of redistributive programs to middle and upper-class voters. However, from the perspective of reducing clientelism, when local officials are asked to monitor behaviors like school and health clinic attendance to determine a family's continued receipt of program benefits, this opens the door to political manipulation. It is

---

[24] The MDS website provides more details about this monitoring process here: http://www.mds.gov.br/ bolsafamilia/cadastrounico/monitoramento.

[25] See Lindert et al. (2007, 72) for a similar point.

worth noting that, although the Bolsa Familia program is considered a model CCT in many respects, the actual enforcement of the supposed conditions has been and continues to be very weak. The government treats initial episodes of noncompliance as evidence that a family is likely in need of additional services to help them comply, rather than as an opportunity to take punitive measures (Lindert et al., 2007, 55). The weakness of conditionality might be portrayed as a shortcoming of the program. From the perspective of reducing clientelism, however, it is actually a quite positive development, reducing local incumbents' ability to engage in "shenanigans" around the compliance stage (McGuire, 2011, 15).

The experience of Brazil and Mexico points to centralization as perhaps the most effective tool for eliminating local clientelism. Such centralization certainly offers a more direct path to accountability than the uneven experience portrayed in the preceding chapters. In the absence of highly centralized program administration or when, as in Brazil, a centralized program is complemented by a continued role for local officials, a focus on curbing clientelism yields some interesting and surprising policy implications for social safety nets. It particular, it suggests that universal coverage and weak, rather than strong, conditionality, are likely to help a program avoid clientelism. In a context of scarce resources, a program might be more effective in eliminating clientelism if it were to offer universal coverage to citizens in selected municipalities, rather than attempt to cover fewer citizens across a larger number of municipalities. And, when conditionalities are not or cannot be enforced by neutral parties with limited political roles or incentives, clientelism is more likely to be avoided by eliminating conditionalities rather than enforcing them. Finally, the comparison with Argentina suggests that other features of these programs, such as a formal role for civil society input and controls, which exists in all three countries studied here, are unlikely to affect the likelihood they might be used in clientelism.

7.3 PROSPECTS FOR CHANGE IN ARGENTINA

For much of the past two decades, targeted social programs in Argentina lacked the desirable characteristics that I argue might limit clientelism. However, since that time, both the PNSA itself and the broader landscape of social safety net policy in Argentina have undergone a number of changes. In this section, I outline these changes and speculate about whether they will fundamentally challenge the appeal of clientelism at the local level in Argentina.

Since the time of most of the field work for this study, the PNSA has undergone an important transition in the way in which it delivers benefits. In the program's first years, benefits were distributed almost entirely in the form of physical boxes of food, of the type described in detail in earlier chapters.

The program has since seen a steady transition away from the distribution of benefits in kind and toward the distribution of either debit cards or "tickets alimentarios," which are vouchers that can be used to purchase foodstuffs directly from stores. According to recent figures, of the 1.8 million families now benefiting from the PNSA, only about 20% receive physical boxes of food (Diaz Langou et al., 2010, 78). This is undoubtedly a positive development; at a minimum, it gives beneficiaries greater autonomy over consumption. It also has possible consequences for clientelism. For those receiving their benefits in the form of debit cards, this also attenuates the ability of local officials to act as intermediaries for the receipt of benefits.[26]

On the other hand, this change has taken place in a context where the PNSA's decentralized organizational structure remains fundamentally unchanged. The selection and dismissal of beneficiaries continues to be the purview of subnational officials. As documented earlier, the concentration of discretion over benefits at the local level lends itself readily to clientelist manipulation. A change in the form of benefit delivery, therefore, is unlikely to fundamentally alter the appeal of clientelism to municipal officials charged with implementing the PNSA.

Though the PNSA has retained most of its defining characteristics, recent years have also seen the implementation of a new social safety net program in Argentina that appears to hold more promise for breaking with clientelist practices. The *Asignación Universal por Hijo*, or AUH, is a semi-conditional cash transfer program designed to deliver a monthly monetary payment to all families who are outside the established public contributory system of child transfers in Argentina – namely, the unemployed, informal workers making below minimum wage, and domestic workers.[27] In contrast to Brazil and Mexico's CCT programs, which are stand-alone programs, the AUH is designed to be a noncontributory counterpart to an already existing, contributory benefit for low and moderate-income families working in the state and private sectors.[28] Created by decree in October 2009, the program rapidly expanded. As of April 2010, it had more than 1.6 million beneficiary households and a larger budget than all of Argentina's other major social safety net programs combined (Diaz Langou et al., 2010, Agis et al., n.d.).[29]

The AUH has two crucial design innovations that distinguish it from the PNSA and most other Argentine safety net programs. First, the program is

---

[26] Depending on how they are administered, vouchers may or may not have the same effect. Debit cards, once acquired, are refilled remotely. In contrast, vouchers may require ongoing contact with local officials to procure the regular benefit.

[27] The program formally excludes informal workers who make more than the minimum wage, though this is difficult to enforce. It is semi-conditional because only a portion of the transfer is tied to compliance with particular behaviors.

[28] Families with incomes above a certain level receive a tax break, but no monetary benefit.

[29] Program data indicates that as of 2013, it had approximately 3.5 million beneficiaries. See http://www.anses.gob.ar/destacados/asignacion-universal-por-hijo-1.

highly centralized. It is almost entirely run by ANSES, the Argentine Social Security Administration, by the same arm that administers the contributory benefit. Prospective beneficiaries sign up for benefits directly from local ANSES offices and receive their benefits using a debit card obtained directly from a bank. The program thus fundamentally eliminates any facilitating role for local elected officials. Like the Brazilian and Mexican programs already reviewed, the AUH does rely on local actors to monitor family compliance with health and schooling conditions. However, this compliance is monitored by health and school officials, rather than more directly by municipal officials. Second, the program is designed to provide universal coverage among the targeted population. As noted before, where universal or near universal coverage is achieved, this should sharply reduce the credibility of any threats to withdraw benefits and, along with it, the viability of clientelist strategies.

Some challenges remain to fully implement the program as designed. As of yet, the coverage of eligible families has not yet reached 100%. In addition, although AUH benefits are supposed to be exclusionary vis-à-vis other cash benefits (though not the PNSA), the Argentine government has not gone the way of Brazil and consolidated its various programs under one umbrella. It is unclear whether the supposedly exclusionary nature of the AUH is being enforced and/or whether the continuity of other benefits might provide a point of leverage for local politicians who would benefit from clientelism. Finally, some policy uncertainty remains over the staying power of the benefits, particularly because the program was created via executive decree, rather than through a law passed by Congress. Its funding structure also raises some questions about durability. The AUH is funded from social security revenue and interest earned on a fund composed of individual contributions to a state pensions fund controlled by ANSES.[30] As Gasparini and Cruces (2010, 36–37) point out, the reliance on these funds in the long term is unlikely to be sustainable and subjects the program's funding structure to the volatility of the business cycle. In spite of these challenges, the AUH may mark a point of departure in the extent to which noncontributory social welfare programs in Argentina are compatible with local level clientelism.

7.4 THE CHANGING STATE AND CLIENTELISM

Argentina's experience with clientelism and social policy, especially when compared with that of Brazil and Mexico, raises broader questions about the relationship between the nature of the state, political accountability, and the quality of government. A long intellectual tradition associates a larger

---

[30] As Diaz Langou et al. (2010) point out, most Argentine social welfare programs of recent years (with the exception of the PNSA) were created via executive decree. At the time the decree establishing the AUH was promulgated, a variety of similar proposals were before the legislature.

state role in the economy with greater particularism and corruption. A large state, particularly one that includes numerous parastatal agencies and is deeply involved in regulating many aspects of daily life, creates many opportunities for particularistic exchanges. At the most basic level, a large state means many jobs that may be (at least potentially) doled out in exchange for political support, whereas a smaller state eliminates some opportunities for particularism. In a large state, many other sorts of benefits and favors might be exchanged for political support, as well. The aid of a politician or his local representative might be needed to obtain a permit to open a business, avoid a cumbersome tax, or carry out a simple transaction with the bureaucracy. A small state, by comparison, would seem to offer fewer opportunities for a politician to extort political support in return for access to some needed benefit, concession, or favorable treatment from the state.

On the other hand, a different logic suggests that a large state should be associated with *less* particularism. This is particularly the case if we consider that larger states may be more likely to distribute universal benefits. As noted above, where benefits are truly universal, politician discretion over who gets what is eliminated, also removing the discretion on which successful clientelism relies and the power that politicians can wield over the lives of individual voters. Wolfinger (1972, 384) nicely presents this view with reference to the American case, saying, "From the time of the New Deal, government has assumed the burden of providing for the minimal physical needs of the poor, thus supposedly preempting a major source of the machines' appeal. The growth of the welfare state undeniably has limited politicians' opportunities to use charity as a means of incurring obligations that could be discharged by political support."[31] In this view, it is the small state that should encourage particularism, by fostering competition for the limited benefits it offers as well as by creating the opportunity for politicians to offer conditional or privately funded benefits to fill in the gaps left by a small state.

The research presented over the course of these pages suggests that neither a uniformly optimistic nor pessimistic view about the relationship between the nature of the state and the prevalence of particularism may be appropriate. Instead, it calls attention to the influence of policy design and the political and social context in which policies are implemented. As Evans (1995, 10) elegantly states with respect to the role of states in industrial development, "[t]he appropriate question is not 'how much' but 'what kind.'" Similarly, the extent to which the state facilitates clientelism may depend not on the size of the state, but on the nature and context of its policies.

With respect to policy design, this book has focused on a highly decentralized food program. Decentralized policy design may allow programs to take

---

[31] Though Wolfinger does go on to argue that political machines may still offer other types of aid, such as help dealing with the bureaucracy, that certain constituencies may find very valuable.

advantage of better local knowledge and improve responsiveness to voters, as advocates suggest. However, the findings discussed here also show that decentralization can be highly compatible with clientelism. An examination of the PNSA as implemented across a sample of Argentine municipalities demonstrates that the promise of decentralization to break with personalist politics is unlikely to be realized as long as poverty is pervasive. Only as poverty declines should we be optimistic that decentralization, when coupled with political competition, will encourage politicians to depart from clientelistic implementation. The comparison with other country cases in this final chapter shows that centralization seems to hold out more promise for the elimination of clientelism. To the extent it severs the ties between decision makers and those in close proximity to voters, centralization is likely to make clientelism substantially harder. At the same time, centralization is no magic bullet. It presumes that national agencies are out of the reach of influence of local actors, which may or may not be the case. Furthermore, centralization does not tell us anything about the quality of program implementation on dimensions apart from clientelism. Errors of exclusion and inclusion may still occur, even when clientelism is limited. This points to the need for continued exploration of how policy design and political and social circumstances interact to affect the actual practice of politics.

References

Acemoglu, Daron, and Robinson, James A. 2001. A theory of political transitions. *American Economic Review*, **91**(4), 938–963.

Adato, Michelle, and Hoddinott, John. 2010. *Conditional Cash Transfers in Latin America*. Baltimore: Johns Hopkins University Press.

Adserá, Alicia, Boix, Carles, and Payne, Mark. 2003. Are you being served? Political accountability and quality of government. *Journal of Law, Economics, and Organization*, **19**(2), 445–490.

Agis, Emmanuel, Cañete, Carlos, and Panigo, Demian. n.d. *El impacto de la asignación universal por hijo en Argentina*. Typescript. CEIL-CONICET. Buenos Aires, Argentina.

Alconada, Hugo. 2009. *Obras y clientelismo, dos claves para sumar votos*. La Nación. April 12.

Aldrich, John H. 1995. *Why Parties? The Origin and Transformation of Party Politics in America*. Chicago: University of Chicago Press.

Alves, Jorge. 2012. *Coordinating Care: State Politics and Intergovernmental Relations in the Brazilian Healthcare Sector*. Ph.D. thesis, Brown University.

Ames, Barry, Machado, Fabiana, Renno, Lucio, Samuels, David, Smith, Amy, and Zucco, Cesar. 2013 (April). *Brazil Electoral Panel Studies: Brazilian Public Opinion in the 2010 Election*. IADB Technical Note IDB-TN-508. Washington, DC: IADB.

Ansolabehere, Stephen, and Snyder, James M. 2000. Valence politics and equilibrium in spatial election models. *Public Choice*, **103**(3), 327–336.

Ansolabehere, Stephen, and Snyder, James M. 2006. Party control of state government and the distribution of public expenditures. *The Scandinavian Journal of Economics*, **108**(4), 547–569.

Argentina, Ministry of Social Development. 2009. *Rendimos cuentas. Diciembre 2007–Mayo 2009*. http://www.desarrollosocial.gob.ar/Uploads/i1/biblioteca/5.pdf.

Argentine Congress. 2002. *Ley 25.724. Programa de nutrición y alimentación nacional*. http://infoleg.mecon.gov.ar/infolegInternet/anexos/80000-84999/84523/texact.htm.

Attanasio, Orazio, Battistin, Erich, Fitzsimons, Emla, Mesnard, Alice, and Vera-Hernandez, Marcos. 2005. *How effective are conditional cash transfers? Evidence from Colombia*. Institute for Fiscal Studies Briefing Note 54. London.

Auyero, Javier. 2000a. The logic of clientelism in Argentina: An ethnographic account. *Latin American Research Review*, 35(3), 55–81.

Auyero, Javier. 2000b. *Poor People's Politics: Peronist Survival Networks and the Legacy of Evita*. Durham, NC: Duke University Press.

Auyero, Javier. 2011. Patients of the state. An ethnographic account of poor people's waiting. *Latin American Research Review*, 46(1), 5–29.

Bailey, F. G. 1963. *Politics and Social Change*. Berkeley and Los Angeles: University of California Press.

Baldwin, Kate. 2013. Why vote with the chief? Political connections and public goods provision in Zambia. *American Journal of Political Science*, 57(4), 794–809.

Banfield, Edward C., and Wilson, James Q. 1963. *City Politics*. Cambridge, MA: Harvard University Press and MIT Press.

Bardhan, Pranab K., and Mookherjee, Dilip. 2002. Relative capture of local and central governments: An essay in the political economy of decentralization. *Center for International and Development Economics Research, Working Paper Series*.

Bardhan, Pranab, and Mookherjee, Dilip. 2006a. Decentralisation and accountability in infrastructure delivery in developing countries. *The Economic Journal*, 116(508), 101–127.

Bardhan, Pranab, and Mookherjee, Dilip (eds). 2006b. *Decentralization and Local Governance in Developing Countries*. Cambridge, MA: MIT Press.

Bardhan, Pranab K., and Mookherjee, Dilip. 2006c. Decentralization, corruption, and government accountability. In Rose-Ackerman, Susan (ed.), *International Handbook on the Economics of Corruption*, pp. 161–188. Northhampton, MA: Edward Elgar.

Barro, Robert J. 1973. The control of politicians: An economic model. *Public choice*, 14(1), 19–42.

Beer, Caroline. 2001. Assessing the consequences of electoral democracy: Subnational legislative change in Mexico. *Comparative Politics*, 33(4), 421–440.

Boas, Taylor C., and Hidalgo, F. Daniel. 2011. Controlling the airwaves: Incumbency advantage and community radio in Brazil. *American Journal of Political Science*, 55(4), 869–885.

Boudon, Lawrence. 1996. Guerrillas and the state: The role of the state in the Colombian peace process. *Journal of Latin American Studies*, 28(2), 279–297.

Bourdieu, Pierre. 2000. *Pascalian Meditations*. Stanford, CA: Stanford University Press.

Brader, Ted A., and Tucker, Joshua A. 2008. Reflective and unreflective partisans? Experimental evidence on the links between information, opinion, and party identification. Manuscript. New York University.

Bratton, Michael. 2008 (June). Vote buying and violence in Nigerian election campaigns. AfroBarometer Working Paper No. 99.

Brinks, Daniel M. 2003. Informal institutions and the rule of law: The judicial response to state killings in Buenos Aires and São Paulo in the 1990s. *Comparative Politics*, 36(1), 1–19.

Brinks, Daniel M. 2008. *Inequality and the rule of Law: The judicial response to police killings in Latin America*. New York: Cambridge University Press.

Britos, Sergio, O'Donnell, Alejandro, Ugalde, Vanina, and Clacheo, Rodrigo. 2003 (November). *Programas alimentarios en Argentina*. Centro de Estudios Sobre Nutricion Infantil.

Brock, Timothy C. 1968. Implications of commodity theory for value change. In A. Greenwald, T.C. Brock, and T.M. Ostrom (eds.), *Psychological foundations of attitudes*. New York: Academic Press.

Brown, Vonda. 2011 (October). *How Governments Abuse Advertising in Latin America*. Open Society Institute. http://www.opensocietyfoundations.org/voices/how-governments-abuse-advertising-latin-america.

Brusco, Valeria, Nazareno, Marcelo, and Stokes, Susan C. 2004. Vote buying in Argentina. *Latin American Research Review*, 39(2), 66–88.

Brusco, Valeria, Nazareno, Marcelo, and Stokes, Susan C. 2005 (November). *La manipulación política de los recursos públicos: Réditos y costos electorales en Argentina*. Presented at the Seventh National Congress of Political Science, Argentina.

Brusco, Valeria, Nazareno, Marcelo, and Stokes, Susan C. 2006. Réditos y peligros electorales del gasto público en la Argentina. *Desarrollo Economico*, 46(181), 63–88.

Bueno de Mesquita, Bruce, Morrow, James D., Siverson, Randolph M., and Smith, Alastair. 2002. Political institutions, policy choice and the survival of leaders. *British Journal of Political Science*, 32(4), 559–590.

Bueno de Mesquita, Bruce, Smith, Alastair, Siverson, Randolph M., and Morrow, James D. 2003. *The Logic of Political Survival*. Cambridge, MA: MIT Press.

Burki, Shahid Javed, Perry, Guillermo E., and Dillinger, William R. 1999. *Beyond the Center: Decentralizing the State*. Washington, DC: World Bank.

Bussell, Jennifer. 2010. Why get technical? Corruption and the politics of public service reform in the Indian states. *Comparative Political Studies*, 43(10), 1230–1257.

Calvo, Ernesto, and Murillo, María Victoria. 2004. Who delivers? Partisan clients in the Argentine electoral market. *American Journal of Political Science*, 48(4), 742–757.

Calvo, Ernesto, and Murillo, María Victoria. 2007 (October). *How Many Clients Does It Take to Win an Election? Estimating the Size and Structure of Political Networks in Argentina and Chile*. Unpublished manuscript.

Calvo, Ernesto, and Murillo, María Victoria. 2010 (December). *Selecting Clients: Partisan Networks and the Electoral Benefits of Targeted Distribution*. Unpublished manuscript.

Calvo, Ernesto, and Murillo, María Victoria. 2013. When parties meet voters: Assessing political linkages through partisan networks and distributive expectations in Argentina and Chile. *Comparative Political Studies*, 46(7), 851–882.

Camacho, Adriana, and Conover, Emily. 2011. Manipulation of social program eligibility. *American Economic Journal: Economic Policy*, 3(2), 41–65.

Campos, Jose Edgardo, and Hellman, Joel S. 2005. Governance gone local: does decentralization improve accountability? In *East Asia Decentralizes*, 237–252. Washington, DC: World Bank.

Castles, Francis G. 2002. Developing new measures of welfare state change and reform. *European Journal of Political Research*, 41(5), 613–641.

Chandra, Kanchan. 2004. *Why Ethnic Parties Succeed: Patronage and Ethnic Head Counts in India*. Cambridge and New York: Cambridge University Press.

Chandra, Kanchan. 2007. Counting heads: A theory of voter and elite behavior in patronage democracies. In Kitschelt, Herbert, and Wilkinson, Steven I. (eds.), *Patrons, Clients, and Policies: Patterns of Democratic Accountability and Political Competition*, pp. 84–109. New York: Cambridge University Press.

Chang, Eric C.C., and Golden, Miriam A. 2006. Electoral systems, district magnitude, and corruption. *British Journal of Political Science*, **37**(1), 115–137.

Chhibber, Pradeep, and Nooruddin, Irfan. 2004. Do party sytems count? *Comparative Political Studies*, **37**(2), 152–187.

Chubb, Judith. 1981. The social bases of an urban political machine: The case of Palermo. *Political Science Quarterly*, **96**(1), 107–125.

Chubb, Judith. 1982. *Patronage, Power, and Poverty in Southern Italy: A Tale of Two Cities*. New York: Cambridge University Press.

Cleary, Matthew R. 2007. Electoral competition, participation, and government responsiveness in Mexico. *American Journal of Political Science*, **51**(2), 283–299.

Cleary, Matthew R. 2010. *The Sources of Democratic Responsiveness in Mexico*. South Bend, IN: University of Notre Dame Press.

Cornelius, Wayne. 1977. Leaders, followers, and official patrons in urban Mexico. In Guasti, Laura, Lande, Carl H., and Scott, James C. (eds.), *Friends, Followers, and Factions*, pp. 337–353. Berkeley and Los Angeles: University of California Press.

Cornelius, Wayne, Craig, Ann, and Fox, Jonathan (eds). 1994. *Transforming State-Society Relations in Mexico: The National Solidarity Strategy*. La Jolla: Center for US–Mexican Studies.

Cox, Gary W. 2010. Swing voters, core voters, and distributive politics. In Shapiro, Ian, Stokes, Susan C., Wood, Elizabeth Jean, and Kirshner, Alexander S. (eds.), *Political Representation*. New York: Cambridge University Press.

Cox, Gary W., and McCubbins, Matthew D. 1986. Electoral politics as a redistributive game. *Journal of Politics*, **48**(2), 370–389.

Cox, Gary W., and McCubbins, Matthew D. 1993. *Legislative Leviathan: Party Government in the House*. Berkeley: University of California Press.

Cox, Gary W., and Munger, Michael C. 1989. Closeness, expenditures, and turnout in the 1982 U.S. House elections. *American Political Science Review*, **83**(1), 217–231.

Cox, Gary W., Rosenbluth, Frances M., and Thies, Michael F. 1998. Mobilization, social networks, and turnout: Evidence from Japan. *World Politics*, **50**(3), 447–474.

Crook, Richard C., and Manor, James. 1998. *Democracy and decentralisation in South Asia and West Africa*. New York: Cambridge University Press.

Cruces, Guillermo, Rovner, Helena, and Schijman, Agustina. 2007 (December). *Percepciones sobre los planes sociales en Argentina*. World Bank Southern Cone Office. Serie de Docmentos de Trabajo Sobre Politicas Sociales No. 2.

De la O, Ana L. 2013. Do conditional cash transfers affect electoral behavior? Evidence from a randomized experiment in Mexico. *American Journal of Political Science*, **57**(1), 1–14.

De la O, Ana L. 2014 (October). *Crafting Pro-Poor Policies: The Politics of Conditional Cash Transfers in Latin America*. Unpublished manuscript, Yale University.

de Soto, Hernando. 1989. *The Other Path: The Invisible Revolution in the Third World*. New York: Harper & Row/Perennial Library. Translated by June Abbott.

Della Porta, Donatella. 2001. A judges' revolution? Political corruption and the judiciary in Italy. *European Journal of Political Research*, 39(1), 1–21.

DePaulo, Bella M., Kashy, Deborah A., Kirkendol, Susan E., Wyer, Melissa M., and Epstein, Jennifer A. 1996. Lying in everyday life. *Journal of Personality and Social Psychology*, 70(5), 979–995.

DePaulo, Bella M., and Kashy, Deborah A. 1998. Everyday lies in close and casual relationships. *Journal of Personality and Social Psychology*, 74(1), 63.

Dercon, Stefan. 2003 (September). *Poverty Traps and Development: The Equity-Efficiency Trade-Off Revisited*. European Development Research Network.

Desposato, Scott W. 2006. How informal electoral institutions shape the Brazilian legislative arena. In Helmke, Gretchen, and Levitsky, Steven (eds.), *Informal Institutions and Democracy: Lessons from Latin America*, pp. 56–68. Baltimore: Johns Hopkins University Press.

Desposato, Scott W. 2007. How does vote buying shape the legislative arena? In Schaffer, Frederic Charles (ed.), *Elections for Sale: The Causes and Consequences of Vote Buying*, pp. 101–122. Boulder, CO: Lynne Rienner.

Diaz-Cayeros, Alberto, Magaloni, Beatriz, and Weingast, Barry. 2003. Tragic brilliance: Equilibrium party hegemony in Mexico. Working Paper. Stanford University.

Diaz-Cayeros, Alberto, Magaloni, Beatriz, and Estévez, Federico. 2012. Strategies of Vote Buying: Democracy, Clientelism and Poverty Relief in Mexico. Unpublished manuscript, Stanford University.

Diaz Langou, Gala, Potenza dal Masetto, Fernanda, and Forteza, Paula. 2010 (July). *Los principales programas nacionales de proteccion social. Estudio sobre los efectos de las variables politico-institucionales en la gestion*. CIPPEC Documento de Politicas Publicas.

Dillinger, William. 1994. *Decentralization and Its Implications for Urban Service Delivery*. Washington, DC: World Bank.

Dixit, Avinash, and Londregan, John. 1996. The determinants of success of special interests in redistributive politics. *Journal of Politics*, 58(4), 1132–1155.

Downs, Anthony. 1957. *An Economic Theory of Democracy*. New York: Harper.

Dresser, Denise. 1994. Bringing the poor back in: National Solidarity as a strategy of regime legitimation. In Cornelius, Wayne, Craig, Ann, and Fox, Jonathan (eds.), *Transforming State-Society Relations in Mexico*, pp. 143–166. La Jolla, CA, Center for US-Mexican Studies.

Druckman, James N., and Kam, Cindy D. 2011. Students as experimental participants. A defense of the "Narrow Data Base." In Druckman, James N., Green, Donald P., Kuklinski, James H., and Lupia, Arthur (eds.), *Cambridge Handbook of Experimental Political Science*, pp. 41–57. New York: Cambridge University Press.

Druckman, James N., Green, Donald P., Kuklinski, James H., and Lupia, Arthur. 2006. The growth and development of experimental research in political science. *American Political Science Review*, 100(4), 627–635.

Dugger, Celia W. 2004. To help poor be pupils, not wage earners, Brazil pays parents. New York Times. January 3.

Eaton, Kent. 2004. *Politics Beyond the Capital: The Design of Subnational Institutions in South America*. Palo Alto: Stanford University Press.

Eisenstadt, S.N., and Roniger, L. 1984. *Patrons, Clients and Friends. Interpersonal Relations and the Structure of Trust in Society*. New York: Cambridge University Press.

Esping-Anderson, Gosta. 1989. The three political economies of the welfare state. *The Canadian Review of Sociology and Anthropology*, **26**(1), 10–36.

Esping-Anderson, Gosta. 1990. *The Three Worlds of Welfare Capitalism*. Princeton, NJ: Princeton University Press.

Evans, Peter. 1995. *Embedded Autonomy: States and Industrial Transformation*. Princeton, NJ: Princeton University Press.

Fafchamps, Marcel. 2003. *Rural Poverty, Risk and Development*. Cheltenham, UK: Edward Elgar.

Faguet, Jean-Paul. 2004. Does decentralization increase government responsiveness to local needs? Evidence from Bolivia. *Journal of Public Economics*, **88**(3/4), 867–893.

Falleti, Tulia G. 2010. *Decentralization and Subnational Politics in Latin America*. New York: Cambridge University Press.

Faughnan, Brian M., and Zechmeister, Elizabeth J. 2011. *Vote Buying in the Americas*. Americas Barometer Insights Series.

Fearon, James D. 1994. Domestic political audiences and the escalation of international disputes. *American Political Science Review*, **88**(3), 577–592.

Fenwick, Tracy Beck. 2009. Avoiding governors: The success of *Bolsa Familia*. *Latin American Research Review*, **44**(1), 102–131.

Ferejohn, John. 1986. Incumbent performance and electoral control. *Public choice*, **50**(1), 5–25.

Ferraz, Claudio, and Finan, Frederico. 2008. Exposing corrupt politicians: The effects of Brazil's publicly released audits on electoral outcomes. *Quarterly Journal of Economics*, **123**(2), 703–745.

Finan, Frederico, and Schechter, Laura. 2012. Vote-buying and reciprocity. *Econometrica*, **80**(2), 863–881.

Fiorina, Morris P. 1976. The voting decision: Instrumental and expressive aspects. *Journal of Politics*, **38**(2), 390–413.

Fiorina, Morris, and Noll, Roger G. 1978. Voters, bureaucrats and legislators: A rational choice perspective on the growth of bureaucracy. *Journal of Public Economics*, **9**(2), 239–254.

Fisman, Raymond, and Gatti, Roberta. 2002. Decentralization and corruption: Evidence across countries. *Journal of Public Economics*, **83**(3), 325–345.

Fiszbein, Ariel, and Schady, Norbert. 2009. *Conditional Cash Transfers: Reducing Present and Future Poverty*. Washington, DC: The World Bank.

Folke, Olle, Hirano, Shigeo, and Snyder, James M. 2011. Patronage and elections in US states. *American Political Science Review*, **105**(3), 567–585.

Fox, Jonathan. 1994. The difficult transition from clientelism to citizenship: Lessons from Mexico. *World Politics*, **46**(2), 151–184.

Fried, Brian J. 2012. Distributive politics and conditional cash transfers: The case of Brazil's *Bolsa Familia*. *World Development*, **40**(5), 1042–1053.

Fundación Grupo Innova. 2003. *Ranking Nacional de Municipios*. Tech. rept. Fundación Grupo Innova, Buenos Aires.

Gaines, Brian J., Kuklinski, James H., and Quirk, Paul J. 2007. The logic of the survey experiment reexamined. *Political Analysis*, **15**(1), 1–20.

Gasparini, Leonardo. 2004 (January). *Poverty and Inequality in Argentina*. https://www.depeco.econo.unlp.edu.ar. CEDLAS-Universidad Nacional de La Plata.

Gasparini, Leonardo, and Cruces, Guillermo. 2010 (July). *Las asignaciones universales por hijo: Impacto, discusion y alternativas*. CEDLAS-Universidad Nacional de La Plata.

Gay, Robert. 1994. *Popular Organization and Democracy in Rio de Janeiro: A Tale of Two Favelas*. Philadelphia: Temple University Press.

Geddes, Barbara. 1994. *Politician's Dilemma*. Berkeley and Los Angeles, CA: University of California Press.

Gelman, Andrew, and Hill, Jennifer. 2007. *Data Analysis Using Regression and Multilevel/Hierarchical Models*. New York: Cambridge University Press.

Gerber, Alan S., Huber, Gregory A., Doherty, David, and Dowling, Conor M. 2009. Is there a secret ballot? Ballot secrecy perceptions and their implications for voting behavior. Presented at the Annual Meeting of the American Political Science Association.

Gerring, John, and Thacker, Strom C. 2004. Political institutions and corruption: The role of unitarism and parliamentarism. *British Journal of Political Science*, 34(2), 295–330.

Gibson, Christopher. 2012. *Civilizing the State: Civil Society and the Politics of Primary Public Health Care in Urban Brazil*. Ph.D. thesis, Brown University.

Gibson, Edward, and Calvo, Ernesto. 2000. Federalism and low-maintenance constituencies: Territorial dimensions of economic reform in Argentina. *Studies in Comparative International Development*, 35(3), 32–55.

Giraudy, Agustina. 2007. The distributive politics of emergency employment programs in Argentina (1993–2002). *Latin American Research Review*, 42(2), 33–55.

Goel, Rajeev K., and Nelson, Michael A. 1998. Corruption and government size: A disaggregated analysis. *Public Choice*, 97(1), 107–120.

Golden, Miriam A. 2003. Electoral connections: The effects of the personal vote on political patronage, bureaucracy and legislation in postwar Italy. *British Journal of Political Science*, 33(2), 189–212.

Golden, Miriam A., and Chang, Eric C.C. 2001. Competitive corruption: Factional conflict and political malfeasance in postwar Italian Christian Democracy. *World Politics*, 53(4), 588–622.

Golden, Miriam A., and Picci, Lucio. 2008. Pork-barrel politics in postwar Italy, 1953–94. *American Journal of Political Science*, 52(2), 268–289.

Golden, Miriam A., and Tiwari, Devesh. 2009. Criminality and malfeasance among national legislators in contemporary India. Presented at the Annual Meeting of the American Political Science Association.

Gonzalez Ocantos, Ezequiel, de Jonge, Chad Kiewiet, Meléndez, Carlos, Osorio, Javier, and Nickerson, David W. 2012. Vote buying and social desirability bias: Experimental evidence from Nicaragua. *American Journal of Political Science*, 56(1), 202–217.

Gonzalez Ocantos, Ezequiel, de Jonge, Chad Kiewiet, and Nickerson, David W. 2014. The conditionality of vote-buying norms: Experimental evidence from Latin America. *American Journal of Political Science*, 58(1), 197–211.

Gordin, Jorge P. 2002. The political and partisan determinants of patronage in Latin America 1960–1994: A comparative perspective. *European Journal of Political Research*, 41(4), 513–549.

Greene, Kenneth F. 2007. *Why Dominant Parties Lose: Mexico's Democratization in Comparative Perspective.* New York: Cambridge University Press.

Grindle, Merilee S. 2000. The social agenda and the politics of reform in Latin America. In Tulchin, Joseph, and Garland, Alison (eds.), *Social Development in Latin America,* pp. 17–52. Boulder, CO: Lynne Rienner.

Grindle, Merilee S. 2007. *Going Local: Decentralization, Democratization, and the Promise of Good Government.* Princeton, NJ: Princeton University Press.

Grosh, Margaret, del Ninno, Carlo, Tesliuc, Emil, and Ouerghi, Azedine. 2008. *For Protection and Promotion: The Design and Implementation of Effective Safety Nets.* Washington, DC: World Bank.

Gruenberg, Christian, and Pereyra, Victoria. 2009. *El clientelismo en la gestión de programas sociales contra la pobreza.* CIPPEC Documento políticas públicas y análisis.

Grzymala-Busse, Anna. 2007. *Rebuilding Leviathan: Party Competition and State Exploitation in Post Communist Democracies.* New York: Cambridge University Press.

Haggard, Stephan, and Kaufman, Robert R. 2008. *Development, Democracy, and Welfare States: Latin America, East Asia, and Eastern Europe.* Princeton, NJ: Princeton University Press.

Hagopian, Frances. 1996. *Traditional Politics and Regime Change.* New York: Cambridge University Press.

Hale, Henry E. 2007. Correlates of clientelism: Political economy, politicized ethnicity, and post-communist transition. In Kitschelt, Herbert, and Wilkinson, Steven I. (eds.), *Patrons, Clients, and Policies: Patterns of Democratic Accountability and Political Competition,* pp. 227–250. New York: Cambridge University Press.

Hall, Anthony. 2006. From Fome Zero to *Bolsa Familia*: Social policies and poverty alleviation under Lula. *Journal of Latin American Studies,* 38(4), 689–709.

Hall, Anthony. 2008. Brazil's *Bolsa Familia*: A double-edged sword? *Development and Change,* 39(5), 799–822.

Hellman, Joel, S. 1998. Winners take all: The politics of partial reform in postcommunist transitions. *World Politics,* 50(02), 203–234.

Helmke, Gretchen, and Levitsky, Steven (eds.) 2006. *Informal Institutions and Democracy: Lessons from Latin America.* Baltimore: Johns Hopkins University Press.

Hicken, Allen. 2011. Clientelism. *Annual Review of Political Science,* 14(1), 289–310.

Holzner, Claudio A. 2003. *End of clientelism: changing political practices among the poor in Mexico.* Presented at the Latin American Studies Association Congress.

Holzner, Claudio A. 2010. The Poverty of Democracy. The Institutional Roots of Political Participation in Mexico. Pittsburgh, PA: University of Pittsburgh Press.

Huber, Evelyne. 1996. Options for social policy in Latin America: Neoliberal versus social democratic models, In Esping-Anderson, Gosta, (ed.), *Welfare States in Transition: National Transitions in Global Economies,* pp. 141–191. London: Sage Publications.

Humphreys, Macartan, Masters, William A., and Sandbu, Martin E. 2006. The role of leaders in democratic deliberations. Results from a field experiment in São Tomé and Príncipe. *World Politics*, 58(4), 583–622.

Huntington, Samuel P. 1968. *Political Order in Changing Societies*. New Haven, CT: Yale University Press.

Huntington, Samuel P. 1991. *The Third Wave: Democratization in the Late Twentieth Century*. Norman, OK: University of Oklahoma Press.

INDEC. 2003 (September). *Aqui se cuenta*. Tech. rept. 7. Instituto nacional de estadística y censos, Argentina, Buenos Aires.

Independent Evaluation Group. 2011. *Social Safety Nets: An Evaluation of World Bank Support, 2000–2010*. Washington, DC: Independent Evaluation Group, the World Bank Group.

Jones, Mark P., Saiegh, Sebastian, Spiller, Pablo T., and Tommasi, Mariano. 2002. Amateur legislators–professional politicians: The consequences of party-centered electoral rules in a federal system. *American Journal of Political Science*, 46(3), 656–669.

Kaufman, Robert R., and Trejo, Guillermo. 1997. Regionalism, regime transformation, and PRONASOL: The politics of the National Solidarity Programme in four Mexican states. *Journal of Latin American Studies*, 29(3), 717–745.

Keefer, Philip. 2002 (October). *The Political Economy of Corruption in Indonesia*. Washington, DC: World Bank.

Keefer, Philip. 2007. Clientelism, credibility, and the policy choices of young democracies. *American Journal of Political Science*, 51(4), 804–821.

Kemahlioglu, Ozge. 2006. *When the Agent Becomes the Boss: The Politics of Public Employment in Argentina and Turkey*. Ph.D. thesis, Columbia University.

Kerkvliet, Benedict J. 1991. Understanding politics in a nueva ecija rural community. In Kerkvliet, Benedict J., and Mojares, Resil B. (eds.), *From Marcos to Aquino: Local Perspectives on Political Transition in the Philippines*, pp. 226–246. Honolulu: University of Hawaii Press.

Key, V.O. 1949. *Southern Politics in State and Nation*. New York: Alfred A. Knopf.

Keyssar, Alexander. 2009. *The Right to Vote*. Revised 1st ed. New York: Basic Books.

King, Gary, Keohane, Robert O., and Verba, Sidney. 1994. *Designing Social Inquiry*. Princeton, NJ: Princeton University Press.

King, Gary, Tomz, Michael, and Wittenberg, Jason. 2000. Making the most of statistical analyses: Improving interpretation and presentation. *American Journal of Political Science*, 44(2), 341–355.

Kitschelt, Herbert. 2000. Linkages between citizens and politicians in democratic polities. *Comparative Political Studies*, 33(6/7), 845–879.

Kitschelt, Herbert. 2007. The demise of clientelism in affluent capitalist democracies. In Kitschelt, Herbert, and Wilkinson, Steven I. (eds.), *Patrons, Clients, and Policies: Patterns of Democratic Accountability and Political Competition*, pp. 276–297. New York: Cambridge University Press.

Kitschelt, Herbert, and Kselman, Daniel M. 2012. Economic development, democratic experience, and political parties' linkage strategies. *Comparative political studies*, 46(11), 1453–1484.

Kitschelt, Herbert, and Wilkinson, Steven I. 2007a. Citizen–politician linkages: An introduction. In Kitschelt, Herbert, and Wilkinson, Steven I. (eds.), *Patrons, Clients, and Policies: Patterns of Democratic Accountability and Political Competition*, pp. 1–49. New York: Cambridge University Press.

Kitschelt, Herbert, and Wilkinson, Steven I. (eds.) 2007b. *Patrons, Clients, and Policies: Patterns of Democratic Accountability and Political Competition*. New York: Cambridge University Press.

Kitschelt, Herbert, Freeze, Kent, Kolev, Kiril, and Wang, Yi-Ting. 2009. Measuring democratic accountability: An initial report on an emerging data set. *Revista de Ciencia Poítica*, 29(3), 741–773.

Knight, Alan, and Pansters, Wil (eds.) 2005. *Caciquismo in Twentieth-Century Mexico*. London: Institute for the Study of the Americas.

Kramon, Eric. 2011 (December). Why do politicians buy votes when the ballot is secret? Theory and experimental evidence from Kenya. Presented at WGAPE meeting, Stanford University.

Krishna, Anirudh. 2007. Politics in the middle: mediating relationships between the citizens and the state in rural North India. In Kitschelt, Herbert, and Wilkinson, Steven I. (eds.), *Patrons, Clients, and Policies: Patterns of Democratic Accountability and Political Competition*, pp. 141–158. New York: Cambridge University Press.

Kunicova, Jana, and Rose-Ackerman, Susan. 2005. Electoral rules and constitutional structures as constraints on corruption. *British Journal of Political Science*, 35(4), 573–606.

Lambsdorff, Johann Graf. 2006. Causes and consequences of corruption: What do we know from a cross-section of countries? *In International Handbook on the Economics of Corruption*, pp. 3–51. Northampton, MA: Edward Elgar.

Lande, Carl H. 1983. Political clientelism in political studies: Retrospect and prospects. *International Review of Political Science*, 4(4), 435–454.

Lawson, Chappell. 2009 (March). *The Politics of Reciprocity: Trading Selective Benefits for Popular Support*. Typescript. MIT.

Lawson, Chappell, and Greene, Kenneth F. 2013. *Self-Enforcing Clientelism*. Unpublished manuscript. MIT.

Lázaro, Lucas. 2003. *De clientes a ciudadanos. La transición de modos clientelares a modos programáticos de movilización poliítica. Estudio de un caso en la provincia de Córdoba*. Undergraduate thesis, Universidad Empresarial Siglo Veintiuno.

Leal, Victor Nunes. 1977. *Coronelismo: The Municipality and Representative Government in Brazil*. Cambridge: Cambridge University Press.

Lederman, Daniel, Loayza, Norman, and Reis Soares, Rodrigo. 2001 (November). Accountability and corruption: Political institutions matter. World Bank Policy Research Working Paper No. 2708.

Levitsky, Steven. 2003. *Transforming Labor-Based Parties in Latin America: Argentine Peronism in Comparative Perspective*. New York: Cambridge University Press.

Levitsky, Steven, and Murillo, María Victoria. 2006. *Argentine Democracy: The Politics of Institutional Weakness*. University Park, PA: Pennsylvania State University Press.

Levy, Santiago. 2006. *Progress against Poverty: Sustaining Mexico's Progresa-Oportunidades program*. Washington, DC: Brookings Institution Press.

Levy, Santiago, and Rodríguez, Evelyne. 2004. *Economic Crisis, Political Transition and Poverty Policy Reform: Mexico's Progresa-Oportunidades Program*. Washington, DC: Inter-American Development Bank.

Lindbeck, Assar, and Weibull, Jorgen W. 1987. Balanced-budget redistribution as the outcome of political competition. *Public Choice*, 52(3), 273–297.

Linder, Anja. 2012. *Do Accountability Mechanisms in Safety Nets Improve Access to Social Services? The case of Brazil's Bolsa Familia.* Manuscript. Stockholm: International Institute for Democracy and Electoral Assistance.

Lindert, Kathy, and Vincensini, Vanina. 2010 (December). Social policy, perceptions, and the press: An analysis of the media's treatment of conditional cash transfers in Brazil. Washington, DC: World Bank. SP Discussion Paper No. 1008.

Lindert, Kathy, Skoufias, Emmauel, and Shapiro, Joseph. 2006 (August). Redistributing income to the poor and the rich: public transfers in Latin America and the Caribbean. SP Discussion Paper No. 0605. Washington, DC: World Bank.

Lindert, Kathy, Linder, Anja, Hobbs, Jason, and de la Brière, Bénédicte. 2007 (May). The nuts and bolts of Brazil's Bolsa Familia program: Implementing conditional cash transfers in a decentralized context. SP Discussion Paper 0709. Washington, DC: World Bank.

Lipset, Seymour M. 1959. Some social requisites of democracy: Economic development and political legitimacy. *American Political Science Review*, 53(1), 69–105.

Lipsky, Michael. 1980. *Street-Level Bureaucracy.* New York: Russell Sage Foundation.

Lladós, José Ignacio. 2007. *En la campaña riojana reparten dinero, inodoros y remedios.* La Nación. With Arturo Ortiz Sosa, Jr. August 16.

Lodola, Germán. 2005. Protesta popular y redes clientelares en la Argentina: El reparto federal del Plan Trabajar (1996–2001). *Desarrollo Económico*, 44(176), 515–536.

Londregan, John, and Romer, Thomas. 1993. Polarization, incumbency, and the personal vote. In *Political Economy: Institutions, Competition, and Representation: Proceedings of the Seventh International Symposium in Economic Theory and Econometrics*, pp. 355–377.

Lupu, Noam, and Stokes, Susan C. 2009. The social bases of political parties in Argentina: 1912–2003. *Latin American Research Review*, 44(1), 58–87.

Lyne, Mona M. 2007. Rethinking economics and institutions: The voter's dilemma and democratic accountability. In Kitschelt, Herbert, and Wilkinson, Steven I. (eds.), *Patrons, Clients and Policies: Patterns of Democratic Accountability and Political Competition*, pp. 159–181. New York: Cambridge University Press.

Lyne, Mona M. 2008. *The Voter's Dilemma and Democratic Accountability: Latin America and Beyond.* University Park, PA: The Pennsylvania State University Press.

Madison, James. 1788. *Federalist 57.* http://thomas.loc.gov/home/fedpapers/.

Magaloni, Beatriz. 2006. *Voting for Autocracy: Hegemonic Party Survival and its Demise in Mexico.* New York: Cambridge University Press.

Magaloni, Beatriz, Diaz-Cayeros, Alberto, and Estévez, Federico. 2007. Clientelism and portfolio diversification: a model of electoral investment with applications to Mexico. In Kitschelt, Herbert, and Wilkinson, Steven I. (eds.), *Patrons, Clients, and Policies. Patterns of Democratic Accountability and Political Competition.* pp. 182–205. Cambridge University Press.

Mainwaring, Scott. 2003. Introduction: Democratic accountability in Latin America. In Scott Mainwaring and Christopher Welna, (eds.), *Democratic Accountability in Latin America*, pp. 3–33. New York: Oxford University Press.

Maister, David H. 1985. The psychology of waiting lines. In Czepiel, John A., Solomon, Michael R., and Suprenant, Carol F. (eds.), *The Service Encounter: Managing Employee/Customer Interaction in Service Businesses*, pp. 113–126. Lexington, MA: Lexington Books.

Manin, Bernard, Przeworski, Adam, and Stokes, Susan C. 1999. *Introduction*. In Przeworski, Adam, Stokes, Susan C., and Manin, Bernard, (eds.), *Democracy, Accountability, and Representation*, pp. 1–26. New York: Cambridge University Press.

Manor, James. 1999. *The Political Economy of Democratic Decentralization*. Washington, DC: World Bank.

Manzetti, Luigi, and Wilson, Carole J. 2007. Why do corrupt governments maintain public support? *Comparative Political Studies*, 40(8), 949–970.

Mares, Isabela. 2004. Economic insecurity and social policy expansion: Evidence from interwar Europe. *International Organization*, 58(4), 745–774.

Matsusaka, John G, and Palda, Filip. 1993. The Downsian voter meets the ecological fallacy. *Public Choice*, 77(4), 855–78.

Mayhew, David R. 1974. *Congress: The Electoral Connection*. New Haven, CT: Yale University Press.

McDermott, Rose. 2002. Experimental methods in political science. *Annual Review of Political Science*, 5(1), 31–61.

McGuire, James W. 1997. *Peronism without Perón: Unions, Parties, and Democracy in Argentina*. Stanford, CA: Stanford University Press.

McGuire, James W. 2011. Social policies in Latin America: Causes, characteristics, and consequences. *ACSPL Working Paper Series*, 1(1).

Medina, Luis Fernando, and Stokes, Susan C. 2002. Clientelism as political monopoly. Presented at the Annual Meeting of the American Political Science Association.

Mesa-Lago, Carmelo. 1978. *Social Security in Latin America*. Pittsburgh, PA: University of Pittsburgh Press.

Mexican Panel Survey. n.d. *Embedded experiments in the 2006 Mexican panel survey*. http://web.mit.edu/clawson/www/polisci/research/mexico06/Assets/Survey_ Innovations.pdf.

Midre, Georges. 1992. Bread or solidarity? Argentine social policies, 1983–1990. *Journal of Latin American Studies*, 24(2), 343–373.

Milazzo, Annamaria, and Grosh, Margaret. 2008 (May). Social safety nets in World Bank lending and analytical work: FY2002–2007. SP Discussion Paper No. 0810. Washington, DC: World Bank.

Min, Brian. 2010. *Distributing Power: Electrifying the Poor in India*. Unpublished manuscript, University of Michigan.

Molinar, Juan, and Weldon, Jeffrey. 1994. Electoral determinants and consequences of national solidarity. In Cornelius, Wayne, Craig, Ann, and Fox, Jonathan (eds.), *Transforming State–Society Relations in Mexico: The National Solidarity Strategy*. San Diego: Center for U.S.–Mexican Studies, University of California.

Montero, Alfred P., and Samuels, David J. (eds.) 2004. *Decentralization and Democracy in Latin America*. Notre Dame, IN: University of Notre Dame Press.

Montinola, Gabriela R., and Jackman, Robert W. 2002. Sources of corruption: A cross-country study. *British Journal of Political Science*, 32(1), 147–170.

Moore, Barrington. 1966. *Social Origins of Dictatorship and Democracy: Lord and Peasant in the Making of the Modern World*. Boston: Beacon Press.

Mora y Araujo, Manuel. 2002 (September). *La estructura social de la Argentina: Evidencias y conjeturas acerca de la estratificación actual*. CEPAL: Serie Politicas Sociales 59. Santiago.

Mora y Araujo, Manuel, and Llorente, Ignacio (eds.) 1980. *El voto peronista. Ensayos de sociología electoral Argentina*. Buenos Aires: Editorial Sudamericana.

Morley, Samuel, and Coady, David. 2003. From social assistance to social development: Targeted education subsidies in developing countries. Washington, DC: Center for Global Development.

Munro, William A. 2001. The political consequences of local electoral systems: Democratic change and the politics of differential citizenship in South Africa. *Comparative Politics*, 33(3), 295–313.

National Endowment for Democracy. 2010. *Political Clientelism, Social Policy, and the Quality of Democracy: Evidence from Latin America, Lessons from Other Regions*. Tech. rept. Network of Democracy Research Institutes, http://www. ned.org/sites/default/files/QuitoConferenceReportFINAL.pdf.

National League of Cities. 2005. *Partisan vs Non-partisan elections*. http://www. nlc.org/build-skills-and-networks/resources/cities-101/city-officials/partisan-vs-non partisan-elections.

Nelson, Joan M. 2000. Reforming social sector governance: A political perspective. In Tulchin, Joseph, and Garland, Alison (eds.), *Social Development in Latin America*, pp. 53–70. Boulder, CO: Lynn Reinner.

Nichter, Simeon. 2008. Vote buying or turnout buying? Machine politics and the secret ballot. *American Political Science Review*, 102(1), 19–31.

Nichter, Simeon. 2009. Declared choice: Citizen strategies and dual commitment problems in clientelism. Presented at the Annual Meeting of the American Political Science Association.

Niño-Zarazúa, Miguel Angel. 2010. Mexico's Progresa-Oportunidades and the emergence of social assistance in Latin America. University of Manchester: BWPI Working Paper 142.

Nyblade, Benjamin, and Reed, Steven R. 2008. Who cheats? Who loots? Political competition and corruption in Japan, 1947–1993. *American Journal of Political Science*, 52(4), 926–941.

Oates, Wallace E. 1972. *Fiscal Federalism*. New York: Harcourt Brace Jovanovich.

O'Donnell, Guillermo. 1993. On the state, democratization and some conceptual problems: A Latin American view with glances at some postcommunist countries. *World Development*, 21(8), 1355–1369.

O'Donnell, Guillermo A. 1994. Delegative democracy. *Journal of Democracy*, 5(1), 55–69.

O'Donnell, Guillermo. 1996. Illusions about consolidation. *Journal of Democracy*, 7(2), 34–51.

O'Dwyer, Conner. 2006. *Runaway State-Building: Patronage Politics and Democratic Development*. Baltimore: Johns Hopkins University Press.

Oliveros, Virginia. 2013. *A Working Machine: Patronage Jobs and Political Services in Argentina*. Ph.D. thesis, Columbia University.

Olken, Benjamin A. 2007. Monitoring corruption: Evidence from a field experiment in Indonesia. *Journal of Political Economy*, 115(2), 200–249.

Olson, Mancur. 1993. Dictatorship, democracy, and development. *American Political Science Review*, 87(3), 567–576.

O'Neill, Kathleen. 2003. Decentralization as an electoral strategy. *Comparative Political Studies*, 36(9), 1068–1091.

Open Society Institute. 2005. *Una censura sutil: Abuso de publicidad oficial y otras restricciones a la libertad de expresión en Argentina*. Open Society Institute.

Pasotti, Eleanora. 2009. *Political Branding in Cities: The Decline of Machine Politics in Bogotá, Naples, and Chicago*. New York: Cambridge University Press.

Pereira, Carlos, and Rennó, Lucio. 2003. Successful re-election strategies in Brazil: The electoral impact of distinct institutional incentives. *Electoral Studies*, 22(3), 425–448.

Persson, Torsten, and Tabellini, Guido. 2000. *Political Economics: Explaining Economic Policy*. Cambridge, MA: MIT Press.

Persson, Torsten, Tabellini, Guido, and Trebbi, Francesco. 2003. Electoral rules and corruption. *Journal of the European Economic Association*, 1(4), 958–989.

Peruzzotti, Enrique, and Smulovitz, Catalina. 2006. *Enforcing the rule of law: Social Accountability in the New Latin American Democracies*. Pittsburgh, PA: University of Pittsburgh Press.

Petersen, Javier Rodriguez. 2011. *Con alimentos o una carga de celular, las viejas practicas clientelisticas siguen presentes en Salta*. Clarín. April 9.

Piattoni, Simona. 2001a. Clientelism in historical and comparative perspective. In Piattoni, Simona (ed.), *Clientelism, Interests, and Democratic Representation: The European Experience in Historical and Comparative Perspective*, pp. 1–30. Cambridge: Cambridge University Press.

Piattoni, Simona (ed.) 2001b. *Clientelism, Interests, and Democratic Representation: The European Experience in Historical and Comparative Perspective*. Cambridge: Cambridge University Press.

Plotkin, Mariano Ben. 2002. *Mañana es San Perón: A cultural history of Perón's Argentina*. Wilmington, DE: Scholarly Resources Inc.

Posner, Daniel, and Kramon, Eric. 2013. Who benefits from distributive politics? How the outcome one studies affects the answer one gets. *Perspectives on Politics*, 11(2), 461–474.

Powell, G. Bingham. 2004. The chain of responsiveness. *Journal of Democracy*, 15(4), 91–105.

Przeworski, Adam, Stokes, Susan C., and Manin, Bernard (eds.) 1999. *Democracy, Accountability, and Representation*. New York: Cambridge University Press.

Putnam, Robert D. 1973. The political attitudes of senior civil servants in Western Europe: A preliminary report. *British Journal of Political Science*, 3(3), 257–290.

Putnam, Robert. 1994. *Making Democracy Work: Civic Traditions in Modern Italy*. Princeton, NJ: Princeton University Press.

Reinikka, Ritva, and Svensson, Jakob. 2005. Fighting corruption to improve schooling: Evidence from a newspaper campaign in Uganda. *Journal of the European Economic Association*, 3(2–3), 259–267.

Remmer, Karen. 2007. The political economy of patronage: Expenditure patterns in the Argentine provinces, 1983–2003. *Journal of Politics*, 69(2), 363–377.

Remmer, Karen L., and Wibbels, Erik. 2000. The subnational politics of economic adjustment. Provincial Politics and Fiscal Performance in Argentina. *Comparative Political Studies*, 33(4), 419–451.

Riker, William, and Ordeshook, Peter. 1968. A theory of the calculus of voting. *American Political Science Review*, 62(1), 25–42.

Rivera, Juan A., Sotres-Alvarez, Daniella, Habicht, Jean-Pierre, Shamah, Teresa, and Villalpando, Salvador. 2004. Impact of the Mexican program for education, health, and nutrition (Progresa) on rates of growth and anemia in infants and young children. *Journal of the American Medical Association*, 291(21), 2563–2570.

Robinson, James A, and Verdier, Thierry. 2002 (Feb.). The political economy of clientelism. CEPR Discussion Papers 3205.

Rocha Menocal, Alina. 2001. Do old habits die hard? A statistical exploration of the politicisation of Progresa, Mexico's latest federal poverty-alleviation programme, under the Zedillo administration. *Journal of Latin American Studies*, 33(3), 513–538.

Rodden, Jonathan, and Rose-Ackerman, Susan. 1997. Does federalism preserve markets? *Virginia Law Review*, 83(7), 1521–1572.

Rodríguez, Victoria E., and Ward, Peter M. 1994. *Political changes in Baja California: Democracy in the making?* La Jolla: Center for U.S-Mexican Studies, University of California, San Diego.

Rodrik, Dani. 1997 (December). *Democracy and Economic Performance*. Manuscript. Harvard University.

Roniger, Luis. 1987. Caciquismo and Coronelismo: Contextual dimensions of patron brokerage in Mexico and Brazil. *Latin American Research Review*, 22(2), 71–99.

Rose-Ackerman, Susan. 1978. *Corruption: A study in Political Economy*. New York: Academic Press.

Rosenzweig, Mark, and Wolpin, Kenneth. 1993. Credit market constraints, consumption smoothing, and the accumulation of durable production assets in low-income countries: Investment in bullocks in India. *Journal of Political Economy*, 101(2), 223–44.

Rueschemeyer, Dietrich, Stephens, Evelyne Huber, and Stephens, John D. 1992. *Capitalist Development and Democracy*. Chicago: University of Chicago Press.

Samuels, David J. 2000. The gubernatorial coattails effect: Federalism and congressional elections in Brazil. *Journal of Politics*, 62(1), 240–253.

Samuels, David J. 2002. Pork barreling is not credit claiming or advertising: Campaign finance and the sources of the personal vote in Brazil. *Journal of Politics*, 64(3), 845–863.

Sarat, Austin. 1990. Law is all over: Power, resistance and the legal consciousness of the welfare poor. *Yale Journal of Law and the Humanities*, 2(2), 343.

Schaffer, Federic Charles (ed.) 2007a. *Elections for Sale: The Causes and Consequences of Vote Buying*. Boulder, CO: Lynne Rienner.

Schaffer, Federic Charles. 2007b. Why study vote buying? In Schaffer, Federic Charles (ed.), *Elections for Sale: The Causes and Consequences of Vote Buying*, pp. 1–16. Boulder, CO: Lynne Rienner.

Schaffer, Federic Charles, and Schedler, Andreas. 2007. What is vote buying? In Schaffer, Federic Charles (ed.), *Elections for Sale: The Causes and Consequences of Vote Buying*, pp. 17–32. Boulder, CO: Lynne Rienner.

Scheiner, Ethan. 2007. Clientelism in Japan: The Importance and Limits of Institutional Explanations. In Kitschelt, Herbert, and Wilkinson, Steven I. (eds.), *Patrons, Clients, and Policies: Patterns of Democratic Accountability and Political Competition*, pp. 276–297. New York: Cambridge University Press.

Schelling, Thomas C. 1960. *The Strategy of Conflict*. Cambridge, MA: Harvard University Press.

Schumpeter, Joseph A. 2012 (1943). *Capitalism, Socialism and Democracy*. New York: Routledge.

Schwartz, Barry. 1975. *Queuing and Waiting: Studies in the Social Organization of Access and Delay*. Chicago: University of Chicago Press.

Scott, James C. 1969. The analysis of corruption in developing nations. *Comparative Studies in Society and History*, 11(3), 315–341.

Scott, James C. 1972. Patron-client politics and political change in Southeast Asia. *American Political Science Review*, 66(1), 91–113.

Segura-Ubiergo, Alex. 2008. *The Political Economy of the Welfare State in Latin America: Globalization, Democracy, and Development*. New York and Cambridge: Cambridge University Press.

Shefter, Martin. 1977. Party and patronage: Germany, England, and Italy. *Politics and Society*, 7(4), 403–451.

Singer, Matthew. 2009. Buying voters with dirty money: The relationship between clientelism and corruption. Presented at the American Political Science Association Annual Meeting.

Singerman, Diane. 1995. *Avenues of Participation: Family, Politics, and Networks in Urban Quarters of Cairo*. Princeton, NJ: Princeton University Press.

Singh, Prerna. 2010. *Subnationalism and Social Development: A Comparative Analysis of Indian States*. Ph.D. thesis, Princeton University.

Skoufias, Emmanuel, Davis, Benjamin, and de la Vega, Sergio. 2001. Targeting the poor in Mexico: An evaluation of the selection of households into PROGRESA. *World Development*, 20(10), 1769–1784.

Smulovitz, Catalina, and Clemente, Adriana. 2004. Decentralization and social expenditure at the municipal level in Argentina. In Tulchin, Joseph S. and Selee, Andrew, (eds.), *Decentralization and Democratic Governance in Latin America*, pp. 3–36. Washington, DC: Woodrow Wilson Center.

Sniderman, Paul M., and Grob, Douglas B. 1996. Innovations in experimental design in attitude surveys. *Annual Review of Sociology*, 22, 377–399.

Snyder, Richard. 2001. Scaling down: The subnational comparative method. *Studies in Comparative International Development*, 36(1), 93–110.

Soss, Joe. 2002. *Unwanted Claims: The Politics of Participation in the US Welfare System*. Ann Arbor: University of Michigan Press.

Spiller, Pablo T., and Tommasi, Mariano. 2003. The institutional foundations of public policy: A transactions approach with application to Argentina. *The Journal of Law, Economics, and Organization*, 19(2), 281–306.

Spiller, Pablo T., and Tommasi, Mariano. 2007. *The Institutional Foundations of Public Policy in Argentina*. New York: Cambridge University Press.

Stein, Ernesto, Tommasi, Mariano, Echebarria, Koldo, Lora, Eduardo, and Payne, Mark (eds.) 2006. *The Politics of Policies: Economic and Social Progress in Latin America. 2006 Report*. Washington, DC: IADB.

Stokes, Donald E. 1963. Spatial models of party competition. *American Political Science Review*, **57**(2), 368–377.

Stokes, Susan C. 2001. *Mandates and Democracy: Neoliberalism by Surprise in Latin Amerca*. New York: Cambridge University Press.

Stokes, Susan C. 2005. Perverse accountability: A formal model of machine politics with evidence from Argentina. *American Political Science Review*, **99**(3), 315–325.

Stokes, Susan C. 2007a. Is vote buying undemocratic? In Schaffer, Frederic Charles (ed.), *Elections for Sale: The Causes and Consequences of Vote buying*, pp. 81–100. Boulder, CO: Lynne Reinner.

Stokes, Susan C. 2007b. Political clientelism. In Boix, Carles, and Stokes, Susan C. (eds.), *The Oxford Handbook of Comparative Politics*, pp. 604–627. Oxford: Oxford University Press.

Stokes, Susan C. 2009. Pork, by Any Other Name...Building a Conceptual Scheme of Distributive Politics. Presented at the Annual Meeting of the American Political Science Association.

Stokes, Susan C., and Dunning, Thad. 2008. Clientelism as persuasion and as mobilization. Presented at the Annual Meeting of the Midwest Political Science Association.

Stokes, Susan C., Dunning, Thad, Nazareno, Marcelo, and Brusco, Valeria. 2013. *Brokers, Voters, and Clientelism: The Puzzle of Distributive Politics*. New York: Cambridge University Press.

Sugiyama, Natasha B. 2008. Theories of policy diffusion. *Comparative Political Studies*, **41**(2), 193.

Szwarcberg, Mariela L. 2007. Strategies of electoral mobilization in comparative perspective: Lessons from the Argentine case. Presented at the Latin American Studies Association Congress.

Szwarcberg, Mariela L. 2008 (April). Counting heads and votes: authoritarian and democratic strategies of electoral mobilization in Argentina. Prepared for delivery at the Comparative Politics Workshop, Yale University.

Szwarcberg, Mariela L. 2009. *Making Local Democracy: Political Machines, Clientelism, and Social Networks in Argentina*. Ph.D. thesis, University of Chicago.

Takahashi, Yuriko. 2006. *Neoliberal Manipulation (or Politization) of Social Spending in Latin America: Evidence from Mexico*. Typescript, Cornell University.

Tarrow, Sidney. 1967. *Peasant Communism in Southern Italy*. New Haven, CT: Yale University Press.

Tavits, Margit. 2007. Clarity of responsibility and corruption. *American Journal of Political Science*, **51**(1), 218–229.

Teixeira, Tomaz. 1985. *A outra face da oliguarquia do Piaui (Depoimento)*. Fortaleza, Brazil: Stylus Comuncaçaes Ltda.

Tendler, Judith. 1997. *Good Government in the Tropics*. Baltimore, MD: Johns Hopkins University Press.

Tendler, Judith. 2000. Safety nets and service delivery: What are social funds really telling us? In Tulchin, Joseph, and Garland, Alison (eds.), *Social Development in Latin America*, pp. 53–70. Boulder, CO: Lynne Rienner.

Tiebout, Charles M. 1956. A pure theory of local expenditures. *Journal of Political Economy*, **64**(5), 416–424.

Torre, Juan Carlos. 1990. *La vieja guardia sindical y los orígenes del Peronismo.* Buenos Aires: Editorial Sudamericana.

Treisman, Daniel. 2000. The causes of corruption: A cross-national study. *Journal of Public Economics,* 76(3), 399–457.

Treisman, Daniel. 2002 (October). *Decentralization and the Quality of Government.* Unpublished manuscript, UCLA.

Treisman, Daniel. 2007. *The Architecture of Government: Rethinking Political Decentralization.* New York: Cambridge University Press.

Tsai, Lily L. 2007. *Accountability without Democracy: Solidary Groups and Public Goods Provision in Rural China.* New York: Cambridge University Press.

Vaishnav, Milan. 2012. *The Merits of Money and "Muscle": Essays on Criminality, Elections and Democracy in India.* Ph.D. thesis, Columbia University.

Valenzuela, Arturo. 1977. *Political Brokers in Chile: Local Politics in a centralized Polity.* Durham, NC: Duke University Press.

van de Walle, Nicholas. 2007. "Meet the new boss, same as the old boss"? The evolution of political clientelism in Africa. In Kitschelt, Herbert, and Wilkinson, Steven I (eds.), *Patrons, Clients, and Policies: Patterns of Democratic Accountability and Political Competition,* pp. 50–67. New York: Cambridge University Press.

Velíz, Claudio. 1980. *The Centralist Tradition in Latin America.* Princeton, NJ: Priceton University Press.

Wang, Chin-Shou, and Kurzman, Charles. 2007. The logistics: how to buy votes. In Schaffer, Federic Charles (ed.), *Elections for Sale: The Causes and Consequences of Vote Buying,* pp. 61–80. Boulder, CO: Lynne Rienner.

Wantchekon, Leonard. 2003. Clientelism and voting behavior: Evidence from a field experiment in Benin. *World Politics,* 55(3), 399–422.

Ward, Peter M. 1998. From machine politics to the politics of technocracy: Charting changes in governance in the Mexican municipality. *Bulletin of Latin American Research,* 17(3), 341–365.

Weber Abramo, Claudio. 2004. *Vote Buying in Brazil: Less of a Problem than Believed?* In *Transparency International Global Corruption Report,* pp. 78–79. Sterling, VA: Pluto Press.

Weingast, Barry R. 1995. The economic role of political institutions: Market-preserving federalism and economic development. *Journal of Law, Economics, and Organization,* 11(1), 1–31.

Weingrod, Alex. 1968. Patrons, patronage, and political parties. *Comparative Studies in Society and History,* 10(4), 377–400.

Weitz-Shapiro, Rebecca. 2006. Partisanship and protest: The Politics of Workfare distribution in Argentina. *Latin American Research Review,* 41(3), 122–148.

Weitz-Shapiro, Rebecca. 2008a. Clientelism and the middle class: Results of a survey experiment in Argentina. Presented at the Annual Meeting of the American Political Science Association.

Weitz-Shapiro, Rebecca. 2008b. The local connection: Local government performance and satisfaction with democracy in Argentina. *Comparative Political Studies,* 41(3), 85–308.

Weitz-Shapiro, Rebecca. 2012. What wins votes: Why some politicians opt out of clientelism. *American Journal of Political Science,* 56(3), 568–583.

Weyland, Kurt (ed). 2004. *Learning from Foreign Models in Latin American Policy Reform*. Baltimore: John Hopkins University Press.

Wibbels, Erik. 2005. *Federalism and the Market: Intergovernmental Conflict and Economic Reform in the Developing World*. New York: Cambridge University Press.

Wibbels, Erik. 2006. Madison in Baghdad? Decentralization and federalism in comparative politics. *Annual Review of Political Science*, 9(1), 165–188.

Wilkinson, Steven I. 2006 (July). *The politics of Infrastructural Spending in India*. Typescript, University of Chicago.

Williamson, John. 1990. What Washington means by policy reform. In *Latin American Adjustment: How Much Has Happened?*, pp. 7–20. Washington, DC: Institute for International Economics.

Willis, Eliza, da C. B. Garman, Christopher, and Haggard, Stephan. 1999. The politics of decentralization in Latin America. *Latin American Research Review*, 34(1), 7–56.

Winters, Matthew S. 2013. *Social Capital and the Allocation of Development Projects*. Unpublished manuscript, University of Illinois.

Wolfinger, Raymond E. 1972. Why political machines have not withered away and other revisionist thoughts. *Journal of Politics*, 34(2), 365–298.

Wolfinger, Raymond E. 1974. *The Politics of Progress*. Englewood Cliffs, NJ: Prentice-Hall.

Wood, Geof. 2003. Staying secure, staying poor: the Faustian Bargain. *World Development*, 31(3), 455–471.

World Bank. 2005. *East Asia Decentralizes*. Washington, DC: World Bank.

World Bank. 2004. World Development Report. *Making Services Work for Poor People*. Washington, DC: World Bank.

Wrong, Michela. 2009. *It's Our Turn to Eat. A Story of a Kenyan Whistleblower*. New York: Harper Collins.

Yaschine, Iliana, and Orozco, Monica. 2010. *The Evolving Antipoverty Agenda in Mexico: The Political Economy of PROGRESA and Oportunidades*. Baltimore: Johns Hopkins University Press.

Ybarra, Gustavo. 2011. *Misiones: el kirchnerismo busca eternizarse con Closs*. La Nación. June 24.

Zucco, Cesar. 2013. When payouts pay off: conditional cash transfers and voting behavior in Brazil 2002–2010. *American Journal of Political Science* 57(4): 810–822.

Author Index

Subject Index